DAVID E. MARKLE

THE AUTHORITATIVE WORD

Essays on The Nature of Scripture

edited by
DONALD K. McKIM

GRAND RAPIDS
WM. B. EERDMANS PUBLISHING COMPANY

Library of Congress Cataloging in Publication Data
Main entry under title:

The Authoritative word.

  Bibliography: p. 265.
    1. Bible — Evidences, authority, etc. — Addresses,
essays, lectures. 2. Bible — Inspiration — Addresses,
essays, lectures. 3. Bible — Canon — Addresses, essays,
lectures. I. McKim, Donald K.
BS480.A97 1983   220.1'3   82-20919
ISBN 0-8028-1948-6

To my parents: Keith and Mary McKim
  —who taught me to love the Scriptures

To the congregation of the Wampum United
Presbyterian Church of Wampum, Pennsylvania
  —which nurtured the love of Scripture in me

CONTENTS

INTRODUCTION

Our knowledge about the Bible has greatly increased in recent years. Biblical scholars, historians, and theologians have all contributed to our better understanding of the nature and formation of the Scriptures. The following essays represent some of the best theological thought in this area. Although they come from varied sources and perspectives, all these writings deal fundamentally with the authority of the Bible and its nature as God's written Word. Together they give an overview of how the Scriptures have been formed, canonized, regarded in history, and interpreted. They show how the Bible functions theologically in the life of the Christian church. Thus, many aspects of the church's doctrine of Scripture are addressed here.

The essays are divided into three major categories. The first section deals with the authority of Scripture in terms of the sources of Scripture and the church's canon. These pieces deal with fundamental issues such as where the Bible came from, how it was assembled, and why the church has regarded these certain books as authoritative.

Paul J. Achtemeier's "How the Scriptures Were Formed" traces the production of the biblical books from early oral traditions. These traditions were reused and reinterpreted to meet new needs in the life of the early church.

The essay by Robert M. Grant on "Jesus and the Old Testament" provides insight into how Jesus Christ cited the Old Testament Scriptures and how He regarded them as authoritative. Grant, in "Paul and the Old Testament," then compares the interpretations of Jesus with those of the apostle Paul, and he shows the interpretive principles Paul used when citing and exegeting the Old Testament.

A fuller discussion of "The Interpretation of the Old Testament in the New" is offered by C. K. Barrett. Barrett writes not only of the exegetical methods used by various New Testament writers but also of the content and purpose of their exegesis of the Old Testament.

In "Tradition and the Canon of Scripture," F. F. Bruce describes how the canons of both the Old and New Testaments came into being. He also discusses how the Protestant Reformers as well as twentieth century churches view the body of authoritative Scripture called the "canon."

The essays in the second section of this collection focus on the doctrine of the authority of Scripture and its historic development from the Scriptures themselves. Theological dimensions of the Bible are explored, and past scholars' differing understandings of these theological aspects of Scripture are examined.

Dewey M. Beegle offers an analysis of "The Biblical Concept of Revelation." Beegle studies the biblical terms for revelation, its channels, and its range and means. He then describes the concept of revelation itself.

In "The Bible," Donald G. Miller writes of the authority of the biblical revelation. Miller probes the question of how Scripture functions as a self-revelation of God and then writes of how readers of Scripture hear God speaking therein.

Scripture's authority as the written Word is further expounded by Donald G. Bloesch in "The Primacy of Scripture." Bloesch cites a number of contemporary theologians who give expression to Scripture's divine authority, and argues for the Bible's primacy over the church and all religious experience. He also offers insights for hermeneutics and biblical interpretation.

G. C. Berkouwer in "The Testimony of the Spirit" explains the Holy Spirit's role in relation to Scripture. This witness of the Holy Spirit is crucial to the doctrine of Scripture. The work of the Holy Spirit is the only means through which acceptance of Scripture's authority comes.

Clarifications of terms such as "authority," "inspiration," and "inerrancy" — frequently used in discussions about the Bible — are made in H. N. Ridderbos's essay on "The Inspiration and Authority of Holy Scripture." Ridderbos insists on the trustworthiness of Scripture as God's self-revelation expressed through human language, concepts, and images.

Jack B. Rogers explores "The Church Doctrine of Biblical Authority" with an historical survey of the nature of biblical authority and how this authority is known. Rogers moves from the early church through the Reformation period and up to the present day in describing theological formulations about the purpose and form of Scripture.[1]

The third section of this collection surveys current views of biblical authority. Scholars differ on how Scriptural authority

---

[1]This essay is developed much further in Jack B. Rogers and Donald K. McKim, *The Authority and Interpretation of the Bible: An Historical Approach* (San Francisco, 1979).

should be construed and how the Bible should be appropriately interpreted. The flavor of this diversity is given in the presentations of this section.

"The Theological Significance of Historical Criticism" by James D. Smart examines the positive contributions made by historical-critical studies of the Bible. Smart sees historical criticism as opening up the richness and diversity of biblical faith so that the church itself might be renewed.

Finally, Avery Dulles, in "Scripture: Recent Protestant and Catholic Views," details how contemporary Protestant and Roman Catholic theologians view Scripture. His canvass of contemporary theological thought focuses on those writings that accept Scripture as the primary source of God's Word and as the indispensable norm for both church and theology.

It is hoped this collection will be helpful to all who seek a fuller understanding of important issues connected with the current study of Scripture. The essays serve as resources; they provide basic data from which further study can begin, and they focus attention on Scripture as God's revelation of Himself and as His written Word to us.

DONALD K. MCKIM

ABBREVIATIONS

BJRL	*Bulletin of the John Rylands University Library of Manchester*
DS	Denzinger, H., *Enchiridion Symbolorum Definitionum et Declarationum de Rebus Fidei et Morum.* 33d ed. by A. Schönmetzer, S.J., Freiburg, 1965
DV	The Constitution on Divine Revelation of Vatican II *(Dei Verbum)*
ET	English Translation
GD	Bavinck, Herman. *Gereformeerde Dogmatiek*, 4 vols. 4th ed. Kampen, 1928-30
Hist. Eccl.	The *Historia ecclesiastica* of Eusebius
Inst.	Calvin, John. *Institutes of the Christian Religion*
JBC	Brown, R. E. et al. *The Jerome Bible Commentary*
JTS	*Journal of Theological Studies*
NTS	*New Testament Studies*
RGG	*Religion in Geschichte und Gegenwart*
W.A.	*Weimarer Ausgabe.* The "Weimar Edition" of the writings of Luther

AUTHORITY:
Sources
and Canon

1 HOW THE SCRIPTURES WERE FORMED

PAUL J. ACHTEMEIER

Perhaps the most important single issue that separates the modern critical view of Scripture from that of the conservatives lies in the fact that critical scholars take Scripture far more literally. That is, critical scholars are not so much perturbed by discrepancies and errors which a preconceived notion of the nature of Scripture would force them to explain away or harmonize, as they are interested in accounting for them. The difference between the critical view of Scripture and the conservative view is therefore not that the conservatives take the text "literally" while others do not. When discrepancies would result from the literal, face-value reading of the text, the conservative has recourse immediately to a harmonizing process in which one or both of the texts have their literal meaning subordinated to an explanation of the text that will preserve inerrancy: the copyist has made an error, ancient standards of accuracy were different from ours, some event can be constructed which allows both accounts to be true as parts of the total event. These and other explanations are adopted to account for the phenomena of Scripture which, on their face, would render difficult if not untenable the idea of inerrancy.

BIBLE BOOKS FROM EARLIER SOURCES

Instead of constructing such explanations of Scripture to save some prior notion of what Scripture is like, critical scholars, noting that secular literature from the ancient world frequently developed from oral accounts, or from the combination of a number of sources, ask whether that may not also be the case with the literature contained in our Bible. When discrepancies exist, could it be that the discrepant details come from differing accounts, or

---

different sources, which have been combined in our biblical books? When accounts in the Synoptic Gospels differ, could it be that further theological reflection by the community has found a way to phrase an account which allows the point to be made in such a way that irrelevant questions are avoided? When, for example, Mark says that Jesus went to share in John's baptism of repentance for the remission of sin (Mark 1:4– 5, 9), would one not assume Jesus too shared such repentance for sins he had committed? Yet that surely is not what the story intends to say. When Matthew then records John's objections to his baptizing Jesus (Matt. 3:13– 15), the reformulation may be aimed precisely at eliminating speculation about what sins Jesus might have committed that led him to be baptized. Again, when Genesis 17:25 says Ishmael was thirteen years old when Isaac was born, but Genesis 21:14– 15 assumes Ishmael was a babe in arms when Hagar was driven into the wilderness after the birth of Isaac, we have rather clear evidence that the account of Abraham and Hagar has been constructed of various stories that originated independently of one another. In such ways, taking the text "literally" leads to the suggestion that discrepancies in the various accounts are due to combinations of sources, and to their further theological development.

Before we investigate further evidence to support the critical hypothesis that such phenomena as we find in Scripture are best accounted for on the supposition that our biblical books are composed of varieties of traditions which have received differing formulations and interpretations, two points need to be made clear. First, the point of the biblical material is not primarily historical. It is primarily theological. Such historical accounts as there are, are told for the theological point they help to make. This is as true of the patriarchal accounts in Genesis as it is of the Gospels and Acts. Biblical materials are closer in intent to sermons than they are to textbooks of history. That is not to say that historical accounts are not present and that they are not on occasion remarkably accurate. It is simply to say that the traditions were formulated and the biblical books composed not to pass on historical information, but to say something about the ways of God with humankind: in the Old Testament through the fate of the chosen people, in the New Testament with the nascent church. To try to make the Bible speak as a historical chronicle is therefore to pervert its intention and to distort its point.

The second point that needs to be made clear is simply that both critical and conservative scholars formulate constructs in the course of their exegesis. It is not the case that the conservatives take the Bible at its plain and literal meaning, while critical scholars impose theories of source development on Scripture. One can see clearly enough the willingness, even eagerness, of conservative scholars to construct hypothetical events that would then allow them to resolve to their satisfaction discrepancies that occurred in the text. One need think only of the proposal made to resolve the discrepancies of the four Gospel accounts about Peter's denial of Jesus (six times, rather than the unanimous Gospel witness of three times) to realize that conservatives are quick to construct explanations for Scripture which are different from the present text of Scripture. The difference between critical scholars and conservative scholars therefore does not lie in the willingness of one and the unwillingness of the other to impose alien constructs on Scripture. The difference lies in the kind of constructs that are created to account for the present shape of Scripture. Conservative constructs are dictated by the prior assumption that Scripture is inerrant, and whatever is necessary to produce to protect that assumption is produced. Critical scholars assume that when the same phenomena appear in the Bible and in other ancient literature, they have the same cause, and thus the scholars seek to isolate the various traditions which have been woven together in our Bible. Therefore, since both conservative and critical scholars are willing to construct hypotheses to account for the phenomena found in Scripture, the difference between them lies in the assumptions each brings to that Scripture. It is the burden of this chapter to attempt to show that the critical assumptions are truer both to the nature and to the intention of Scripture.

The assumption, then, which critical scholars feel has been forced upon them by the nature of the biblical literature, is that that literature has been composed in many instances of the combination of earlier traditions; that in the transmission of those traditions as well as in their combination, theological reflection and appropriation have continued to occur; and that Scripture therefore reflects the dynamic process at work in the community of Israel, and in the church, as those who stood within these communities sought to understand the significance of their God-directed history. The evidence leading to such an assumption the critical scholar finds overwhelming. We can review only a small fraction of it.

The fact that the biblical books are based on prior sources is in some instances stated by the biblical book itself. Thus, for example, we learn that some of the material in I and II Kings was drawn from the "Annals of the Kings of Israel" (I Kgs. 15:31; 16:20; II Kgs. 10:34; 13:8) and that what was taken was only a selection from that literature. Closer analysis of those books has shown that the historical material is used in the service of a larger, theological purpose, namely, to show that the fate of kings and nations is determined more by their faithfulness to God than by the extent of their national wealth or the size of their armies. The selection from the sources therefore had theological rather than historical intent. Again, the Gospel of Luke begins with an account of the source material available (Luke 1:1 — from the material in Luke it seems apparent that one of those "many" narratives was the Gospel of Mark) and hints that, for this author, that material was in some sense deficient (1:3—4). Recent research on Luke has made abundantly clear that the purpose of that Gospel also is theological rather than simply historical.

In other instances, careful analysis of the biblical book itself gives clear indication that it has been assembled from traditions which have been worked and reworked over a period of time by a variety of authors. The Book of Judges is a clear example of such a process. From a variety of older stories about various heroes of the several tribes of Israel, an account has been constructed to show that neglect of the true God has fearsome consequences for his chosen people. That theme is set out in Judges 2:16— 23. The careful reader will note the recurring pattern of disobedience, disaster, repentance, and rescue. From time to time there are hints that a king would solve such problems, since regal absence produces such chaos. That is the gist, for example, of the closing sentence of the book. From such evidence, scholars have concluded that individual tribal stories were collected and arranged to make a theological point (obedience to God is the critical issue), as well as a political point (kings ensure stability). That political point itself, however, has theological implications, namely, that kings (David is the prime example) who obey God rescue their people.[1]

One can observe the same process at work in the Book of Exodus. There is, for example, a remarkable tension contained in a series of regulations found in Exodus 21 to 23. One finds, on the one hand, regulations that regard slaves as property of their master (21:1— 11, 21), that deny to female slaves the right to be released after six years of service (21:7), that imply women are the property of their fathers, or, if married, of their husbands (22:16— 17, 22), and that regard the value of a human being as

---

[1]This example of Judges, like all the others, has been greatly simplified because of the limitations of space. The evidence itself can be found in any good commentary, such as Robert G. Boling, *Judges*, Anchor Bible series (Garden City, N.Y., 1975), pp. 29— 33.

related to his or her status as slave or free (21:23–25, 26–27, 29–31, 32). On the other hand, one finds regulations that show compassion to aliens (22:21; 23:9), that are especially concerned with widows and fatherless children (22:22–24), that insist the poor are not to be exploited (22:25–27) or suffer injustice (23:6), that are even concerned lest animals be maltreated (23:11–12). Such a contrast is probably best explained by assuming the combination of two sources of regulations, the first tied to the status quo of the society, and reflecting normal cultural values of that time and place, while the second, grounded in the special history of Israel (e.g., 23:9), transcends such regulations and locates the basis of society in the same mercy and justice of God which Israel has experienced in its own national life as chosen people. The clash of divine mercy with conventional social values points not to a static Scripture of eternal immutable laws, but rather to a process whereby God's revelation of himself and his will is taking command of Hebraic national life, the same process we can observe in the prophets.[2]

In some cases, some books are simply rewritten forms of other biblical books, done in an effort to make a new point. The books of Chronicles, for example, are largely a recasting of I and II Kings, done in an effort to accent the importance of the Temple in Jerusalem and in general to claim for Judah priority over the north in religious matters. In an analogous way, Matthew and Luke can be understood as the earliest commentaries on the Gospel of Mark, since they not only add material to Mark's general content, but reorder and in some cases recast that Marcan material. The prophetic books also, as we shall see in more detail, are made up of collected traditions associated with a given prophet, and the books in the New Testament bearing the name "John" (Gospel, Epistles, Revelation) may well be materials produced by those who identified closely with the disciple John and who sought to preserve the traditions associated with his proclamation of the faith.

OLD MATERIAL USED IN NEW WAYS

As is clear from all of this, the biblical authors are by no means enslaved to their traditions. As new situations develop, old traditions are used in new and different ways. For example, the

---

[2]I have excerpted and summarized here the excellent work contained in George W. Coats and Burke O. Long, eds., *Canon and Authority* (Philadelphia, 1977), especially pp. 115–25.

same tradition can be interpreted in quite different ways in two biblical writings. The tradition concerning the selection and blessing of Abraham (Gen. 12:1–3; 17:1–8), whose progeny became great and possessed the Land of Canaan, is cited both in Ezekiel (Ezek. 33:23–29) and in Isaiah (Isa. 51:1–3), yet for diametrically opposed reasons. While the promise is reaffirmed in Isaiah, and is used as the basis for the promise of restoration to Israel, in Ezekiel it is specifically denied and countermanded by God, who through Ezekiel announces that the people may not cite those traditions as a basis for hope and comfort.[3] Again, it is clear from the context in which Mark has placed the saying of Jesus about his true family (Mark 3:31–35) that he means the tradition to cast a negative light on the familial reaction to Jesus: Mark has coupled it with the scribal denunciation of Jesus as demonic (Mark 3:21–35; Mark has inserted the Beelzebul controversy, vv. 23–30, into the story of familial reaction, vv. 21, 31–35). Luke, on the other hand, gives this tradition a positive interpretation by including it in a context that emphasizes the need to seek out Jesus and hold fast to him (Luke 8:4–21). In that setting, the fact that mother and brothers seek him out is an example of the correct attitude toward Jesus. The exclusive tone of the saying in Mark (Mark 3:33–34) is transformed into an inclusive tone in Luke (Luke 8:20–21). Similarly, Matthew and Luke have made different use of the parable of the lost sheep. In Matthew, as wording and context make clear (Matt. 18:10–17), the point is the need for church members to exert every effort to return an erring fellow Christian to the church, whereas in Luke, wording and context show that that author understood the point to be the need to reach out even to those who in that cultural context would be socially unacceptable. The parable in Luke thus points to the missionary need of the church to reach out to sinners and bring them into the Christian fellowship (Luke 15:1–10, especially vv. 2, 10).[4]

It is clear from this that not even the sayings of Jesus were regarded as immutable and unalterable by the authors of the Gospels. Far from having one fixed meaning which remained the

[3] I owe this example to ibid., pp. 31–32.

[4] If, as most scholars agree, one of Luke's sources was Mark, we can speak of Luke's altering the point of the material he got from Mark. In the case of Matthew and Luke, since it appears that neither knew the other's Gospel, it is likely that the parable of the lost sheep appeared in their sources with no context, and Matthew and Luke have provided the kind of context each thought best suited to that parable. Although some scholars think the Lucan context is closer to the original, we are not in a position to make any firm judgments.

same for all time, the sayings of Jesus were evidently regarded as capable of quite different meanings in different situations, and the author who collected those traditions used them to make the theological point he or she thought necessary for those who would read that Gospel. The composition of the Gospels rather clearly proceeds, therefore, along the lines of the collection and interpretation of traditions rather than along the lines of a minutely accurate chronicle of the events of Jesus' life. The purpose is theological rather than chronological or historiographic, as such comparisons of the Gospels with one another make clear.

Again, it is evident that what would on a more rigid view of the nature of the biblical books have to be regarded as discrepancies, and thus as a threat to a view of the Bible as the timeless formulation of unchanging truth, can be explained in a more satisfactory way when one understands that the biblical authors are relying on a variety of traditions as they compose and arrange. On such a view, further, what would under other circumstances appear to be outright contradictions can be understood, if one understands the freedom with which biblical authors could use their traditions, as an interpretative method employed to make a new point in a new situation. Thus, for example, when the author of Psalm 139 feels that the major need is comfort, a tradition of ascent to heaven and descent to Sheol can be used to show the futility, even impossibility, of finding any location that is beyond the sustaining power of God (Ps. 139:8– 10). In another context, the prophet Amos is remembered as having used those very same figures to indicate the futility of finding any place that would be out of reach of the punishment of God (Amos 9:2– 3). Clearly, to expect a tradition to have one, and only one, meaning wherever it appears is to expect something of the biblical materials that they do not intend to provide.[5]

The dynamic nature of biblical traditions is further demonstrated when Amos can take the tradition of the exodus of Israel, which is the chief example and proof of the love and care of God for Israel (e.g., Deut. 7:7– 8), and equate it with the way God rules the fate of other nations, to show that Israel is not immune from her impending doom. Israel can no more point to the land given her as a sign of special divine protection than could the Cushites, the Philistines, or the Arameans (Amos 9:7). Similarly, traditions that remembered the Lord fighting for, and giving vic-

---

[5]An excellent study of this mode of employing traditions can be found in W. Brueggemann and H. W. Wolff, *The Vitality of Old Testament Traditions* (Atlanta, 1975).

tory to, David in his battles against the Philistines are used in another context as evidence that the Lord as holy warrior will fight against Israel and will bring her low. Thus, when there are references in Isaiah 28:21 to the Lord's having arisen at Mount Perazim, where God gave victory over the Philistines (II Sam. 5:17–20), and to God's rage at the valley of Gibeon, where God also told David how to overcome the same foe (I Chr. 14:13–16), they are not, as one would expect, assurances that God will again arise to defend Israel and defeat her enemies. Rather, they are cited as examples of the way God will now turn on Israel and deliver her to her enemies.[6]

Such a reversal of traditions does not always render formerly positive judgments negative in intent. In the course of being produced, some prophetic books were edited in such a way that prophetic oracles which clearly pronounced doom on Israel are used to speak of her eventual restoration. Thus, in Hosea, after the prophet's children are named "Not loved" and "Not my people" to illustrate the fate of Israel (Hos. 1:6–9), a second tradition was introduced, using those same phrases, but this time without the negatives ("You are my people," "You are loved"), to make just the opposite point. Similarly, an appendix was added to Amos (Amos 9:8b–15) which again promised restoration to Israel by directly contradicting the words that had gone before (compare v. 8a with 8b). Thus, a later editor did with the traditional oracles of Amos what Amos in his turn had done with the traditions of comfort and positive promise he had used. In that way, traditions were used and reused, transformed and retransformed in the process of giving to our biblical books the shape in which we now have them.

This same process goes on in the New Testament as well. A clear example can be found in the way the parable of the sower is used in various Gospels. Linguistic hints make it rather clear that Mark is responsible for putting it into its present framework in chapter 4, along with other parables and parabolic sayings. The vocabulary of the explanation of the parable (Mark 4:13–20) makes it likely that it arose at a later time than the parable itself, since the explanation is given in missionary vocabulary that developed after Jesus' resurrection and the subsequent ever widening outreach of Christian proclamation. That explanation, with its emphasis on the fate of the seed in various soils, began a process of turning a parable designed to caution against under-

---

[6]I owe this example to Coats and Long, eds., *Canon and Authority*, pp. 36–37, although it is used there to make a slightly different point.

estimating the importance of Jesus[7] into a statement about missionary expectations: do not become discouraged if some efforts meet with failure (4:15– 19), since the promise of fruitful success is always there and outweighs any failure (v. 20). Luke then uses the parable and explanation as the first of a series of traditions that emphasize the missionary imperative for the church (Luke 8:4– 21) and carries out the account of that missionary activity in the second volume of his work, namely, Acts.

Such use of traditions for different purposes than they originally had can be found not only within the Old and New Testaments but also when the Old Testament is used in the New. When Paul, in his effort to show that faith in Christ rather than performance of the law is now the way God wishes human beings to pursue righteousness, quotes Deuteronomy 30:12– 13, he gives it a meaning quite different from that which it bore in its original setting. Instead of using this passage to show, as Deuteronomy did, that superhuman efforts are not necessary in order to fulfill the commands of the law, since it is not some reality remote from the covenant community, Paul uses the passage to justify his claim that it is precisely that performance of the law which the coming of Christ has rendered useless in God's eyes.[8] In using the tradition from the Old Testament with such freedom, Paul is doing nothing different from the way we have seen other biblical authors and compilers use older traditions. That new meanings are found in old traditions, even meanings which were not those originally intended, is a phenomenon that can be observed repeatedly in both Old and New Testaments, as our examples have shown. Thus, when New Testament authors appear to quote an Old Testament text in a form which differs from that which we find in current texts of the Old Testament or when they discern in a text a meaning other than it may have borne in its original context, they are doing what biblical authors have regularly done in their use of traditions. Far from creating a problem, as such use of texts does for those who want to emphasize an inerrant and hence basically static biblical text, such a practice on the part of New Testament authors simply follows the precedent established by prophets and chroniclers, psalmists and

---

[7]On the meaning of the parable, see my *Invitation to Mark* (Garden City, N.Y., 1978), pp. 69– 70; cf. also my *Mark* in the Proclamation Commentaries Series (Philadelphia, 1975), pp. 65– 69.

[8]An excellent discussion of this point can be found in C. T. Rhyne, *Faith Establishes the Law: A Study of the Continuity Between Judaism and Christianity, Romans 3:31* (Th.D. Dissertation, Union Theological Seminary in Virginia, 1979); see especially p. 18.

narrators in earlier times. It is one more example of the dynamic nature of traditions which is evident in the literature that makes up our Scriptures.

GOD NOT BOUND TO THE PAST

The basic problem which is being exposed here concerns whether or not God works by means of discontinuity as well as continuity. Put in other terms, it concerns the question as to whether God is a God of the past, and hence bound to the history he has created, or whether he is a God of the future, whose future acts can change the significance of history itself. The way in which the prophets used the traditions of the past clearly indicates that they saw God in the latter mode. He is God of the future and is free to re-create the meaning of the past by what he does in the future. That is essentially the difference between the "true" and the "false" prophets. When Hananiah confronted Jeremiah with the message that God would quickly restore Israel and return what had been pillaged by the Babylonians, Hananiah was simply applying to his time the message of Isaiah: God's wrath will be visited upon his chosen people, but when it passes, God will restore his people (Isa. 9:8 to 12:6). That was the prophetic tradition upon which Hananiah called, and it was precisely that which made him a false prophet. Jeremiah was compelled by the Word of God to denounce Hananiah because the traditions upon which he called were precisely the wrong ones for the new time (see Jer. 28). Evidently a rigid adherence to the form that sacred traditions assumed in the past is precisely the wrong way to honor the Word of a God who is living and who is thus the God of the present and the future as well as of the past.[9]

This same use of traditions characterizes the preaching of Jesus. Not only does he set aside divine commands from the past (e.g., Matt. 5:38; cf. Lev. 24:20), he is also quite willing to contradict them, in his words (Mark 10:2–9) as well as in actions he encouraged among his followers (Luke 5:33–38). It was precisely faithfulness to holy traditions of the past that caused Peter to miss the point of a direct Word of God to him about what he was permitted to eat, a Word that he misunderstood though it was repeated three times (Acts 10:9–17).

Clearly, in all of this, it is evident that the Word of God is a

[9]For more on this point, see the work of James A. Sanders, especially *Torah and Canon* (Philadelphia, 1972), and his essay in Coats and Long, eds., *Canon and Authority*.

dynamic reality which does new things in new times and which is therefore not bound to the past. That dynamism of the Word is clearly evident in the way in which traditions themselves are used in the various books of the Bible. Traditions can be used in new ways; they can be altered, then can be reformulated, even contradicted. It is precisely those figures in the biblical literature who find their certainty in the traditions from the past who with alarming regularity find themselves opposed to the will and Word of God.

The kind of examples we have given on the preceding pages could be multiplied into the hundreds. It is the recognition of their existence, and the meaning they have for the nature of Scripture, and therefore the way we understand it, which lies behind the emergence in the past century of the "critical" view of Scripture.[10] Again, we must be clear that the difference between the conservative view of the nature of Scripture and the critical view is not the difference between the imposition of a prior set of constructs on the text, on the one hand (as conservatives accuse critical scholars of doing), and the willingness to take the text seriously as it presently stands, on the other (as conservatives like to claim they do). Conservatives are quite as willing as critical scholars to construct hypotheses to account for Scriptural evidence, and they do it regularly in an effort to defend the prior assumption of inerrancy. Every time a conservative scholar harmonizes discrepancies by appealing to some historic event behind the reports in Scripture, an event which supposedly explains the differences, that scholar is using a construct based on a prior assumption (inerrancy) to account for the present shape of Scripture. It is not a question, as we indicated above, of whether or not a construct is to be permitted to explain the present shape of our Scriptures. It is rather a question of which construct most adequately represents the reality of the Scripture it seeks to understand.[11]

[10]The word "critical" as used in this context does not mean that one is critical of the content of Scripture, but rather that one is critical of one's own prejudices about what it can and cannot mean. Critical scholarship arose in an effort to free interpretation of the Bible from prior understandings of what it could or could not say. The task must obviously still be carried on, and scholars must be critical of their own views as well as of the views of others.

[11]All human understanding involves the construction of hypotheses that enable us to organize and make sense of the phenomena we confront in our daily lives as well as in our scholarly endeavors. In this area, it is the conservative, not the critical scholar who is open to the charge of imposing a prior category onto the understanding of Scripture (viz., that it is inerrant by modern standards).

ONGOING INTERPRETATION

Viewed in that perspective, it becomes clear that to understand
the varied witness in Scripture as the result of continuing attempts to fathom God's will for new times is to understand the
Bible as the product of a living attempt, never ended, to determine into what kind of future the God of Israel and of the church
is leading his people. To understand Scripture in that way, rather
than as a timeless deposit of the will of God that never changes,
is to recognize that the task of interpreting God's will for a new
time is never finished. It is to realize that the creative period for
Scripture is not simply the point of origin, as though God spoke
to his people once and then withdrew again into some cloud of
unknowing that forever after hid his face. Rather, the creative
period of perceiving God's will continues as traditions are interpreted and reinterpreted, as theological reflection on the impact
of a holy God on a sinful world struggles to achieve some clarity
of expression. As that reflection continues, traditions shift, as we
saw, and take on new meanings. Such shifting of tradition can
be simply the adaptation of stories to differing environments.
When Luke, for example, retells the story of the paralytic brought
by friends to Jesus, he describes the roof they dismantle not as
the mud roof of the Palestinian house, as in Mark 2:4, but as the
roof made of tiles familiar to his own readers (Luke 5:19). Such
shifting of traditions, however, can also be as far reaching as the
basic recasting of national traditions. For example, the idea of a
golden age for Israel during the period of desert wandering, known
to Hosea and Jeremiah (Hos. 2:14– 15; 11:1– 3; Jer. 2:2– 3), is
lost in the final casting of that tradition and becomes, instead,
a period of rebellion and apostasy. Even as they wait at the foot
of God's holy mountain, the Israelites profane themselves with
an idol (Exod. 32), and that sets the tone for the whole period,
an interpretation represented in the New Testament when Stephen rehearses the history of Israel as one of such apostasy (Acts
7:2– 53). Similar major recastings occur when the Mosaic covenant tradition finally achieves ascendancy in our canon over the
Davidic covenantal tradition which played so strong a role in the
Isaianic prophecies.[12]
   All of our biblical texts are therefore the products of interpretation of the will of God as that is illumined in a new time by
earlier traditions. Struggling to understand new revelations of
God's purpose for them, Israel and the church turn to older

[12]On this last point, see especially James A. Sanders, pp. 44– 45, 56– 59.

traditions to find some clue to how they may cope with such a dynamic God. Our Scriptures reflect that process, and enshrine that quest. The real threat to a proper understanding of the Bible is therefore to fail to see it in the light of its own origins in this process of interpretation and reinterpretation. To eliminate, through harmonizing and explaining away, the tensions that inevitably result from such struggles to understand God's will for new times is to lose the dynamic witness of the Scriptures to that God. To consider the chief verification of our Gospels some imagined history which one has to reconstruct in order to understand them is to lose the Jesus to whom the Gospels point. The attempts to write a life of Jesus show clearly enough that where historical data are absent and speculation provides it, the result is not the Jesus of history but a Jesus of the pious imagination. What is recovered then is a Jesus as the writer would like him to have been. To consider the chief value of Acts to be a chronicle of the development of the early church, rather than as a theological reflection on what that period had to say for a church which in the author's time was already feeling the stress of division and disunity, is to rob that account of its value for our own similar situation. To harmonize Paul with Acts, in the quest for such a "history," is, as such attempts all too clearly show, to lose Paul as he appears in his letters, with his uncompromising "by faith alone" and his understanding of the radical freedom-responsibility polarity within the Christian faith. To lose the dynamic tensions in the biblical witness, or to want to eliminate them through harmonizing, is thus precisely to lose the witness of Scripture to the dynamic God, who never allows his people to become complacent, or to canonize a holy past.

A further implication of the nature of Scripture as we have outlined it consists in the realization that Scripture has been produced out of the experience of a community as it sought to come to terms with a God whose nature was totally beyond that community's human perceptions and who therefore acted in ways unaccountable by contemporary social or political customs. Scripture reflects not only God's Word to the community but also that community's response, both positive and negative, to that Word. Scripture did not drop as a stone from heaven. It grew out of the life of a community chosen by a God it barely understood and often did not want to follow, yet who would not release his people to their own devices. On the other hand, if the community produced Scripture out of its struggle to shape its life to the will of God, that Scripture also sustained the community in times of severe crisis. If one cannot imagine the Bible without the community whose life and struggle of faith it records, one cannot imagine the community without the traditions that helped it understand and sustain itself. The Christian faith, therefore, is not the response to a holy book. Church and Scripture grew up alongside each other — the traditions shaping the life of the church and the church interpreting and reshaping the traditions in the light of its own proclamation of those traditions. The struggle within the primitive church concerning the question as to whether or not a Gentile had first to become a Jew in order to be a Christian is clearly recorded in Paul's letter to the church in Galatia. When the question was resolved, the resolution itself became a part of the Christian tradition and influenced not only further Scripture (that Gentiles do not need first to become Jews is clearly taken for granted in Acts) but even some of the traditions of the sayings and deeds of Jesus (Mark 7 is clearly intended for Gentile readers who are unaware of Jewish customs — vv. 3–4 — yet who are expected to read and understand Jesus' words). What the traditions in Galatians portray as unresolved conflict the later traditions in Mark (and the other Gospels) and Acts portray as further Christian tradition, now resolved in favor of Gentile converts.

In such ways, the form of Scripture that we have is the form used and shaped by the community as it struggled with its own traditions, whose very struggles in turn were shaped by those same traditions. Scripture is thus the record of the faith and the self-realization of the Christian community as it struggled to understand its own identity and the role God expected it to play in his plan of redemption for a sinful world.

The tensions within Scripture have a further point to make. If the Bible represents the self-understanding of the community that produced it, it is by no means an idealized statement of Christian propaganda. Rather, the Bible, Old and New Testaments alike, is a series of critiques of the very community that produced it. If the New Testament is the product of the church, it is also the church's harshest critic. A cursory reading of the letters of Paul makes clear that they contain a higher proportion of criticism than commendation, and even so irenic a book as Acts betrays the fact that all was not well with the community out of which that book was produced.[13]

It becomes apparent from all of this that the major significance of the Bible is not that it is a book, but rather that it reflects the life of the community of Israel and the primitive church, as those

---

[13]See, e.g., Acts 6:1; 15:1–2; 16:36–39.

communities sought to come to terms with the central reality that God was present with them in ways that regularly outran their ability to understand or cope. Our understanding of the inspiration of that Scripture must therefore take into account the living reality to which the Bible points. We must take into account the church's affirmation that the Bible is the result of the experience of Israel and of the early church with the God who invaded their world and forced them to come to terms with that fact. In some way or other, our understanding of inspiration must reckon with the interrelation of community and Scripture, as well as the continuing process of reinterpretation imposed on Scriptural traditions by the theological reflections of the communities whose life is mirrored in those writings. We must take seriously Paul's insight that the Spirit is given to the community, and that only as members of that community can individuals, themselves bearers of spiritual gifts, enjoy the full range of those gifts (I Cor. 12).

We have now seen, in brief summary, a sketch of the modern critical view of Scripture and the evidence upon which it is based.[14] We have seen how the evidence presented by Scripture itself, the so-called "phenomena," points to an explanation of Scripture as a process in which traditions are formulated and reformulated, interpreted and reinterpreted. This will have a profound effect on the way we understand the inspiration of the writings produced by such a process.

[14] In addition to specific references, I have drawn insight for various points in this chapter from Rahner, *Inspiration in the Bible*, trans. C. H. Henkey (New York, 1961); Leander E. Keck, *The Bible in the Pulpit* (Nashville, 1978), especially chap. 3, "The Bible in the Church"; Leander E. Keck, "The Presence of God Through Scripture," *Lexington Theological Quarterly*, 10 (1975); John L. MacKenzie, "The Social Character of Inspiration" in *Catholic Biblical Quarterly*, 24 (1962); and the work of James Sanders.

2 JESUS AND THE OLD TESTAMENT

ROBERT M. GRANT

Naturally enough, the interpretation of the Bible in Christianity begins with Jesus. This fact might seem sufficiently obvious not to require notice, were it not for the tendency of many modern historical critics to assume that Jesus must have conformed completely to what they call "normative" Judaism. Therefore, they go on to conclude, he must have interpreted the Old Testament, the Bible of Judaism, just as any other Jewish exegete of his day would have expounded it. There is no novelty in his message, at least insofar as it is an interpretation of the Old Testament. And since a great deal of his message is built upon the foundations of Old Testament theology, there can hardly be any novelty in the methods of interpretation which he employed.

Yet there is a saying in the tractate Sanhedrin of the Babylonian Talmud which ought to give these critics pause. "He who says, 'The Torah is not from God,' or even if he says, 'The whole Torah is from God with the exception of this or that verse which not God but Moses spoke from his own mouth' — that soul shall be rooted up."[1] To the Jewish mind every word of scripture had been spoken by God. There could be no question of its inspiration or authenticity. And anyone who uttered such a question clearly revealed his own separateness from the holy congregation of Israel. Here speaks the voice of "normative Judaism." But Jesus, on the other hand, finds a distinct difference between the words by which God joined together Adam and Eve in an enduring bond of marriage and the words by which Moses temporized with the people's hardheartedness and permitted divorce (Mark 10:2ff.). This view would have been intolerable in the "normative Judaism" of Jesus' day and later.

[1]Sanhedrin 99a; B. H. Branscomb, *Jesus and the Law of Moses* (New York, 1930), p. 156.

Clearly Jesus, while he is a Jew and while his mission is primarily to his own people and is expressed in the terms of their thought, does not hesitate to go beyond Judaism and distinguish between parts of scripture in which God is more or less fully revealed. It is this discrimination which underlies all later Christian developments of the theory of interpretation. And yet we must not overemphasize the difference between Jesus and his contemporaries. There are significant resemblances as well.

To Jesus, as to his contemporaries in Judaism, the scriptures were authoritative and inspired. To his opponents, whether human or superhuman, he can quote scripture and say, "It is written . . ." (Mark 11:17; Matt. 4:4; Luke 4:4, and so on). He can ask them, "Have you not read . . . ?" (Mark 2:25). And he can stress the divine source of inspiration of scripture by saying, "David himself said in the Holy Spirit" (Mark 12:36). This is an especially interesting passage, for we find in the contemporary writings of Philo of Alexandria the concept of the inspired writer as an instrument of God. The Holy Spirit of God uses him as a flute and breathes through him. Jesus' expression is not so mechanical. It is the Holy Spirit which inspires David; but it is David who speaks. This is the same emphasis on the human side of inspiration which we find in Jesus' discussion of Moses' bill of divorcement.

Like his contemporaries, Jesus regards Moses as the author of the Pentateuch and David as the author of the Psalms. He was not a literary or historical critic; indeed, it would be incredible if the tradition had reported any interest on his part in literary questions. He regards the events of the Old Testament times as real events. God made man male and female (Mark 10:6); Abel was murdered (Matt. 23:35; Luke 11:51); and so on. And yet they are more than historical events. They have direct relevance to the times in which Jesus stands. When David was hungry he ate the showbread; the regulations of cult must be subordinated to human needs; the Sabbath was made for man (Mark 2:25ff.). With such an appeal to the religious content of scripture as against its merely literal or legal form, Jesus sweeps away the accumulated dust of tradition; he teaches "as one with authority, and not as the scribes" (Mark 1:22). And we are therefore not surprised when he attacks the authoritative exegetes of his day with the ironic statement: "You do well to set aside the commandment of God in order to keep your tradition" (Mark 7:9).

In Jesus' view of scripture there was a strong emphasis on the importance of the vitally religious portions as contrasted with the lesser value of merely cultic prescriptions. His attitude toward the Sabbath and the legal requirement of ritual cleanliness (Mark

7:1ff.) is illustrative of this emphasis. And it can be shown that he quoted definite passages of scripture to support his point of view. In Hosea 6:6 he finds the expression, "I desire mercy and not sacrifice" (Matt. 9:13, 12:7). Or again, in Isaiah 29:13 he finds his opponents described: "This people honors me with their lips, but their heart is far from me; in vain they worship me, teaching as doctrine the ordinances of men" (Mark 7:6f.). And finally, he finds the present state of the temple foretold in Isaiah 56:7 and Jeremiah 7:11: "My house shall be called a house of prayer of all nations; but you have made it a den of thieves" (Mark 11:17). The prophetic reinterpretation of religion is close to that of Jesus himself. And when he comes to express in a single sentence the key to the meaning of the whole law of the Old Testament, he makes use of a passage from Deuteronomy, the "Shema" which every Israelite recited daily: "Hear, Israel, the Lord our God is one Lord, and thou shalt love the Lord thy God . . ." (Mark 12:29f.). With this passage he joins the other "law of love" from the Holiness Code of Leviticus: "Thou shalt love thy neighbor as thyself" (Mark 12:31). Jesus' statement is clear and explicit: "There is no other commandment greater than these." The evangelist Matthew reinterprets it only slightly when he says, "On these two commandments hang all the Law and the prophets" (Matt. 22:40).

The systematic arrangement of the Sermon on the Mount doubtless owes much to the evangelist Matthew.[2] Perhaps the series of antitheses beginning: "You have heard . . . but I say," is not so closely knit as Matthew would have us believe; but as a whole the passage (Matt. 5:21 – 48) reproduces accurately the attitude of Jesus toward the legal portions of the Old Testament. He is a highly independent teacher. He might accurately be called a non-conformist. He does not set aside the Law, however; he deepens it, reinforces it, raises it all to its own highest level. It is sometimes said that the expression, "You have heard . . . but I say," is characteristic of Jewish exegesis; but the examples adduced are not very convincing.[3] The expression is far more characteristic of Jesus himself, whose teaching is a teaching with personal authority. His exegesis is more unlike than like that of his contemporaries.

We have not yet mentioned the way in which Jesus' interpretation of the Old Testament is most strikingly individual. Jesus not only proclaims the imminent and somehow already present

[2]E. v. Dobschütz, "Matthäus als Rabbi und Katechet," *Zeitschrift für die neutestamentliche Wissenschaft* 27 (1928), 338– 48.

[3]J. Bonsirven, *Exégèse rabbinique et exégèse paulinienne* (Paris, 1939), p. 24.

reign of God; he proclaims the fact that it is the fulfillment of the predictions of the great prophets. "The time is completed and the reign of God has drawn near" (Mark 1:15). This knowledge is not esoteric. It is not a mystery known only to Jesus and his disciples. "How do the scribes say that Elijah must come first? Elijah does come first and renews all things. And how is it written of the Son of Man, that he suffers many things and is set at nought?" (Mark 9:11f.). Here Jesus points out that the Elijah who was to precede the reign of God, according to the scribes, is known to him and to them. But what the scribes cannot understand is a figure who suffers. They cannot believe that Isaiah 53 can refer to an individual as well as to the nation. Indeed, Jewish exegesis of Isaiah 53 never interpreted messianically the passages referring to suffering and rejection.[4] Here Jesus' interpretation is unique. He goes beyond contemporary Judaism and interprets the prophecies of the Old Testament in reference to his movement and to himself. It is fairly clear in another passage (Matt. 11:5; Luke 7:22) that Jesus regarded his "signs" as fulfillments of the prophecy of Isaiah. And at the end of his life, in the Last Supper in the upper room, he sealed with his disciples a new covenant which fulfilled the prophecy of Jeremiah (Mark 14:24). Whether or not some of these examples may properly be regarded as influenced more by the theological outlook of the early Church than by the remembrance of Jesus, the idea that he regarded prophecy as somehow fulfilled in himself lies deep in the tradition.

Such an interpretation of scripture was thoroughly repugnant to Jesus' contemporaries. His interpretation of Daniel 7:13 as referring to himself, if we can rely on the somewhat confused testimony of his investigation by the authorities, was called "blasphemy" by the high priest (Mark 14:64). And his free attitude toward the Law brought the accusation that his mission was its destruction (Matt. 5:17). Yet there are passages, not only in the somewhat Judaistic Gospel of Matthew but also in the Gospel of the gentile Luke, which represent Jesus as upholding a rigorous doctrine of scripture like that held by contemporary rabbis. "All scripture is inspired and helpful for teaching" (II Tim. 3:16); this is the Jewish doctrine. And it is reflected in Matthew 5:18 (Luke 16:17): "Until heaven and earth pass away, one *yodh* [the smallest letter of the Hebrew alphabet] or one corner of a letter shall not pass away from the Law." Not even one of the least of the commandments can be "loosed" (Matt. 5:19). And in conformity with this doctrine, Jesus orders a healed leper to show himself to the priest and make the offering which Moses commanded (Mark 1:44).

This paradoxical attitude of Jesus toward the scriptures is in part due to the way in which his sayings were remembered by conservative groups within Jewish Christianity.[5] But to a greater extent it comes from his own double relation to the Old Testament. The Law in itself is what Paul was to call "holy"; the commandment was "holy and righteous and good" (Rom. 7:12). But "love is the fulfillment of the Law" (Rom. 13:10). Moreover, the holy history of the Old Testament is significant not only in itself but also in relation to the greater thing which was to come (Matt. 12:38ff.; Luke 11:29ff.). "You have heard that it was said to the ancients"—and for their time it was the word of God to them—"but I say"—I who speak with all the authority of the prophets, and more.

Ancient Christian analysis and more than a century of modern critical study make it impossible for us to employ the Gospel of John in interpreting the thought of Jesus himself. The ideas which we find expressed in this gospel are often derived from genuine tradition of the sayings of Jesus; but they have been transposed into another key by those who handed down the tradition. They do not represent so much what Jesus taught as what the Church taught in his name. It is the Spirit of truth which comes later and interprets Jesus to a new generation (John 16:13f.). Nevertheless, the attitude of the Johannine Jesus toward the Old Testament is very close to that reported in the synoptic tradition. With his contemporaries in Judaism he knows that Moses gave the Law (John 10:35). And yet Jesus' attitude toward the scriptures is ambiguous. The Law is not all on the same plane. In the Law there is not only the Sabbath but also circumcision; and circumcision takes precedence of the Sabbath (John 7:22). Therefore healings are also permissible on the Sabbath. There is a higher way than simple legalism. Moreover the Jews search the scriptures because they believe that by them they can attain eternal life. These very scriptures contain an element of prophecy which bears witness to Jesus himself (John 5:39), and this is their true and ultimate meaning. The Jews who do not turn to Jesus are without excuse, for Moses himself has pointed the way. "If you believed Moses, you would believe me; for he wrote concerning me. But if you do not believe his writings, how will you believe my words?" (John 5:46f.). It is the Law without its proper prophetic interpretation to which Jesus refers as "your" Law

[5]B. T. D. Smith, *S. Matthew* (Cambridge, 1926), p. 96; Branscomb, p. 216.

(John 8:17, 10:34). It is mere law, misunderstood without the Spirit.

In this question of the true meaning of the Law we come close, as we shall see, to the thought of Paul, especially as it is set forth in II Corinthians, and it is probable that John was not immune to the insights of his great forerunner to the gentiles. And yet we must avoid mechanical distinctions and over-subtle analyses. Jesus and Paul are not unlike in their attitude toward the question of the Old Testament; and any investigation into the relation of their outlooks which results in sharp antitheses between a Jewish Jesus and a Greek Paul can hardly be correct. Both of them faced the final question of the meaning of the Old Testament for the new Israel of God; and their answers were not dissimilar.

A final question requires our attention. What was the relation of this new understanding of the Old Testament to the exegesis of contemporary rabbis? Let us consider an example in which the form and content of Jesus' interpretation lies close to that of his contemporaries. "You have heard that it was said to the ancients, 'Do not swear falsely, but pay your oaths to the Lord' [Lev. 19:12; Exod. 20:7; Num. 30:2]. But I say to you, Do not swear at all; not by heaven, for it is the throne of God; not by earth, for it is the footstool of his feet [Isa. 66:1]; not by Jerusalem, for it is the city of the great king [Ps. 48:2]; not by your head shall you swear, for you cannot make one hair white or black" (Matt. 5:33ff.). The content of this example of exegesis is Jewish; we may compare Sirach 23:9: "Accustom not thy mouth to an oath, and be not accustomed to the naming of the Holy One." The form is also Jewish; it is what the rabbis called *halakah,* from the verb *halak,* to "walk," in the sense of following a way of life.

Another example of Jesus' teaching method which is characteristically Jewish may be found in Mark 12:26f. "Concerning the resurrection of the dead, have you not read in the book of Moses how God spoke to him at the bush and said, 'I am the God of Abraham and the God of Isaac and the God of Jacob' [Exod. 3:6]? He is not the God of the dead but of the living." According to Luke 20:39 some of the scribes said, "Teacher, you have spoken rightly." The answer was typical of the exegesis called *haggada,* theological and mythological interpretation; a very similar example is to be found in IV Maccabees. It illustrated the statement of the oldest midrash on Deuteronomy; "Those who search out the intimations of scripture say, 'If you wish to know the Creator of the world, learn *haggada*; from it you will come to know God and cleave to his ways.' "[6]

These sayings of Jesus have a strong claim to be regarded as genuine, for while they are thoroughly Jewish in form and content, they are preserved in Greek books by Christians to whom the Jewish form was gradually becoming meaningless. And yet they are not simply Jewish. They must be understood in the wider context of all Jesus' sayings. And it must be remembered that there is a striking difference between the underlying eschatological emphasis of Jesus' mission and the rabbis' concentration upon the Law. He looks forward for his inspiration; they look back. Their task has been well described by George Foot Moore in these words:

> To discover, elucidate, and apply what God ... teaches and enjoins [in the Law] is the task of the scholar as interpreter of scripture. Together with the principle that in God's revelation no word is without significance this conception of scripture leads to an atomistic exegesis, which interprets sentences, clauses, phrases, and even single words, independently of the context or the historical occasion, as divine oracles; combines them with other similarly detached utterances; and makes large use of analogy of expressions, often by purely verbal association.[7]

This is not the exegesis of Jesus.

In summary we may say that while often the form and sometimes the content of the sayings of Jesus is very similar to that of contemporary rabbis, his underlying outlook is different from theirs. In the first place he does not hesitate to criticize scripture and to interpret it in relation to its own highest utterances, which are words of God. Love of God and love of neighbor are the two great commandments in whose light the rest must be regarded. In the second place, he frequently points to the fulfillment of the prophecies of scripture in his mission. The messianic interpretation of scripture is not novel. We find something closely resembling it in the Dead Sea Scrolls, with their interpretations of prophetic passages as referring to the Teacher of Righteousness. What is novel is Jesus' proclamation that the reign of God is at hand and is being inaugurated in his own work.

Indeed, the story of the paradoxical "triumphal entry" into Jerusalem seems to show that Jesus was consciously fulfilling the prophecy of Zechariah 9:9: "Behold, thy king cometh unto thee,

---

[6]Sifre Deuteronomy, 49 end, cited by G. F. Moore, *Judaism in the Age of the Tannaim*, Vol. I (Cambridge, 1927), p. 319.

[7]Moore, p. 319; reprinted by permission of the Harvard University Press.

lowly, and riding upon an ass, even upon a colt the foal of an ass." Neither Mark nor Luke refers to the prophecy of the peaceable king; Matthew (21:4) says that the entry took place so that what was spoken through the prophet might be fulfilled; and John (12:16) states that "his disciples did not know these things at first, but when Jesus had been glorified they then remembered that these things had been written of him and that people had done these things for him." Scholars have often suspected that the literary evidence shows that the relating of Zechariah to the entry was the creation of the early Church. The evidence suggests just as strongly that the relating was the Church's discovery of the real intention of Jesus.

At this point there is a difference between ancient and modern understandings of Jesus' mission. An ancient Christian would conclude that Jesus was simply indicating, in a veiled manner, that he was the king whose coming was predicted by the prophet. A modern student of the gospels might go on to consider the events which, according to Mark and Matthew, follow the entry. He might be impressed by the relation of the cleansing of the temple to the prediction of cleansing in Zechariah 14:21. He might find the saying about the casting of "this mountain" into the sea (Mark 11:23) related to the prediction of Zechariah 14:4 that the Mount of Olives would be split "toward the east and toward the west" (in Hebrew, "toward the sea"). He could then suggest that as Jesus fulfilled one part of the prophecy, either he or his disciples, or both, expected that the rest of the events predicted would take place; since the events did not take place and the fig tree did not bear fruit out of season, Jesus realized that the cup of suffering was not to be taken away from him (Mark 14:36) and that his way could be only the way of the cross. Such a picture of Jesus' attitude toward prophecy remains conjectural, but it cannot be excluded on dogmatic grounds. For "of that day or that hour no one knows, neither the angels in heaven nor the Son, but only the Father" (Mark 13:32). With ancient theologians, modern students of the gospels have to accept what the New Testament tells them of the humanity of Jesus.

The saying in Matthew 13:52 about the Christian scribe, as Klostermann pointed out,[8] can well be applied to Jesus himself:

> Every scribe instructed in the kingdom of heaven is like a householder who brings out of his treasure-chest things new and things old.

[8] E. Klostermann, *Jesu Stellung zum Alten Testament* (Kiel, 1904), p. 28.

3 PAUL AND THE OLD TESTAMENT

ROBERT M. GRANT

At the end of the nineteenth century it was customary for critics to distinguish sharply between "the religion of Jesus" and "the religion about Jesus." The first was the highest form of Judaism; the second was Christianity. Sometimes the question was asked, "Jesus or Paul?"—for Paul was the founder of the Christian faith. More recent study has come to reject this dichotomy and to insist on the continuity between Jesus and his greatest apostle. This continuity is evident in the attitudes of Jesus and of Paul toward the interpretation of the Old Testament.

Paul was acquainted with collections of sayings of the Lord,[1] and through these he was aware of what Jesus had taught in regard to the Old Testament. The new covenant of the Lord had fulfilled the prophecies of the Old Testament (I Cor. 11:25). Moreover, the early Church before Paul had contributed its own interpretations of the suffering and victory of Christ. His death for our sins and his resurrection on the third day took place "according to the scriptures" (I Cor. 15:3f.). It is difficult for us to determine how much of his exegetical theory Paul owes to his predecessors in the Christian faith. In any event, the general interpretation of the Old Testament in terms of Christ is due to them.

In the rejection of legalism, Paul's thought resembles the teaching of Jesus. He knows that the Law as a book of legal ordinances was our enemy. It brought a curse even to those who tried to keep its commandments, for in Deuteronomy 27:26 it says, "Cursed is everyone who does not abide in all the things written in the book of the law to do them" (Gal. 3:10). Paul takes the Christian understanding of the Law from Jesus. It is summed

---

[1]See my note in *Harvard Theological Review* 39 (1946), 71ff.

Reprinted with permission of Macmillan Publishing Co., Inc. from A Short History of the Interpretation of the Bible *by Robert M. Grant, pp. 28–42. Copyright © 1948, 1963 by Macmillan Publishing Co., Inc., renewed 1976 by Robert M. Grant.*

up in a single sentence: "Thou shalt love thy neighbor as thyself" (Gal. 5:14; Rom. 13:9).

Both to Jesus and to Paul, the Old Testament is a book of hope. But Paul, who lives after the death and resurrection of Jesus, is able to discover many messianic allusions which could hardly have been found earlier. For example, his interpretation of Christ as the second Adam is not given him by Jesus himself, but by a combination of current Jewish speculation with Christian awareness of the significance of redemption. The experience of the Church, the body of Christ, was also prefigured in the story of Israel. The fathers were "baptized" in the cloud and in the sea at the Exodus, and they ate "spiritual" food and drank "spiritual" drink in the desert. These were foreshadowings of the Eucharist (I Cor. 10:2ff.).

There are striking differences between the exegetical thought of Jesus and of Paul. Paul lives after the crucifixion. He sees the tragedy of legalism. Christ himself had become "a curse" for us when he was crucified; for the Law says, "Cursed is everyone who hangs on a tree" (Deut. 21:23; Gal. 3:13). While Jesus criticized the Law he did not carry his criticism to the point of absolute rejection. Again, Jesus is not a theologian; indeed, he is the despair of theologians. No systematic treatment can do justice to the richness and variety of his thought. Paul, on the other hand, has a naturally theological mind. His is not our type of theology, to be sure. More often than not, his mind moves allusively, intuitively, by verbal association rather than by any obvious logical process. He was not a Greek, trained in a Platonic or Stoic school; he was a Jew, brought up at Jerusalem at the feet of Gamaliel (Acts 22:3). "Philosophy" for him means only "vain deceit" (Col. 2:8).

There are several passages in his letters where Paul makes some effort to express systematically his conceptions of exegesis. In the first place, we may consider the words which he uses in setting forth the relation between the history contained in the Old Testament and the history of new Israel, the Church. The word "type," which he employs several times, ordinarily means simply "example"; in I Thessalonians 1:7 the church at Thessalonica is described as "an example to all the believers in Macedonia and Achaea," while in II Thessalonians 3:9 the apostle himself is an example for them to imitate. In I Corinthians 10:6 the word is used in what was to become a semitechnical expression. The whole story of the Exodus took place on behalf of us who are Christians: "these things were our types, so that we should not be desirers of evil." In an earlier passage the same thought is expressed without the use of the word. "In the law of

Moses it is written: Thou shalt not muzzle the plowing ox. Does God care for oxen? or does he speak, doubtless, on our account? For us it was written" (I Cor. 9:9f.). Here the idea is not so much of an obvious example, or type, as of a hidden mystery, which might almost be called allegory.[2] In Romans 5:14 Adam is called "a type of one to come." He is not simply an example, for he corresponds to Christ not only by resemblance but also by difference. In many instances Christ comes to reverse his work; Paul emphasizes this relationship in I Corinthians 15.

Another word lies close to Greek rather than to Jewish exegetical theory, and yet when we examine Paul's use of the expression, we see that it lies within the limits of Judaism. He employs the word in his letter to the Galatians:

> It is written, Abraham had two sons, one from the slave girl and one from the free [Gen. 16:15]. The one from the slave girl was born according to the flesh, but the one from the free, through the promise. These things are *meant allegorically:* for they are two covenants, one from Mount Sinai in Arabia; but it is parallel to the present Jerusalem, for it is in slavery with its own children. But the Jerusalem above is free; which is our mother (Gal. 4:22–26).

The words *meant allegorically* (*allegoroumena*) are from a verb commonly used by Greek interpreters, especially by Stoics who interpreted allegorically and explained away the myths concerning the gods. According to these exegetes, some of whom were Paul's contemporaries, "saying one thing and signifying something other than what is said is called allegory."[3] They proceeded to interpret Homer, for example, as if it were an allegory. They looked for hidden mysteries under the outward forms. Similarly Paul goes far beyond the literal or historical understanding of the story in Genesis when he finds in it prefigured the enslaved Israel and the free. He is reading into it a theory which the story cannot literally bear. But his interpretation is not the same as allegorization. He does not deny the reality of the Old Testament history. Moreover, there is a sense in which the figures of the Old Testament were actually intended to be examples, and if it is proper to look for such examples in Exodus or Deuteronomy, it is also proper to find them in the story of Abraham's two sons. Paul's theory is not entirely forced.[4]

Our understanding of Paul's interpretation of the Old Testa-

---

[2]It should be observed that Deuteronomy 25:4 is entirely unrelated to its context. Thus the idea of a hidden meaning could arise, as in the case of Melchizedek.

[3]Pseudo-Heraclitus, *Quaestiones homericae,* 6.

[4]J. Bonsirven, *Exégèse rabbinique et exégèse paulinienne* (Paris, 1939), pp. 309f.

ment does not depend merely on the words which he uses in setting it forth. More important is the content which he is able to find in scripture. His exegesis is Christocentric. To him Jesus is the promised Messiah, and not only the passages which explicitly foretell his coming but the scriptures as a whole are full of references to him. We have already seen that Paul finds the death and resurrection of Christ pretypified in scripture. He does not say where the types are to be found, but we may suspect that in Isaiah 53 he found the death of Christ and in Hosea 6:2 (or perhaps in the book of Jonah) he found his resurrection.

For Paul, as for ancient Christians generally, the meaning of Christ was not to be understood apart from the history of God's plan of redemption which, beginning with the old Israel, found its culminating point in the creation of a new Israel, the Church. Paul shares with other Christians an understanding of the mystery of God's working in history. This understanding is both based on and largely responsible for his exegesis. In the light of his experience of the crisis of human history which confronted him in Christ, he finds other crises in the history of Israel and believes that they are types which prefigure the events of his own day. The first crisis is that of Adam's fall, by which sin and death entered the world (Rom. 5:12). The second crisis is the faithfulness of Abraham, which was "reckoned to him for righteousness" (Gal. 3:6). The third crisis is the giving of the Law through angels to Moses, "because of transgressions" (Gal. 3:19). The fourth crisis is the crucifixion and resurrection of Christ. Each of these crises is meaningful for us, for each took place on behalf of us who are Christians. "As in Adam all die, so in Christ all shall be made alive" (I Cor. 15:22). The promise of blessing which God made to Abraham and to his seed applies to Christ and therefore to Christians (Gal. 3:16). Christ has redeemed us from the Law (Gal. 3:13); "the law of the Spirit of life in Christ Jesus has freed you from the Law of sin and death" (Rom. 8:2). And the crucifixion and resurrection of Christ point forward to our own death and resurrection with him (Rom. 6:3f.; Col. 3:1ff.).[5]

A significant example of Paul's rabbinic exegesis is to be found in one of the proofs which he gives for his interpretation of the biblical history:

> The promises were spoken to Abraham and to his seed. It does not say, And to seeds, as in the case of many, but, as in the case of one, And to thy seed—who is Christ (Gal. 3:16).

[5]Cf. W. Morgan, *The Religion and Theology of Paul* (Edinburgh, 1917), pp. 3ff.; E. Stauffer, *Die Theologie des Neuen Testaments* (Geneva, 1945), pp. 3ff.

In Genesis 13:15 (17:19) the word "seed" is of course a collective noun. It refers to the heirs of Abraham considered as a whole. By insisting on a rigorous literalism which he elsewhere ignores (II Cor. 11:22), Paul is able to interpret the word in reference to Christ. How can he do so? He is not considering Christ merely as an individual, but as constituting a body with all the righteous who live by faith in him. The blessing of Abraham does not come down to Christ alone, but to us. It might almost be said that "Christ" is a collective noun as well as "seed." While the form of Paul's exegesis is rabbinic and verbal, its underlying thought is more profound.[6]

Another interesting example is set forth in I Corinthians 10:1ff., where the experience of the children of Israel at the Exodus is understood as an example for Christians. In the verse from Galatians cited above, Paul relies on a completely literal and verbal exegesis; in this passage from I Corinthians, his interpretation is very free and his quotation of the Old Testament is not exact:

> I want you to notice, brethren, that our fathers were all under the cloud and all passed through the sea, and were all baptized in Moses' name in the cloud and in the sea, and all ate the same spiritual food, and all drank the same spiritual drink; for they drank from a spiritual rock that followed them, and the rock was Christ.

Here we notice not only the use of Christian terms to describe the spiritual experience of Israel, but also the use of non-biblical elements in the story. In the Bible there is no rock which follows the Israelites. But the theory that such a rock existed is easy to explain on the basis of the biblical accounts. According to the three accounts of the miraculous gift of water (Exod. 17, Num. 20, and 21:16ff.) the water was given at three different places. What could be more natural than to suppose, therefore, that the miracle was still more miraculous? The rock followed the Israelites. And so we find the story told in the Targum of Pseudo-Jonathan.[7] But the rock did not merely follow the Israelites; the rock was Christ. This idea has two possible sources. In the first place, to Paul Christ was the preexistent Wisdom of God, described in the Old Testament, which was God's instrument in the creation and providential care of the world. Now, according to Philo of Alexandria, the rock which gave forth water to the Israelites was to be identified with Wisdom. In the second place, in the Last Supper

---

[6]Bonsirven, pp. 298f. When Paul repeats his argument about the promise in Romans 4, he does not interpret "seed" in this way.

[7]O. Michel, *Paulus und seine Bibel* (Gütersloh, 1929), p. 29.

Christ gave spiritual food and drink to his disciples; this spiritual food and drink is his own body and blood; therefore the rock which gives spiritual drink must be identified with him. Is this exegesis arbitrary? The religious experience of Christians in their redemption from sin and death can be interpreted symbolically in terms of the saving of Israel from Egypt. And if the language of religion is naturally symbolic, we may find Paul's exegesis confirmed, not indeed by logic, but by the imaginative understanding which comes from faith.

With the mention of faith we come to what is perhaps the most important aspect of Paul's interpretation of the Old Testament. Why is it, he asks, that the Jews, to whom God originally gave the scriptures, cannot understand them as Christians do? Why do they not see the types and allegories which lie before them? His answer is set forth in the Second Epistle to the Corinthians. It is based on an Old Testament example. After Moses had spoken with God on Mount Sinai, his face shone so brightly that it was necessary for him to wear a veil with the children of Israel (Exod. 34):

> Until this very day the same veil remains, not taken away, in the reading of the Old Covenant; it is done away in Christ. Even to this day when Moses is read the veil lies on their heart; "but when he returns to the Lord, the veil will be taken off" [Exod. 34:34]. Now "the Lord" means the Spirit; and where the Spirit of the Lord is, there is freedom (II Cor. 3:14ff.).

Here Moses is not only a type of the Old Testament but also a type of the unbelieving Israelite, who must return to the Lord as Moses did. Who is the Lord? He is the Spirit, who interprets the scriptures to the Christian heart, without a veil. The Spirit brings us freedom from the letter of the Old Testament. God has made us "ministers of the New Covenant, not of the letter but of the Spirit; for the letter kills, but the Spirit makes alive" (II Cor. 3:6). The letter is not the Old Testament as such; it is the Old Testament as a legal document, as the unconverted Israelites interpret it. By the aid of the Spirit we are able to understand the Old Testament as a spiritual book.[8]

The reason that others cannot thus understand the Old Testament is simply that they have not received the gift of the Spirit. They have been blinded, indeed blinded by Satan:

> If our gospel is hidden, it is hidden for those who are perishing, in whom the god of this age has blinded the minds of unbelievers,

[8]Ibid., pp. 178f.

so that the light of the glorious gospel of Christ, who is the image
of God, cannot shine (II Cor. 4:3f.).

Here is the ultimate basis of Pauline exegesis. The true understanding of the Old Testament comes from God. Those who do
not possess this true understanding have been blinded. Argument
is possible, even argument on purely rational grounds (II Cor.
4:2; cf. Rom. 2:15); but it can never convince those who do not
share the gift of faith.

What shall we say of the form of Paul's exegesis? We have seen
that its governing principles make it Christian; everything is finally determined by its reference to Christ. But in its outward
aspects his interpretation of the Old Testament is not unlike the
interpretation of some of his rabbinic contemporaries. Such similarities are what we should expect to find when we recall the
statement in the Acts (22:3) that Paul was educated "at the feet
of Gamaliel." And the analysis provided by the best modern
scholars confirms this statement. Here we shall give only a few
examples.

In the first place, Paul takes great liberties with the original
meaning of passages he cites. The context means very little to
him. Consider the quotation of Psalm 69:9 in Romans 15:3:

> Let each one of us please his neighbor for good, for edification;
> for even Christ did not please himself; but as it is written, "The
> reproaches of those who reproached you fell on me."

In the Gospel of John another part of the same verse is interpreted in reference to Christ: "Zeal for your house has consumed
me" (John 2:17). While to us this may appear an improper use
of a single verse out of a psalm which does not seem to be messianic, the early Church found many messianic predictions in the
psalms. And the rabbis often interpreted them in the same way.
To one who knew the story of Christ's ministry, such exegesis
would not seem arbitrary. And Paul goes on to justify his interpretation in the next verse of his letter: "Whatever things were
previously written were written for our instruction, in order that
through patience and through the encouragement of the scriptures we might have hope." This rabbinic principle is cited in
order to justify characteristic rabbinic exegesis.

Another example of exegesis which is Christocentric in content
and rabbinic in form is to be found in the first chapter of Colos-
sians. Of Christ, Paul says:

> He is the image of the invisible God, the firstborn of all creation,
> for *in* him were created all things in the heavens and on the earth,

the visible and the invisible, thrones, lordships, principalities,
powers; all things were created *through* him and *for* him; and he
is *before* all things, and all things have their consistency in him;
and he is the head of the body, the Church; he is the beginning
. . . (Col. 1:15ff.).

At first sight this passage appears to be a rhapsodic description
of the preexistent Christ. But it is actually a typical result of
rabbinic exegesis, with its underlying presuppositions stated only
in part. Paul begins by recognizing Christ prefigured in Proverbs
8:22, where Wisdom describes God's use of her in creation. Since
Christ, the Wisdom of God, is God's agent in creation, we must
naturally look for further light on his meaning in the creation
story of Genesis. There it is stated that "in the beginning God
made heaven and earth" (Gen. 1:1). The well-trained rabbinic
interpreter will endeavor to define more closely the meaning of
the preposition "in." Is it merely locative? Or does it not rather
define the agency of creation? By comparing Proverbs 8:22 we
can see that it must describe the agency used by God, and we
can express this still more clearly by replacing "in" with other
prepositions, all of which seem to be applicable. "Through" this
"beginning" and "for" him God made heaven and earth; he is
"before" them and "with" them. One further deduction can be
made from scripture: since in Paul's native tongue the same word
means "beginning" and "head," there is clearly pretypified the
Christ who is not only the beginning of creation but head of his
body, the Church.[9]
    We may wonder at the way in which so imposing a structure
is raised on what to us may seem so slight a foundation; and yet,
given the general rule of Christocentric interpretation, as well as
the rabbinic principle of the value of every word in scripture, the
demonstration proceeds logically.
    Perhaps the most instructive example of Christocentric inter-
pretation, combined with verbal exegesis, is to be found in Romans 10:5–10. Here, in the light of Paul's certitude of salvation
by faith, he does not hesitate to analyze a passage of the Old
Testament in which salvation by works is set forth and to conclude that it proves salvation by faith! Moses writes (Lev. 18:5)
that the man who does the righteousness which is of the Law
shall live by it (Rom. 10:5). There is another passage in the Law
which states that the performance of the Law is not impossible,
or even difficult; and since this passage is contrary to Paul's own
view (Rom. 7), he finds that he must explain it away. The passage in Deuteronomy (30:11ff.) is as follows:

[9]C. F. Burney, "Christ as the APXH of Creation," *JTS* 27 (1925–26), 160ff.

> For this commandment which I command thee this day, it is not
> too hard for thee, nor is it far off. It is not in heaven, that thou
> shouldst say, Who shall go up for us to heaven, and bring it to
> us, and make us hear it, that we may do it? Nor is it beyond the
> sea, that thou shouldst say, Who shall go over the sea for us, and
> bring it to us, and make us hear it, that we may do it? But the
> word is very near to thee, in thy mouth, and in thy heart, that
> thou mayst do it.

For the legal righteousness of the old covenant, Paul substitutes
the righteousness of faith of the new covenant, and in true rabbinic fashion glosses each phrase to make it conform with this
own thought.

> But the righteousness which is of faith speaks thus: Do not say in
> your heart, Who shall go up to heaven (*that is, to bring Christ down*)
> or, Who shall go down into the deep (*that is, to bring Christ up from
> the dead*)? But what does it say? The word is near thee, in thy
> mouth, and in thy heart (*that is, the word of faith which we preach*).
> For if you confess with your mouth Jesus as Lord, and believe in
> your heart that God raised him from the dead, you will be saved;
> for the heart's belief results in righteousness, and the mouth's
> confession results in salvation.

Paul believes that unless the Old Testament writer had Christ in
mind, his expressions would be meaningless. For it is Christ who
came down from heaven, who rose from the dead, who brought
the gift of salvation. We may compare a similar exposition of
Psalm 68:18 in the fourth chapter of Ephesians. In neither case
are the *gesta Christi* obviously in the text; and as Bonsirven observes, "The strangest thing for us is that they [the examples of
exegesis] take the form of a demonstration."[10]
    These examples must suffice to show us the rabbinic form of
Paul's exegesis of the Old Testament. The most striking feature
of it is its verbalism, its emphasis on single words at the expense
of contexts. And yet, as we have said, once we admit the Christocentric reference of the Old Testament we can understand it
sympathetically. In the light of historical interpretation we should
hesitate to insist on the permanent validity of the way in which
Paul works out his interpretations. But for Christians the Old
Testament is not a self-sufficient book. Its message is not complete. It looks forward beyond its own time to the coming of one
who we believe came in Jesus.
    When we have examined instances of Christians rabbinism in
Paul's letters we have not finished our task. It is obvious that

[10]Bonsirven, p. 307; cf. Philo, *De paenitentia*, p. 183.

there is a striking difference between their work and his. He writes in Greek. The significance of this fact must not be over-valued; there was much Greek in Jewish Palestine; and Greek philosophical thought persistently influenced Judaism. We should, however, compare Paul's exegesis with that of another Jew who wrote in the Greek language. And we shall find a few remarkable similarities between the exegetical work of Paul and that of Philo of Alexandria.

Paul's emphasis on the singular "seed" in Galatians 3:16 finds a parallel in Philo's stress on the singular "child" in Genesis 17:16 (*De mutatione nominum*, 145); again, both Paul and Philo find hidden meanings in names, especially the names of persons important in biblical history. Both Paul and Philo allegorize the name of Hagar (Gal. 4; *Legum allegoriae*, III.244). A more important example is to be found in Paul's identification of the miraculous rock with Christ; Philo identifies it with Wisdom or the Logos (*Legum allegoriae*, II.86; *Quod deterius potiori insidiari soleat*, 118).

Perhaps we may not agree with Michel's conclusion that, in spite of differences, the exegesis of Philo is closer to that of Paul than is that of the rabbis. But we can make his suggestion our own, that both Philo and Paul are dependent on the exegetical tradition of the synagogue.[11] Both differ from the rabbinic exegetical tradition, however, in their outlook. For both Philo and Paul are apostles to the gentiles. Both Philo and Paul make use of the terminology of Greek rhetoric.

Yet Paul cannot be explained merely in terms of his Jewish and Greek sources. His whole personality was changed by his experience of conversion. It is possible that like other converts he somewhat exaggerated the extent of the change; but it is true, especially in regard to his view of the Old Testament, that it is no longer he who lives, but Christ who lives in him (Gal. 2:20). He has died to the Law, through the Law, that he may live to God (Gal. 2:19). His interpretation of scripture cannot possibly be what it was in his pre-Christian life. The Old Testament remains scripture; but it is no longer letter, but Spirit; no longer Law, but a ministry of grace. And in it everywhere is Christ; for Christ is the end of the Law (Rom. 10:4) and we now serve in newness of the Spirit and not in oldness of the letter (Rom. 7:6). A specifically Christian interpretation of the Old Testament has come into existence.

---

[11]Michel, p. 111. Cf. W. L. Knox, *Some Hellenistic Elements in Primitive Christianity* (London, 1944), pp. 34ff.

4 THE INTERPRETATION OF THE OLD TESTAMENT IN THE NEW

C. K. BARRETT

EXEGETICAL METHOD

Most of the writers of the New Testament were Jews, and all were children of their own age. It is therefore not surprising that their work bears many resemblances to that of Philo, the rabbis, and the Qumrân exegetes. It is true that the New Testament contains no formal and continuous commentary on any book of the Old Testament;[1] this serves to underline the fact that we owe the New Testament to a new and creative outburst of religious feeling and theological thinking, an event in which men were deeply conscious of the novelty and spontaneity of their ideas and experiences. Apart however from the absence of such extended expository material, the parallelism between the New Testament and contemporary Jewish use of the Old Testament is close. This will be considered first in respect of form.

In the New Testament, Old Testament material is often introduced without any citation formula, and sometimes without any indication that the Old Testament is being used. The wording of the Old Testament is taken over and woven into narrative or argument. Sometimes the context makes it clear that the Old Testament is employed, as for example in Stephen's speech in Acts 7. Here a good deal of Old Testament history is summarised and, as a glance in a copy of the New Testament where Old Testament words are printed in capitals or heavy type will show, there is frequent use of the wording of scripture, though it is not till verse 42 that a formal quotation occurs (*As it is written in the book of the prophets* . . .). Again, in I Peter 2:1−10, though only verse 6 (Isa. 28:16) is marked down as a quotation (*It is contained*

---

[1]See however pp. 52, 54f., on Testimony Books.

Reprinted from "The Interpretation of the Old Testament in the New" by C. K. Barrett in The Cambridge History of the Bible, *Vol. 1, eds. P. R. Ackroyd and C. F. Evans, pp. 389−411, by permission of Cambridge University Press. Copyright © Cambridge University Press 1970.*

in scripture . . .), the application throughout the paragraph of language dealing with the people of God is sufficient to show that the Old Testament is being used. Often, however, if the reader were not familiar with the Old Testament passages involved, it would be impossible to pick them out from the apparently continuous material which the New Testament presents. There is a notable narrative example in Mark 15:24: "They divided his clothes, casting lots for them" (διαμερίζονται τὰ ἱμάτια αὐτοῦ, βάλλοντες κλῆρον ἐπ' αὐτά). This can be read as a straightforward account of the actions of the soldiers at the crucifixion. Matthew (27:35) and Luke (23:34) use similar words, and give no more indication than Mark that a quotation is involved. John, however (19:24), refers specifically to a passage of scripture (γραφή), and the reader turns to Psalm 22:18: "They divided my clothes among them, and for my clothing they cast lots" (διεμερίσαντο τὰ ἱμάτιά μου ἑαυτοῖς, καὶ ἐπὶ τὸν ἱματισμόν μου ἔβαλον κλῆρον). It is now impossible to doubt that Mark 15:24 was framed (either by Mark or by some earlier editor of the gospel tradition) in terms of the Old Testament and that the reader was intended to pick up the allusion, even though the evangelist did not help him to do so. It was even easier for Old Testament material to be worked into hortatory and theological passages. Thus it would be easy to read Ephesians 4:25f. ("Forsaking falsehood, speak truth, each man with his neighbour, for we are members of one another. Be angry but do not sin; let not the sun go down on your anger") without observing the references to Zechariah 8:16 ("Speak truth, each man to his neighbour") and Psalm. 4:4 ("Be angry but do not sin"). There is, again, nothing to indicate that the last two verses of the Christological hymn of Philippians 2:6–11 rest upon I Kings 19:18 (Septuagint) and Isaiah 45:23.

The use of the Old Testament in the New Testament is thus a much larger matter than direct, indicated quotation. There are, however, such quotations, and they are often marked out by citation formulas. Of these the most common reflect the fact that the Old Testament was known as a written book: *as it is written, for it is written*, and the like (καθὼς γέγραπται, γέγραπται γάρ). These recall the rabbinic use of *that which is written* (kāṯûḇ),[2] and hardly call for comment. Less common in the New Testament is the use of a verb of *saying* (e.g., καθὼς εἴρηται); this recalls the very common Hebrew *as it is said* (šeneʾemar). Both the New Tes-

---

[2] In such expressions as keʾmāh šekāṯûḇ.

tament writers and the rabbis on occasion personify scripture, as in such expressions as *Scripture says* (e.g., Rom. 10:11, λέγει γὰρ ἡ γραφή; cf. *kaṯuḇ 'omēr*). Its authors, or supposed authors, are also represented both as writing and as speaking; for example,

> Mark 12:36. "David himself said in the Holy Spirit" (cf. Luke 20:42, "David said in the Book of Psalms").
> Mark 7:10. "Moses said"; 12:19 "Moses wrote."
> Mark 7:6. "Isaiah prophesied."
> Romans 9:27. "Isaiah cried out" (κράζει).
> Romans 10:20. "Isaiah is so bold as to say."

The supernatural element in scripture is more strongly stressed when its human authors are represented as mere mouthpieces for divine speakers; for example,

> Matthew 1:22. "All this happened in order that what was spoken by the Lord through the prophet might be fulfilled."
> Acts 4:25. ". . . who by the Holy Spirit said through the mouth of our father David . . ."[3]

Many Jewish forms and methods of exegesis recur in the New Testament.

A. The New Testament employs allegory. An outstanding example occurs in Galatians 4, where Paul refers to the story of Abraham and of the sons Ishmael and Isaac born to him by the slave Hagar and the freewoman Sarah respectively, the one in the course of nature, the other as the result of divine promise. "These things," he adds, "are allegories" (ἔστιν ἀλληγορούμενα).[4] The two women are covenants; their children are those who are born under the Law, and those who (as Christians) are born for freedom. Paul is not yet at an end, for he introduces also Mount Sinai in Arabia, the present Jerusalem, the heavenly Jerusalem, and the persecution of the freewoman's offspring by that of the slave. This is the most extended, but not the only, allegory in the New Testament.

B. Occasionally interpretations are found which are cast in a form akin to the *pešer* form of the Qumrân commentaries. Perhaps the best example is the treatment of Deuteronomy 30:12f. in Romans 10:6f.

> Do not say in your heart, Who shall ascend into heaven? that is, to bring Christ down; or, Who shall descend into the deep? that is, to bring Christ up from the dead.

---

[3]The Greek here is notoriously obscure, but the main point is not in doubt.
[4]For the verb cf. Philo, *De Vita Contemplativa*, 28f.

This requires little modification to become:

> Do not say in your heart, Who shall ascend into heaven? The *pēšer*
> of this is, Who shall bring Christ down? Do not say in your heart,
> Who shall descend into the deep? The *pēšer* of this is, Who shall
> bring Christ up from the dead?

C. At least two of the recognised methods of rabbinic interpretation occur in the New Testament.

Arguments *a minori ad maius* are fairly common (and of course
not only in exegetical discussions). These take various forms, but
the transition from less to greater is usually based on a Christological fact or implication. Thus in Mark 2:23–28 Jesus refers
to the Old Testament incident (I Sam. 21:1–6) in which David
and his followers, against the sacred regulation, ate holy bread
from the sanctuary; since this was permissible, it follows that the
disciples of Jesus were free to pluck and eat ears of corn in circumstances (that is, on the Sabbath) in which this was not normally allowed.[5] A more formally theological example occurs at
Hebrews 9:13f. The former verse ("If the blood of bulls and goats
and the ashes of a heifer sprinkling those who have been defiled
sanctify them with a view to cleanness of the flesh") does not
quote a specific passage, but refers in Old Testament language
to a number of Old Testament regulations;[6] the latter verse ("How
much more will the blood of Christ . . . cleanse our conscience
. . .") draws the Christian conclusion. II Corinthians 3:4–18
should be noted here, for though it contains a complication of its
own, it provides a particularly clear illustration of the point at
issue. Paul describes, with the frequent use of Old Testament
language, Moses' descent from Mount Sinai after receiving the
Law, when his face shone, so that he was obliged to cover it. The
Law, in Paul's view, was a ministry of death (II Cor. 3:7; cf.
Rom. 7:10); if it was delivered in circumstances of such glory,
how much more should the life-giving ministry of the Christian
dispensation be accompanied by glory (3:8; cf. 3:17f.). It should
however be observed that that which transfigured Moses into a
figure of glory was the Law, in Jewish estimation the central
element of the Old Testament. Since the ministry of Moses pales
into insignificance beside the Christian ministry and is being
done away (3:11), the Old Testament as a whole is seen to stand

---

[5]Some see here a simple argument from analogy: in each situation this proposition holds, Necessity knows no law. Jesus' disciples, however, were not in
serious need, and Matthew's insertion (12:5ff.) shows that he understood the
argument to be of the *a minori ad maius* kind.

[6]Lev. 16:3, 14f.; Num. 19:9, 17.

within the *a minori ad maius*. It is no longer one precept or institution that is transcended: the whole of sacred scripture is transcended by its fulfilment. "Transcended" does not mean
"discarded," for the figure of Moses, and his writings, retain a
transformed significance; this, however, is a matter that must be
discussed below (cf. pp. 44, 54, 55f.).

The New Testament uses also the second of the *middôt* (*gᵉzêrāh
šāwāh*). The best example of this occurs in Romans 4.[7] Paul quotes
Genesis 15:6, in which it is stated that Abraham's faith in God
was counted (ἐλογίσθη) to him as righteousness. The question
is, in what sense is the word "counted" used? Paul answers this
by means of a second quotation in which the same word is used.
Psalm 32:1 ("Blessed is the man whose sin the Lord will not
count," λογίσηται) shows that "counting" and "not counting"
are not a matter of the balancing of good and bad deeds, but of
forgiveness and reconciliation. Paul has now established the
meaning of the disputed word, but sees the opportunity of drawing further use from his *gᵉzêrāh šāwāh*. The psalm he has quoted
is (he supposes) a psalm of David; David was a Jew; is then the
blessing of forgiveness one that is confined to circumcised Jews?
Not so, for the same verbal link allows us to return to Genesis 15,
where righteousness is counted to Abraham while still un-
circumcised.

D. Inevitably the New Testament uses also the simple and
straightforward kind of interpretation which was in use among
Jews of every sort. The Old Testament is quoted because it says
with authority what the New Testament writer wished to say. It
furnishes, for instance, examples that are to be followed, such as
that of Elijah, the man of prayer (Jas. 5:17f.), and Job, the man
of endurance (5:11), and others that are not to be followed, such
as those of Cain the murderer (I John 3:12) and Esau the profane
(Heb. 12:16). Hebrews 11 is worth noting because of a characteristic double emphasis: the Old Testament believers are held
up as a pattern that should be copied, but at the same time it is
observed that their witness, apart from its fulfilment, is incomplete (11:39f.; see below, pp. 55f.).

The morality of the Old Testament is assumed, and its commandments (notably the commandments to love God and the
neighbour: Deut. 6:4f.; Lev. 19:18) are repeated with added weight
(e.g., Mark 12:28–34 and parallels; Rom. 13:8ff.). Old Testament imagery, usually of a straightforward kind, is taken over

[7]See J. Jeremias, in *Studia Paulina*, ed. J. N. Sevenster and W. C. van Unnik
(Haarlem, 1953), pp. 149ff.

and used in the same, or a very similar, sense. Examples are
given below (pp. 51f., 53f., 55f.).

E. Finally, and most important, there is the parallel between
the conviction which appears in the Qumrân writings that ancient prophecy was being fulfilled in the contemporary experience
of a religious community and the similar conviction which inspired the writers of the New Testament. It cannot however be
said that this parallelism of conviction led to much formal sim-
ilarity, because the Qumrân exegesis of prophecy in terms of
current events is expressed in the *pešer* form, whereas the New
Testament more often narrates the event and adds that it happened in fulfilment of scripture.

CONTENT AND PURPOSE

When the use of the Old Testament made by the New Testament
writers is compared with that of their Jewish contemporaries,
many formal resemblances, and some formal differences, appear.
The same observation holds good with regard to substance as
with regard to form. A simple pointer to this is provided by a
comparison of the relative frequency of quotation of various parts
of the Old Testament. In the list of Old Testament references
given in the Nestle edition of the New Testament, the Pentateuch
occupies about seven columns, the Psalms five, Isaiah nearly five,
the prophets as a whole (including Daniel) nearly twelve. The
Pentateuch is still strongly represented (though Leviticus and
Numbers make but a poor showing), but the Prophets and the
Writings claim a much greater share of the interpreter's attention.
The New Testament is less concerned with the legal, and much
more concerned with the prophetic, element in the Old Testament, in both its religious and predictive aspects. This simple
statistical observation, however, requires further analysis if it is
to lead to useful consideration of the use of the Old Testament
in the New.

The question from which this analysis may proceed is this:
What does the user of a sacred literature hope to find in his
authoritative documents? For Jewish users of the Old Testament
this question can be answered on the basis of the accounts given
above. The rabbis turned to the Old Testament as the basis of
the legal system which they created. Exact and scientific exegesis
of the text made it applicable to new situations which were not
contemplated by the original lawgivers, and permitted trained
legal experts to draw out a full religious, civil, and criminal code
capable of regulating the life of their own society. Philo, his mind

stored with Greek speculative and moral theory, which he accepted as true, went to the Old Testament convinced that he would find this truth there — as he was able to do, by means of the allegorical method. He was thus able to prove to his own satisfaction, and for use in missionary propaganda, that the best Greek thought had been anticipated by Moses. The Qumrân exegetes found in the Old Testament predictions of events which took place in the life of their own sect, and thus they were able to demonstrate both that the Old Testament was true prophecy (since it had manifestly been fulfilled), and that their sect was the messianic fulfilment of God's purpose for Israel, since its story could be found written (somewhat obscurely, it is true) in the pages of the Old Testament.

These statements are only approximately true. There is a speculative (and sometimes surprisingly mystical) element in the rabbinic use of the Old Testament, and the rabbis cherished the messianic hope of their people and busied themselves with messianic texts. Philo, again, was more than a thinly disguised Greek philosopher; he was deeply concerned that the national law should be observed, and that in its literal sense; and occasionally (especially in *De praemiis et poenis*, 163–72) he expresses a straightforward hope for the glorious future of his people. The Qumrân sect separated itself from the main body of Judaism not on account of its messianism, but on account of a divergent interpretation of the biblical basis of the Law. Nevertheless, though it would be mistaken to draw clear-cut distinctions between the exegetical motivation of Philo, the rabbis, and the Qumrân *pešer* commentators, it is correct to take the three exegetical lines that have been mentioned and use them as norms of the exegetical activity of the Jewish people. All reappear within the New Testament.

A. New Testament writers use the Old Testament in order to establish regulations for the Christian life. Examples are numerous, and only a selection can be given here.

One important group deals with the relations between men and women. The treatment of marriage and divorce in Mark 10:2–12 (and parallels) will serve as a useful starting point, for it contains a discussion, which reflects legal exegetical controversy, of the Old Testament evidence. Quotation of Deuteronomy 24:1 suggests the permissibility of divorce; this, however, is countered by passages from Genesis (1:27; 2:24), which show that the original intention of God in creation was the permanent union of one man and one woman, so that revised legal procedure will exclude divorce. It is important that this principle is applied

in Mark 10:12 to a situation which the historical Jesus can hardly
have envisaged,[8] and that Matthew (5:32; 19:9; cf. I Cor. 7:15)
shows that the prohibition was not understood in a strict legalistic sense. The subordination of women to men is grounded by
Paul in the narrative of creation (I Cor. 11:3–12; cf. Gen. 1:27;
2:18, 22f.), though without formal quotation; the author of I Peter
makes a different, moral and haggadic rather than theological
and halakic, use of the Old Testament for a similar purpose when
he notes Sarah's respectful way of addressing her husband (3:6).

A second important field in which Old Testament material
was used as the source and foundation of Christian legislation
was that of the admission of the Gentiles, over which, as is well
known, controversy raged in the middle of the first century. The
controversy is presented in the New Testament by the side which
ultimately caused its view — that Gentiles might be admitted to
the Church without Jewish rites such as circumcision — to prevail. It is however evident that their adversaries must have based
their argument on the Old Testament, and that they had ready
to hand plenty of material which, at least on the surface, appeared to support them. From Abraham onwards, members of
God's people were expected (if men) to be circumcised; the Law
was given to them that it might be kept. An almost unlimited
number of Old Testament texts affirmed this. We possess (at
least) two counterarguments, and both of these are based on the
Old Testament. Luke represents the Apostolic Council of Acts 15
as the scene of the decisive solution of the problem, and the
debate is made to turn on James's quotation of Amos 9:11f. It is
hard to believe that this quotation could have had the decisive
force Luke attributes to it, especially as James is made to give it
in the Septuagint form,[9] and the narrative of the Council raises
other familiar historical problems; but presumably the quotation
was thought by Luke and his contemporaries to be convincing,
or at least to provide important confirmation of a position of the
truth of which they were already satisfied.

The second justification of the admission to the Church of
Gentiles as such is Paul's, and here a solid Old Testament foundation is provided. In Galatians 3, Paul conducts an argument
to show that though the Old Testament promised life to every
one who does the things that are written in the Law (Lev. 18:5),

---

[8] In Jewish law a wife cannot divorce her husband.
[9] B. Gerhardsson, *Memory and Manuscript* (Lund, 1961), p. 260, is not convincing, if the intention is to suggest that James himself made use of the Septuagint
variation in his interpretation.

yet, by affirming that righteousness and life are to be had by faith (Hab. 2:4), it implies that no one in fact does the things that are written in the Law, a conclusion that brings upon all men — Jews equally with Gentiles — the curse pronounced in Deuteronomy 27:26 upon every one who does not abide in all the things that are written in the book of the Law, to do them. Jews and Gentiles thus stand on the same footing before God, and the demand that Gentiles should become Jews by circumcision is not merely baseless but an affront to God. This is certainly not a modern argument, though it is far more profound than the mere citation of a concatenation of texts; it provides however a further example of the use of the Old Testament as the basis and source of Christian regulation and procedure.

Other matters of Christian usage and discipline were, at least in part, regulated by means of the Old Testament, which provided the basis for the requisite $h^a l\bar{a}\underset{.}{k}\hat{o}\underset{.}{t}$. How far were Christians obliged to keep the Jewish Sabbath? Various reasons were given for the new Christian freedom, of which one was the Old Testament precedent of David's freedom from similar religious regulations.[10] Were Christians permitted to eat food sacrificed to idols? Part of the answer is given by the quotation of Psalm 24:1: since God assumes ownership of the whole earth and its contents, it may be deduced that nothing is untouchable. Which is the more valuable gift, speaking with tongues or prophecy? The Old Testament shows (see I Cor. 14:21) that the former will not lead to faith; it is therefore of little value, at least as an evangelistic agency. How ought the collection for the poor saints in Jerusalem to be conducted? The regulation for the collection of manna (Exod. 16:18, quoted in II Cor. 8:15) will supply the clue. Other Old Testament material is cited in II Corinthians 9.

The nature of the Church and the basis of Church discipline are both founded in the Old Testament in the two allusions, in II Timothy 2:19, to Numbers 16: "The Lord knows those who are his," and "Let every one who names the name of the Lord depart from evil." In the same epistle (3:8), Church discipline is further strengthened by an allusion to Moses' treatment of his adversaries in Exodus 7 (with the addition of the apocryphal names Jannes and Jambres). Other New Testament books invoke other parts of the Old Testament for the same purpose, and Revelation makes particularly clear and forceful use of the figures of Jezebel and Balaam (2:14, 20). The appointment of a successor to Judas is given Old Testament grounding, and Paul uses the

---

[10]See above, p. 40.

commandment of Deuteronomy 25:4 to justify the payment of apostles (I Cor. 9:9), but apart from this, surprisingly little use is made of the Old Testament in relation to the developing New Testament ministry — Christian ministers were neither rabbis nor priests.

There is in the New Testament far more halakic development, far more of moral and disciplinary regulation, than is sometimes recognised,[11] and much (though not all) of this is explicitly founded on Old Testament passages, from the principles of which rules relevant to the new situation of the new people of God are deduced. In this respect the New Testament writers stand close to their Jewish contemporaries. The outstanding difference lies in the fact, which is not always apparent, that though the Law continues to provide a framework of argument, authority is found to lie elsewhere. This is expressed sometimes negatively when (as in the argument quoted above from Gal. 3) the Law is used to prove its own incompetence. The positive counterpart to this negative argument is expressed most succinctly in Romans 10:4: Christ is the end of the Law. He is now the final authority under which the life of the people of God is lived.

B. The New Testament writers believed that the life, death, and resurrection of Jesus Christ, under whose authority they lived, had been predicted in the Old Testament. The events to which they themselves bore witness were thus the proof that they were living in the age of fulfilment. This is perhaps the most familiar aspect of the relation between the Testaments, and does not call for detailed illustration. All the main features of the story of Jesus are given Old Testament support.

Matthew[12] marks out the main features of the infancy narrative with quotations. The miraculous conception of Jesus fulfils Isaiah 7:14; he is born in Bethlehem because so it is written in Micah 5:2; his parents flee, taking him with them, into Egypt, in order that later as God's Son he may be called out of Egypt (Hos. 11:1), and thereby he escapes Herod's plot, which nevertheless is successful enough to provoke the lamentation of Jeremiah 31:15. The modern reader may wonder whether the story was constructed on the basis of the Old Testament material; Matthew has no doubt that Jesus was the fulfiller of prophecy.

During his ministry, Jesus was notable as a worker of miracles

[11]See E. Käsemann, "Sätze Heiligen Rechtes im Neuen Testament," *NTS*, I (1955), 248–60, reprinted in *Exegetische Versuche und Besinnungen*, II (Göttingen, 1964), 69–82.
[12]In the Lukan infancy narratives the fulfilment of the Old Testament is differently expressed, through the use of Old Testament language in the hymns.

(in fulfilment of Isaiah 53:4: "He took our sicknesses and bore our diseases," many other Old Testament passages are alluded to), and as a teller of parables (in order to fulfil the prophecy of Ps. 78:2: "I will open my mouth in parables"). Much more in the gospels is written in language that recalls the Old Testament, but the chief weight lies on the announcement that as the Son of man Jesus must suffer, for so it has been foretold. "How is it written of the Son of man that he should suffer much, and be set at nought?" (Mark 9:12). Many of the details are filled in. The combined hostility of Jews and Romans fulfils Psalm 2:1f. (Acts 4:25f.): "Why did the Gentiles rage, and the peoples plot vanity? The kings of the earth stood by, and the rulers were gathered together against the Lord and against his Christ." The betrayal by Judas was foretold not only by Jesus, but also in the Old Testament: John 13:18 (Ps. 41:9): "He that eats my bread has lifted up his heel against me." As the narrative continues, detail after detail is claimed as the fulfilment of prophecy: the division by lot of the clothes of Jesus (John 19:24), his thirst (19:28), the fact that none of his bones was broken, and that his side was pierced (19:36f.).

Paul is as certain that the resurrection took place "according to the scriptures" as that the death of Christ was foretold (I Cor. 15:3f.), but does not find it easy to give precise documentation. This was however supplied for example at Acts 2:25–28, where a careful argument is given to support the exegesis. If David appears to refer to a promise that God's Holy One shall not see corruption, he cannot have been thinking of himself since the existence of his grave proves the corruptibility of his flesh; he must have been speaking of his greater descendant, Christ.

The events that follow and introduce the life of Christians, which rests upon the historic work of Jesus, are also documented. Christ ascended into heaven, as Psalm 68:19 predicted (Eph. 4:8). The gift of the Spirit was a fulfilment of the prophecy of Joel 2:28–32 (Acts 2:16). The Church is the Israel of God (Gal. 6:16), and to it the epithets which had been used of the ancient people may now with even greater propriety be applied (I Pet. 2:1–10).

Not even the Qumrân manuscripts afford a list of fulfilments of scripture that can approach that which has now been outlined. It is clear that the first Christians believed themselves to be witnessing not a few preliminary tokens of God's fulfilment of his age-old purposes, but the central (though not the final) act to which all prophecy pointed. The process of fulfilment was focused upon the historic figure of Jesus: "However many God's promises

may be, in him is the Yes to them" (II Cor. 1:20). But because
Christ was the focus of fulfilment, all who were in Christ were
involved in it.

The Old Testament passages adduced in the New are of vary-
ing degrees of cogency. It is not easy, for example, to believe that
Rachel's weeping for her children (Jer. 31:15) had much to do
with Herod's massacre of the innocents. Yet when this is said, it
must be allowed that the use made of Old Testament passages
in the New is surprisingly appropriate. The age of the New Testament was not an age of historical criticism; certainly it was not
so in the orders of society in which Christianity spread most
rapidly. Yet New Testament thinkers worked their way so suc-
cessfully into the essential meaning of the Old Testament that
they were sometimes at least able to bring to light a genuine
community of thought and feeling between what had been experienced and said in the distant past and the event of Jesus
Christ. The "argument from prophecy" may fairly be stated as
an affirmation of the universal significance of Jesus.

C. It is the characteristically Philonic kind of exegesis that is
hardest to find in the New Testament; and this is true even when
we generalise and look not simply for cases where Greek philosophy is sought and found in the Old Testament, but also for those
in which any kind of contemporary thought is imported into the
sacred text. This is not to say that New Testament exegesis of the
Old Testament is always historical and sound — it has already
been shown that this is not so. It is true, however, that New
Testament interpreters commonly move within the same general
framework of thought as the Old Testament itself.

A notable exception is perhaps to be found in the series of
Christological terms which are qualified in John by the adjective
true (ἀληθινός). Some of these are Old Testament terms — light,
bread, vine. *Light* occurs in a context (John 1:4f.) which recalls
the narrative of creation in Genesis 1; *bread* recalls the story of
the manna; and the figure of the *vine* appears to be based on
several Old Testament passages where the plant serves as a figure
of Israel. The precise meaning that John gives to *true* is too large
a question to be discussed here, but, at least in the view of some
commentators, it owes something to the Platonic notion of the
contrast between the real and the phenomenal. Thus the manna
eaten by the Israelites in the wilderness serves as a figure of the
true, heavenly bread given by God to men in his Son. So far as
this exegesis is justified it may be said that we have an example
of the reading of Greek philosophy into an Old Testament passage.

Many students of the New Testament have held that the same

is true of the use of the Old Testament made by the Epistle to the Hebrews, which has been described as a Platonic reinterpretation of the original New Testament gospel. There is some superficial justification for this view in passages which speak of the Law as having a shadow of good things to come (10:1; cf. Col. 2:17), but it is in fact a misunderstanding of the epistle. The essential sense of its quotations is rooted not in Platonism but in apocalyptic.[13]

Old Testament material is indeed adapted in the New Testament to new circumstances; of this an outstanding example is the use of Old Testament passages (see pp. 44f.) in the controversy about the admission of Gentiles to the Church. Many (though not quite all) of the passages used originally had no connection with the theme of the incorporation of non-Jews into the people of God; this however was the theme of the New Testament writers, and since it was imperative to them to prove their point out of the Old Testament, they read their opinions into the texts they used. Yet even here the New Testament exegesis is not wholly unprincipled. For example, in 1 Peter 2:10 the author draws on the language of Hosea (see 1:6, 9; 2:1, 23) to describe the Gentile Church: "Who formerly were not a people, but now are God's people; who had not received mercy, but now have received mercy." Now it is certain that in Hosea these words apply to Israel, who for her sins had been pitilessly punished so as to be no longer God's people but would in the end be pitied by God so as to become his people once more. The prophecy had nothing to do with non-Jews and is therefore, in a sense, misapplied in the New Testament. Yet in another sense it is used rightly, for it does state the principle that God's people exists as such only by God's mercy, and not at all in virtue of its own merits and qualifications; and this is the ground on which in the end Gentiles came to stand together with Jews as one people under the judgement and mercy of the same God.

It is here that we may make a distinction between the New Testament interpretation of the Old Testament and that current in Judaism, which in many ways it very closely resembled. New Testament Christianity was aware of itself as a prophetic phenomenon. Its members were themselves inspired. This gave them a sense of kinship with the Old Testament writers. Deeper than this, however, was the fact that they conceived themselves to stand in fundamentally similar circumstances. The Law, the Prophets, the Psalms all arose out of situations in which men had

[13]See below, pp. 55ff.

become acutely conscious of the manifestations in history of God's
judgement and mercy. This was often conceived in limited and
limiting terms, but it was the creative factor which produced the
various forms of literature. The New Testament literature itself
was evoked by what its authors believed to be the supreme manifestation in history of the judgement and mercy of God, and the
Old Testament manifestation and the New Testament manifestation interacted in mutual illumination. Sometimes this community of theme was expressed in too mechanically Christological
a form, and reference to particular incidents in the life of Jesus
was found where no such reference was intended. Even so, however, the community of theme is not robbed of its significance
and makes possible for the New Testament writers an understanding of the essential meaning of the Old Testament which it
would be hard to parallel.

VARIETIES OF NEW TESTAMENT EXEGESIS

So far the New Testament has been regarded, in its treatment of
the Old Testament, as a unit. This is a defensible, and indeed an
indispensable, method. It is not however a final method, since
in exegesis as well as in other matters there is much variety within
the New Testament. Though, as has already been observed, all
its authors view the Old Testament with respect, and quote it as
an authority, some use it more than others, and in the various
books different methods of interpretation and application are
employed.

Synoptic Gospels and Acts
These books contain a considerable number of Old Testament
quotations, some of which have already been pointed out, which
are adduced as prophecies fulfilled in the work of Jesus and of
his disciples. An outstanding example is the quotation from Isaiah 61:1f., which is used at Luke 4:18f. to bring out the meaning
of Jesus' proclamation and is sealed with the affirmation, "Today
this scripture has been fulfilled in your ears." These quotations
call for no further comment here. It is also however characteristic
of the Synoptic Gospels to use, in teaching or narrative, Old
Testament language without drawing attention to its source. In
some passages this is unmistakable. Thus in the parable of the
Wicked Husbandmen the steps taken by the owner of the vineyard are described as follows (Mark 12:1): "A man planted a
vineyard, and put a fence round it, and dug a winepress, and
built a tower, and let it out to husbandmen, and went away."

With this should be compared Isaiah 5:1–2: "My beloved had a vineyard on a hilltop in a fruitful place. And I put a fence round it, and put in stakes, and planted a fine vine, and built a tower in the middle of it, and dug a winepress in it." Even when allowance is made for the fact that the preparation and planting of a vineyard was necessarily a stereotyped procedure, it is impossible to doubt that though there is no explicit reference to Isaiah, the language of the New Testament parable is based on that of the Old and that the interpretation of the parable is thereby determined: in the New Testament, as in the Old, the vineyard is Israel (Isa. 5:7).

With somewhat less confidence the miracle of Mark 7:31–37 may be claimed as another example. The narrative records the cure of a man who is deaf and a stammerer (μογιλάλος). This is an uncommon Greek word, but it occurs in the Septuagint version of Isaiah 35:6: The tongue of the stammerers (μογιλάλων) shall be plain. The rarity of the word adds weight to the view that the Marcan narrative was written with the Old Testament prophecy in mind; but there is no explicit reference to it nor any suggestion that Mark himself saw a fulfilment of the Old Testament.[14]

The material we have now considered has not unnaturally given rise to the view that some at least of the gospel narratives arose as midrāšim on Old Testament passages. This may be an exaggerated view, but the influence of the Old Testament on the form in which the traditions about Jesus were repeated should not be underestimated. It is salutary for the modern reader to recall Justin's intention (*Apologies*, I, 30) to demonstrate the divinity of Jesus Christ on the basis of his deeds, trusting rather prophecies given before the event than human reports. The gospel story as a whole differs so markedly from current interpretation of the Old Testament that it is impossible to believe that it originated simply in meditations on prophecy; it originated in the career of Jesus of Nazareth! But the earliest method of evaluating the theological significance of his life was to tell the story of it in terms of the Old Testament, and though the conviction that the story had been foretold arose before it could be documented (see Mark 9:12; 14:21; I Cor. 15:3f.; and see above, pp. 46ff.), it is likely that when Old Testament material was

---

[14]See E. Hoskyns and N. Davey, *The Riddle of the New Testament* (London, 1931), pp. 167f. A further example is to be found in Mark 15:24; see above, p. 38.

adduced, it contributed new details to the stories it was intended to illustrate.

A related suggestion (see further below, pp. 54f.) is that already Testimony Books, or collections of Old Testament texts believed to have been fulfilled in the events of the New Testament, were in circulation in the New Testament period.[15] That such books existed at a rather later time is certain;[16] their existence in the first century can (in the absence of the books themselves) be no more than conjecture, but it is a reasonable conjecture, and is given some support by a special set of quotations peculiar to Matthew (1:23; 2:15, 18, 23; 4:15f.; 8:17; 12:18ff.; 13:35; 21:5; 27:9; cf. 2:6). These are all introduced in similar terms and do not follow the text of the Septuagint; it is possible that they were drawn by the evangelist from a special source.

The speeches in the early chapters of Acts are full of quotations; Stephen's in chapter 7 is little more than a summary of Old Testament history, and even Paul's speech at Athens in chapter 17 is not without its allusions. The quotations are on the whole of the kind that can broadly be described as "messianic"; they are designed to illustrate and support that part of the preaching that asserts that in the life, death, and resurrection of Jesus the Old Testament scriptures were fulfilled, so that with him the new age began to dawn.

John

Like the Synoptic Gospels, the Fourth contains a number of straightforward proof texts; some of these have already been quoted. They are however relatively few, and to their fewness must be added the observation that from time to time John appears to handle the expectations of Judaism in a critical and even negative way. A notable example of this is John the Baptist's denial (1:21) that he is to be identified with Elijah—an identification which the Synoptic Gospels make without hesitation (Matt. 17:11ff.; cf. Mark 9:13; Luke 1:17). It is characteristic both of John's ironical style and of his use of the Old Testament that he places on the lips of unbelieving Jews the Old Testament teaching that the Messiah would be of the seed of David and would come from Bethlehem, the village where David was (7:42); Jesus, therefore, who came from Galilee, could not, in their belief, be the Messiah. It is probable that John was aware of the tradition that though Jesus was brought up in Galilee, he had been

---

[15]See J. R. Harris, *Testimonies*, I (Cambridge, 1916), II (1920).
[16]Notably the *Testimonia ad Quirinum* of Cyprian.

born in Bethlehem; he was thus representing Jewish unbelief as based on inaccurate opinion about Jesus' birthplace. Behind this point, however, appears to lie another: the earthly origin of Jesus, whether in Galilee or Judea, is ultimately irrelevant, since he comes from God, and this divine origin determines the meaning and authority of his mission.

These observations, important as they are, do not lead to the conclusion that John had no use for the Old Testament; what they suggest is that he used it in a way of his own. It is his method to deal not so much with Old Testament texts as with Old Testament themes. One of the clearest examples is provided by his description of Jesus as the Good Shepherd (10:1–16). In this passage, no part of the Old Testament is quoted, but no one familiar with the Old Testament can read it without recalling a number of places where similar imagery is used—for example, Psalms 23; 80; Ezekiel 34; and not least the fact that David, the ancestor and prototype of the Messiah, was a shepherd. Without pinning himself to a particular prophecy, John takes up a central Old Testament theme and familiar Old Testament language and concentrates them upon the figure of Jesus. A similar example is to be found in John 1:29, where the exegete who seeks the background of the description of Jesus as the Lamb of God does not need to decide too nicely between the Passover lamb, the lamb of the daily burnt offering, the lamb of Isaiah 53, the goat of the Day of Atonement, and other Old Testament animals.[17] Whatever they suggest—all of them—in sin-bearing and sin-removing efficacy, Jesus was.

From this point another step may be taken. If Jesus truly *was* whatever lambs, shepherds, and the like may in the pages of the Old Testament suggest, he must have been more than the object of prophecy; it may reasonably be maintained that he was its subject too.[18] Here it must suffice to refer to two passages where this view stands out clearly. In John 12:41, after reference to Isaiah 53:1 and 6:9f., the evangelist comments, evidently with Isaiah 6:1 in mind, "These things Isaiah said because[19] he saw his glory." The next words ("and he spoke about him") show that "his glory" means Christ's glory; that is, the celestial figure whose glory Isaiah saw, and who entrusted to him his prophetic commission and message, was Christ himself. A similar point is

---

[17]See C. K. Barrett, "The Lamb of God," *NTS*, I (1955), 210–18.

[18]For a full discussion of this theme see A. T. Hanson, *Jesus Christ in the Old Testament* (London, 1965).

[19]Accepting the reading ὅτι; the alternatives (ὅτε, ἐπεί) do not affect the point under discussion.

made in John 10:34f. After quoting Psalm 82:6 ("I said, You are gods"), John continues, "If he called them gods to whom the word of God came. . . ." But John has already (1:1f., 14) identified Jesus with the word of God, and if this identification is to be taken seriously, it must be concluded that Jesus, the Word, was in some sense involved in the Old Testament passage.

Paul

As examples given in the general discussion will have shown, Paul manifests so wide a range of the various uses of the Old Testament made by Christian writers that it will scarcely be possible to give special treatment of his peculiarities. He quotes isolated passages, which he held to be fulfilled in the gospel; he demonstrates the great themes of the Old Testament, and shows their significance in a Christian setting, as for example when he proves out of scripture the universal sinfulness of mankind (Rom. 3:9–20); he draws Christian $h^a l\bar{a}\underline{k}\hat{o}\underline{t}$ out of Old Testament data (e.g., I Cor. 9:9; see above, pp. 45f.); and simply reiterates the Old Testament command of love, as Jesus himself had done (Rom. 13:8–10; Lev. 19:18; cf. Mark 12:31). Here two further points may be noted.

When taken with other New Testament writers, Paul may be held to provide further evidence for the Testimony Book theory mentioned above (p. 52). Thus in Romans 9:33 Paul places side by side Isaiah 28:16 ("Behold, I lay in Sion a stone of stumbling and a rock of tripping") and 8:14 ("He that believes in him [that is, in the elect corner-stone] shall not be put to shame"). There is no connection between the Isaiah passages beyond the fact that each refers to a stone. In I Peter 2:4, 6, 8 the same passages are used (with the addition, in v. 7, of Ps. 118:22). Now it is possible that Paul and Peter independently set out to collect possibly messianic passages containing the word *stone*; it is possible that Peter had read, and borrowed from, Romans; but it is at least a reasonable hypothesis (though it can hardly be more than this) that Paul and Peter independently drew upon a ready-made collection of messianic texts, in which one subdivision was "Christ as the Stone."

It is perhaps more important to note that Paul raised in the sharpest form the Christian problem of the Old Testament (see p. 41). The use he made of the Old Testament is credible only on the part of one who believed it to be the word of God, whose authority must always be reverenced. This is backed up by explicit statements. It was the greatest privilege of Israel that they were entrusted with the oracles of God (Rom. 3:1f.). The Law itself was holy, and the commandment it contained was holy, righteous, and good (7:12). It was spiritual, that is, inspired by God's Spirit (7:14). Yet it was also true that the Law was now fulfilled and completed: Christ was the end of the Law (10:4). Moreover, Christians by definition were people who were no longer under the Law (6:14f.), which was unable to modify the covenant of promise, grace, and faith, which God had established—long before the Law was given—as the basis of his relation with his people (Gal. 3:17). This paradox lies at the heart of Christianity, and Paul is content to leave it with his readers. Later generations were to demonstrate their inferior grasp of Christian truth by attempts to cut the knot of the problem—Barnabas, for example, by allegorising the gospel out of the most unlikely pieces of the Law, Marcion by rejecting the Old Testament altogether. Paul could not have accepted either of these expedients, and his example may suggest to theologians a wise caution. It will be better to hold firmly both elements of the problem than to eliminate either of them, or to be satisfied with too easy a synthesis.

Hebrews[20]

The origins of the allegorical method of interpreting a sacred text were discussed above.[21] It has often been maintained that Hebrews is a Christian attempt to apply this method to the Old Testament, and it is true that there are passages in Hebrews that suggest this view. The earthly tabernacle is described as a *parable* (9:9); the true tabernacle is not made with hands and is not of this creation (9:11). It follows that whereas the copies of the heavenly things must be cleansed by the blood of bulls and goats and the like, the heavenly things themselves can be cleansed only by better sacrifices (9:23), and that Christ did not enter into a man-made sanctuary, a mere antitype[22] of the true one, but into heaven (9:24). The Law thus had a shadow of the good things to come (10:1). It is however only on the surface that these passages suggest the Stoic method of allegory and the Platonic contrast between the world of phenomena and the world of heavenly reality. The author's intention (especially in its relation to the Old Testament) is given by chapter 8, which contains in a long quotation from Jeremiah 31:31–34 the prophecy of the new covenant; and the significance of *new* is underlined. "If the first had

---

[20]See C. K. Barrett, "The Eschatology of the Epistle to the Hebrews," in *The Background of the New Testament and its Eschatology*, eds. W. D. Davies and D. Daube (Cambridge, 1956), pp. 363–93, especially pp. 391f.

[21]C. K. Barrett, "The Interpretation of the Old Testament in the New," *The Cambridge History of the Bible*, Vol. I, eds. P. R. Ackroyd and C. F. Evans, pp. 378f.

[22]Hebrews appears to use τύπος of the original, ἀντίτυπος of the copy.

been faultless, no place would have been sought for a second"
(8:7). "By saying *new* he has antiquated the first; and that which
is antiquated and growing old is near to disappearance" (8:13).
The theme of Hebrews is in fact not the relation between con-
trasting but parallel worlds of phenomena and reality, time and
eternity, but (as with the rest of the New Testament) the fulfilment of Old Testament prophecy in time. Some of the verses
quoted above themselves make this point. The tabernacle is a
parable *for the present time* (9:9). The Law had a shadow of good
things *to come* (10:1). Christ as the high priest now remains con-
tinuously in heaven until the time of his second coming (9:28),
but his self-offering and his appearance before the Father in
heaven, though in a sense they represent eternal truths, were
once-for-all acts (e.g., 9:24, 26). In its use of the Old Testament,
Hebrews is nearer to common Christian usage than has sometimes been supposed.

Like Paul, the author of Hebrews also demonstrates the paradox that is involved in the Christian use of the Old Testament,
but he does so in a different way. We have already noted his
conviction, which he shares with New Testament writers generally, that in Christ the promises and prophecies of the Old Testament were fulfilled. Yet in his account of faith he turns without
hesitation to the Old Testament, and produces from it a long list
of men and women who lived by faith. He agrees that they were
seeking a homeland they had not found and did not yet possess
(11:14ff.) and makes the claim that in his dealings with them
God had in mind some better thing for us, so that they could not
reach their goal independently of us (11:40); yet he can say that
Christians too are seeking the city that is not yet here but is still
to come, and represent their life as a pilgrimage, or race, conducted in faith and hope (12:1; 13:14). He thus exposes himself
to the questions, What difference did the coming of Christ make?
What is the difference between life under the old covenant and
life under the new?

The difference lies in the objective act of cleansing (1:3) and
atonement (2:17) made by Christ, who, in his death, discovered
eternal salvation for men (9:12) and set them free from death
and the devil (2:14). Though they must still live by faith, they
have an assurance (10:22), an anchor (6:19), which Old Testament believers could not have. The pattern of the life of faith is
the same in the New Testament as in the Old; but it is marked
out more clearly, and there is no doubt of the goal to which it
leads.

THE NEW TESTAMENT AND THE OLD

There is no single term that adequately describes the relation in which the New Testament stands to the Old. There is no doubt that New Testament writers viewed the Old as prophecy and interpreted it as such; that is, they understood the Old Testament to predict certain events which had duly taken place in the experience of Jesus or of the Church. There is no doubt that they employed the Old Testament also in a variety of ways that may be brought together under the term "allegory"; that is, they believed that the Old Testament, or parts of it, contained hidden meanings that had been concealed from earlier generations but had now come to light with the Christian revelation.

It may be that along with these "prophetic" and "allegorical" interpretations of the Old Testament should be set a third, the typological. This may be distinguished from the other two in that it seeks correspondences between persons and events not (as allegory does) in meanings hidden in language but actually in the course of history, and looks not to the fulfilment of a prediction, but to the recurrence of a pattern.[23] The distinction is useful, but it is probably true that the most characteristic New Testament estimate of the Old sees in it a combination of typology and prophecy. The New Testament writers do see recurrence of patterns of divine activity (since the God of the Old Testament is also, in their belief, the God and Father of the Lord Jesus Christ); but the event of Jesus Christ, itself the fulfilment of the Old Testament as a whole (cf. II Cor. 1:20), is for them so final and radical that after it no pattern could be simply reproduced.

It is doubtful whether any New Testament writer ever formulated for himself the question, What is the authority of the Old Testament? So far as they were Jews, the question was one that could take care of itself. Of course, the Old Testament had the authority of the voice of God himself. This attitude was adopted in turn by Gentile converts to Christianity. Yet the attitude of Christians to the Old Testament was not the same as that of Jews. The change in attitude can be seen in a variety of lights: it was due to a new outburst of prophecy, which brought the interpreters nearer to those whom they interpreted; it was due to a new exegesis, which saw in the Law the end of a legal relationship with God; it was due above all to the conviction that Jesus himself was the fulfilment of the Old Testament and thus

[23]For this definition see H. Nakagawa, in *RGG*, VI (1962), 1095.

the living and abiding Word of God. Out of this complicated but creative attitude to the Old Testament scriptures a new scripture was born, in testimony to the incarnate Word.

5 TRADITION AND THE CANON OF SCRIPTURE

F. F. BRUCE

Let us look at those Scriptures which provide a corrective to unwritten tradition, a standard or "canon" by which it may be tested: in other words, we must consider the relation between our general subject of Christian tradition and the "canon" of Scripture. When we speak of the "canon" of Scripture we use the word in a different sense from that of "rule" or "standard"; the "canon" of Scripture is originally the "list" of books recognized by the church as her sacred writings — a use of the word first attested, it appears, in Athanasius.[1] But inevitably, because of the close relation between Scripture and the rule of faith, something of the sense of authority has come to be attached in common usage to the terms "canon" and "canonical" when they refer to the books of the Bible.

This is an area in which the most biblicist and anti-traditionalist Christian communities rely perforce upon tradition — a tradition which in fact is more essential the more biblicist a community is, for the more dependent it is for its authority on *sola scriptura,* the more necessary it is to define *sola scriptura.* In other words, the more Christians aim at being "people of one book," the more important it is for them to know the limits of that one book.

DELIMITING THE CANON

There are some churches in which the limits of the canon are laid down by authority: their members (formally, at any rate) accept these limits because their church has defined them. This

---

[1]Athanasius, *Thirty-Ninth Festal Letter* (see p. 65). Cf. T. Zahn, *Grundriss der Geschichte des neutestamentlichen Kanons* (Leipzig, 1904), p. 87, cited by H. Oppel, KANΩN (*Philologus*, Suppl. 30, Heft 4, Leipzig, 1937), pp. 70f., cited by R. P. C. Hanson, "Origen's Doctrine of Tradition," *JTS* 49 (1948), 23.

From F. F. Bruce, Tradition: Old and New *(Exeter: The Paternoster Press, 1970) pp. 129–50, reprinted by permission of the publisher.*

is true, for instance, of the Roman Catholic Church, the Church of England, and those churches which adhere to the Westminster Confession of Faith. But what of churches which do not have the canon of Scripture delimited for them in this way? (I write now of my own heritage.) On what authority (say) do we accept the thirty-nine books of the Old Testament, as commonly reckoned, either rejecting the Apocrypha altogether or else relegating them to an inferior or "deuterocanonical" status? "We accept these thirty-nine books," it may be said, "because they make up the Hebrew Bible which our Lord and the apostles acknowledged." True: there seems to have been common ground between our Lord and the Jewish scribes of His day on the content of Scripture, however much they differed on its interpretation and application. We may be sure that He and they accepted the threefold corpus of Law, Prophets, and Writings as it was known from the second century B.C. if not earlier.[2] But, in view of the fact that the precise limits of the third group, the "Writings," do not appear to have been fixed by Jewish authority until the last quarter of the first century A.D., can we be quite sure that our Lord accepted (say) Ecclesiastes or Esther? If (as the argument from silence might suggest) Esther was unknown as a canonical book to the Qumran community,[3] would it be surprising to discover that it was similarly unknown in our Lord's circle? Yet we accept Ecclesiastes and Esther as part of Holy Scripture. Why? Not, in our case, because ecclesiastical authority so directs us — stubborn individualists as many of us are, if ecclesiastical authority did so direct us, that in itself might stimulate us to refuse the direction. No: we accept them, I suppose, because we have "received" them as included in Holy Writ, in other words, because of our tradition. Our tradition is not inviolably sacrosanct, but unless strong reason is shown for rejecting something that we so receive, like the canonicity of these books, we go along with it.

Take an example of another kind: the Book of Enoch.[4] We do

---

[2] The Law comprises the Pentateuch (Genesis-Deuteronomy); the Prophets comprise the Former Prophets (Joshua, Judges, Samuel, Kings) and the latter Prophets (Isaiah, Jeremiah, Ezekiel, the Book of the Twelve Prophets); the Writings comprise Psalms, Proverbs, Job, with the five *Megillōt* or "Rolls" (Canticles, Ruth, Lamentations, Ecclesiastes, Esther) and Daniel, Ezra-Nehemiah, and Chronicles: twenty-four books in all.

[3] Esther is the only book of the Hebrew Bible unrepresented among the Qumran manuscripts.

[4] That is, the "Ethiopic Enoch" (a compilation so called because it is extant in its entirety only in the Ethiopic version), distinguished as I Enoch from the much later II Enoch (the "Secrets of Enoch," originally composed in Greek but extant only in Slavonic) and II Enoch (a Hebrew mystical treatise). Aramaic fragments of I Enoch have been found among the Qumran manuscripts; rather more than one-third of the work is extant in a Greek version.

not accept this book as canonical: it is not so accepted either by western Catholicism (the rock from which *we* were hewn) or by eastern Orthodoxy, although it is part of the Bible of the Monophysite Ethiopic church. Yet it is quoted, and quoted as authoritative, by a New Testament writer.[5] We cannot dismiss Jude's Enoch quotation as on a level with Paul's quotations from Menander[6] or Epimenides;[7] Jude quotes from the Book of Enoch as other New Testament writers quote the Hebrew prophets, treating the words as a divine oracle.[8] No doubt it would put too great a strain on our intellectual agility to defend the divine inspiration of the whole Book of Enoch, even if other parts of it have influenced thought and language elsewhere in the New Testament.[9] But it is not because of the difficulty of defending the inspiration of the Book of Enoch that we do not accept it; it is primarily because our tradition does not recognize it: we have not "received" it. Certainly, if valid arguments were forthcoming for the acceptance of this book, we might revise our tradition and accept it; otherwise we go along with our tradition.

However, Jude's quotation of a passage from the Book of Enoch as a divine oracle might prompt the query whether the Letter of Jude itself should be accepted as canonical. It was one of the "disputed" books in the early church,[10] and Luther put it among the four New Testament books to which he accorded a lower canonical status than the other twenty-three.[11] But this raises the problem of the New Testament canon — a knottier problem than that of the Old Testament canon. Apart from such questions as might be raised about "marginal" books like Ecclesiastes and Esther, the Christian biblicist can properly say that he accepts the Old Testament not on the authority of ecclesias-

---

[5]I Enoch 1:9 is quoted in Jude 14f.

[6]I Cor. 15:33.

[7]Titus 1:12; cf. Acts 17:28a.

[8]As John Bunyan reckoned it his duty to take comfort from Ecclus. 2:10, even if it was an apocryphal work, because it was "the sum and substance of many of the promises" (*Grace Abounding*, 65), so it could be said that I Enoch 1:9 may well rank as a divine oracle, because it is the sum and substance of many of the prophetic warnings of judgement. Tertullian, accepting an antediluvian date for I Enoch, and regarding Jude's quotation as lending authority to the book (since Jude is in his eyes an apostle), adds the further consideration that "nothing which pertains *to* us must be rejected *by* us" (*On the Apparel of Women*, 3).

[9]Not only the references to fallen angels in Jude 6 and II Pet. 2:4 (cf. the "spirits in prison" of I Pet. 3:19) — i.e., to the trespassing "sons of God" of Gen. 6:2, 4, on whose sin and penalty I Enoch enlarges — but also the portrayal of the "Son of Man" in the independent section called the "Similitudes of Enoch" (I Enoch 37–71); cf. M. D. Hooker, *The Son of Man in Mark* (London, 1967), pp. 33ff.

[10]See p. 75.

[11]See p. 78.

tical tradition but on that of our Lord and the apostles. He has no such short answer to the question of the New Testament canon.

These, then, are some of the questions which arise when this subject is under consideration.

THE OLD TESTAMENT CANON

The earliest Christians, as we have seen, found their sacred writings ready to hand in the books of the Hebrew Bible, either in their original text or in the Greek version. The acceptance of the Old Testament was indubitably something which they "received from the Lord" — by example as well as by instruction. For, to reproduce a purple passage from a distinguished Old Testament scholar of a past generation:

> For us its supreme sanction is that which it received from Christ Himself. It was the Bible of His education and the Bible of His ministry. He took for granted its fundamental doctrines about creation, about man and about righteousness; about God's Providence of the world and His purposes of grace through Israel. He accepted its history as the preparation for Himself, and taught His disciples to find Him in it. He used it to justify His mission and to illuminate the mystery of His Cross. He drew from it many of the examples and most of the categories of His gospel. He reenforced the essence of its law and restored many of its ideals. But, above all, He fed His own soul with its contents, and in the great crises of His life sustained Himself upon it as upon the living and sovereign Word of God. These are the highest external proofs — if indeed we can call them external — for the abiding validity of the Old Testament in the life and doctrine of Christ's Church. What was indispensable to the Redeemer must always be indispensable to the redeemed.[12]

In the apostolic age there is no sign that Christians felt the need of a New Testament in the sense of a collection of writings. They had the sacred writings which their Lord used and fulfilled, writings which not only conveyed the way of "salvation through faith in Christ Jesus" but which also, being divinely inspired, were "profitable for teaching, for reproof, for correction, and for training in righteousness, that the man of God may be complete, equipped for every good work."[13] These writings, until well into the second century, constituted the church's Bible, read, of course, through Christian spectacles. From them the apostles of the first

---

[12]G. A. Smith, *Modern Criticism and the Preaching of the Old Testament* (London, 1901), p. 11.
[13]II Tim. 3:15–17.

century and the apologists of the second century drew their basic texts as they proclaimed and defended the gospel; the reading of them was sufficient to convince a number of educated pagans of the truth of Christianity.[14]

One thing which does not seem to have greatly concerned those early Christians was the precise delimitation of their Bible. Actually, there was no particular reason why they should be greatly concerned; they were all agreed about its main contents. It is commonly supposed that the threefold division of the Hebrew Bible corresponds to three stages in the growth of the Hebrew canon.[15] The Law and the Prophets were firmly established as well-defined bodies of canonical literature long before the Christian era, and so were most of the "Writings." The grandson of Jesus ben Sira tells how his grandfather, at the beginning of the second century B.C., was a student of "the law and the prophets and the other books of our fathers."[16] Our Lord apparently knew His Bible as beginning with Genesis and ending with Chronicles,[17] as the Hebrew Bible traditionally does; and He is recorded as speaking of "everything that is written . . . in the law of Moses and the prophets and the psalms" (Luke 24:44). Since the Psalter is the first book of the "Writings," it has sometimes been thought that "the psalms" here might indicate the whole group of documents which it introduces, but this is uncertain. This third group was not authoritatively "closed" until after the catastrophe of A.D. 70, when the rabbis of Jamnia, Yochanan ben Zakkai and his colleagues, undertook the reconstitution of the Jewish polity on a religious basis. But although the "Writings" had remained open until then, so that they could freely discuss the admission of fresh documents or the eviction of others, their final decision seems to have been the confirmation of tra-

---

[14]"One of the extraordinary features of the early Church is the number of men who were converted by reading the Old Testament" (W. Barclay, *The Making of the Bible* [London, 1961], p. 41).

[15]See, e.g., O. Eissfeldt, *The Old Testament: An Introduction*, E. T. (Oxford, 1965), pp. 560ff.

[16]Ecclesiasticus, prologue. It is evident from Ecclus. 48:22–49:10 that Ben Sira knew all the "Latter Prophets"—Isaiah, Jeremiah, Ezekiel, and the Twelve—as canonical. In the first half of the first century A.D. Philo of Alexandria speaks of the Therapeutae as studying "laws, and oracles uttered through prophets, and hymns and the other things by which knowledge and piety are increased and brought to perfection" (*On the Contemplative Life*, 25).

[17]This is the most natural inference from His language about "the blood of all the prophets shed from the foundation of the world . . . from the blood of Abel to the blood of Zechariah" (Luke 11:50f.)—Zechariah being best identified with the martyred prophet of II Chr. 24:20–22.

ditional practice.[18] Josephus, writing towards the end of the first
century, treats the whole canon of Hebrew scripture as closed
and reckons its contents to be twenty-two books in all (a total
designed to coincide with the number of letters in the Hebrew
alphabet).[19]

Christians, however, and particularly Gentile Christians, would
not feel bound by the decrees of Jamnia. The rank and file who
used the Greek version might include among their sacred books
works which were closely associated with those of whose canonicity there was no doubt, although the better informed made
a distinction—in theory, at least—between those which were
part of the Hebrew Bible and those which were not. Here and
there in the New Testament we find introduced by a formula
which normally indicates a Scripture quotation something which
cannot be identified in any Old Testament text known to us (or,
for the matter of that, in any other text known to us).[20] Jude not
only quotes from the Book of Enoch,[21] but also alludes to an
incident which was probably recorded in the *Assumption of Moses*.[22]
It is striking, however, that from "the Books commonly called
Apocrypha" no quotation appears to be made by any New Testament writer.[23]

---

[18]The upshot of their debates was that, in spite of objections, Proverbs, Ecclesiastes, Canticles and Esther were acknowledged as canonical; Ecclesiasticus
was not acknowledged (Babylonian Talmud *Shabbat* 30*b*; Mishnah *Yadaim* 3:5;
Babylonian Talmud *Megillah* 7*a*; Palestinian Talmud *Megillah* 70*a*). The Jamnia
debates "have not so much dealt with the acceptance of certain writings into the
Canon, but rather with their right to remain there" (A. Bentzen, *Introduction to
the Old Testament* i [Copenhagen, 1948], 31). There was some argument earlier
in the school of Shammai about Ezekiel, long since included among the Prophets,
but when an ingenious rabbi showed that he did not really contradict Moses, as
had been alleged, misgivings were allayed (TB *Shabbat* 13*b*).

[19]*Against Apion* I. 37–43. Since Josephus does not name the individual books,
but classifies them in three groups of five, thirteen, and four respectively, we
cannot say positively that his canon coincided precisely with that laid down at
Jamnia, but if he reckoned Ruth as an appendix of Judges and Lamentations of
Jeremiah, his total of twenty-two would correspond with the traditional twenty-
four. Canonicity for him depends on prophetic inspiration, which dried up in the
reign of Artaxerxes I: "Our history has also been written in detail from Artaxerxes
to our own times, but is not esteemed as of equal authority with the books already
mentioned, because the exact succession of prophets failed."

[20]E.g., the utterance of "the Wisdom of God" in Luke 11:49; the passage
beginning "What no eye has seen . . ." in I Cor. 2:9 and the "scripture" quoted
in James 4:5.

[21]See p. 61.

[22]Jude 9; cf. Clement of Alexandria, *Adumbrations on Jude*. (The relevant part
of the *Assumption of Moses* is no longer extant.)

[23]The "Books commonly called Apocrypha" (Westminster Confession I, 3)
are I and II Esdras (III and IV Esdras in the Vulgate), Tobit, Judith, additions

The earliest Christian list of Old Testament books, compiled about A.D. 170 by Melito, bishop of Sardis, was based on information which he received while travelling in Syria;[24] it comprises all the books of the Hebrew Bible except Esther.[25] Just a little later is a list preserved in a manuscript in the Library of the Greek Patriarchate in Jerusalem in which the title of each book is given both in Hebrew (or Aramaic) and in Greek.[26] Origen (c. A.D. 230) also gives us a list of Old Testament books with their Hebrew and Greek titles; the Book of the Twelve Prophets is accidentally omitted from the textual tradition of his list but is required to make up his total. "Outside these," he adds, "are the books of Maccabees."[27] Athanasius (A.D. 367) communicated to his fellow bishops a list of canonical books, including all the books of the Hebrew Bible except Esther; Esther he includes, along with Wisdom, Ben Sira, Judith, and Tobit, among those "other books outside our list which are not canonical, but have been handed down from our fathers as suitable to be read to new converts."[28]

As late as the second half of the fourth century, then, there survived in the church a strong tradition putting the books contained in the Hebrew Bible on a higher level than those not

---

to Esther, Wisdom of Solomon, Ecclesiasticus (Wisdom of Jesus ben Sira), Baruch, Letter of Jeremiah, Additions to Daniel (The Prayer of Azariah and the Song of the Three Young Men, Susanna, Bel and the Dragon), Prayer of Manasseh, I and II Maccabees. There may be allusions to Wisdom in Rom. 1:18–2:16, but if so they express dissent as well as assent. The martyrs of the Maccabaean struggle (cf. II Macc. 6–7) are probably in view in Heb. 11:35b–38, the author of which indeed probably acquainted with IV Maccabees, but IV Maccabees was never accounted a canonical book. If the argument from silence is pressed, it should be realized that one could apply it to Canticles and Esther, which are not quoted in the New Testament (there may be allusions to Ecclesiastes in Rom. 8:20 and I Cor. 15:32).

[24]Quoted by Eusebius, *Hist. Eccl.* IV.26.14.

[25]See p. 61. One objection to the canonical acceptance of Esther was the fact that the name of God makes no appearance in it; another (voiced naturally among Jews rather than among Christians) was its record of the institution of a new festival (Purim), which conflicted with the view that all the festivals were instituted by Moses. Lamentations and Nehemiah are not specifically mentioned by Melito, but they may have been included with Jeremiah and Ezra respectively.

[26]Cf. J. P. Audet, "A Hebrew-Aramaic List of Books of the Old Testament in Greek," *JTS*, NS I (1950), 135ff. Lamentations is not mentioned by name but may have been counted as an appendix to Jeremiah. This list makes the total twenty-seven.

[27]Quoted by Eusebius, *Hist. Eccl.* VI.25.2. Origen's total, like Josephus's, is twenty-two.

[28]Athanasius, *Thirty-Ninth Festal Letter*. His total also is twenty-two. To the five recommended books "outside our list" he adds The Shepherd of Hermas (see p. 60).

contained in it, although doubts persisted regarding the status of Esther.

The question of the Old Testament canon is discussed by Jerome in the prologues to his Latin translation of the books of Samuel (or, as he called them, I and II Kings), of the Solomonic books and of Daniel. Jerome's acquaintance with Hebrew was far in advance of that of any other father of the western church — far in advance, one might say, of that of any other church father in west or east after the time of Origen—and he attached high importance to the "Hebraic verity," as he put it. It was he who first used the adjective "apocryphal" of the books outside the Hebrew canon,[29] indicating not that they were in any sense spurious but that although the church "does not receive them within the canonical scriptures," yet she "reads them for the edification of the people, not to confirm the authority of ecclesiastical dogmas."[30]

But Jerome's careful distinction tended to be forgotten by others who had no direct access, as he had, to the Hebrew Bible and who had received the books which he called the Apocrypha together with those which belonged to the Hebrew canon. Augustine, for example, reckons the Old Testament books as forty-four in number (including Tobit, Judith, Wisdom, Ecclesiasticus, I and II Maccabees),[31] and the same view was accepted in his time by the Synod of Hippo (393) and the Third Synod of Carthage (397).

But the law was not laid down dogmatically about the limits of the Old Testament canon: they remained a matter of tradition until the sixteenth century.[32] It was in the Reformation period

[29]Prologue to Samuel (*Prologus Galeatus*). The adjective "apocryphal" (Gk., ἀπόκρυφος, "hidden") had previously been used to denote books which were esoteric in content or withdrawn from general reading (cf. II Esdras 14:46f.); Jerome uses it of those books which other church fathers called "ecclesiastical" (i.e., suitable for reading publicly in church).

[30]Prologue to books of Solomon. This is the passage referred to in Article VI: "And the other books (as Hierome saith) the Church doth read for example of life, and instruction of manners; but yet doth it not apply them to establish any doctrine."

[31]Augustine points out that the books of the Maccabees (and others) "are held as canonical not by the Jews but by the church" (*City of God* xviii. 36). He further explains that books like I Enoch have no place in the canon "because their antiquity brought them under suspicion, and it was impossible to ascertain whether these were his [Enoch's] genuine writings" (*City of God* xv. 23; cf. xviii. 38).

[32]The distinction between the Apocrypha and the books contained in the Hebrew Bible was preserved by some medieval scholars, especially those who knew Hebrew or at least paid attention to Jerome. Thus Hugh of St.-Victor (died c. 1141) in a chapter *De numero librorum sacri eloquii* enumerates the books of the

that a serious issue was made of them. While the Anglicans and Lutherans generally followed the precedent of Jerome,[33] treating the apocryphal books as unsuitable for the establishment of doctrine, the Council of Trent (1546) ignored his precedent and declared that all the books in the Vulgate were canonical without distinction,[34] and at the opposite extreme the Reformers who followed the pattern of Geneva ultimately took the line that "the Books commonly called Apocrypha, not being of divine inspiration, are not part of the canon of the Scripture; and therefore are of no authority in the church of God, nor to be any otherwise approved, or made use of, than other human writings."[35]

The position taken up at Trent was reaffirmed at Vatican Council I (1869– 70),[36] but in practice the distinction made by Jerome is observed today by many Roman Catholic scholars, who find it convenient to use the old classification of biblical books into "protocanonical" and "deuterocanonical."[37] But po-

Hebrew Bible and adds: "There are also in the Old Testament certain other books which are indeed read [i.e., in church] but are not inscribed in the body of the text or in the canon of authority: such are the books of Tobit, Judith and the Maccabees, the so-called Wisdom of Solomon and Ecclesiasticus" (*De Sacramentis* I, Prologue, chap. 7: *Patrologia Latina* 176, cols. 185– 186 D).

[33]Richard Hooker defends the Anglican attitude in his *Laws of Ecclesiastical Polity*, Vol. V (London, 1597), p. 20.

[34]Sessio IV, *Decretum de canonicis scripturis*. III and IV Esdras and the Prayer of Manasseh are not included in these books: III and IV Esdras (= I and II Esdras of the "Protestant" Apocrypha) are placed in an appendix to the Vulgate and versions translated from it. (The Eastern Church confirmed the canonicity of the apocryphal books included in the Septuagint in 1642 and 1672.)

[35]Westminster Confession of Faith I, 3. The word "ultimately" is used deliberately: earlier representatives of the Geneva tradition are not so uncompromising. Coverdale (1535), who first gathered the apocryphal books together as an appendix to the Old Testament, says he did so because "there be many places in them, that seme to be repugnaunt vnto the open and manyfest trueth in the other bokes of the byble," yet will not "haue them despysed, or little sett by" because if they are read in the light of the canonical books "they shulde nether seme contrary, ner be vntruly & peruersly alledged." The Geneva Bible (1560), following Jerome, says that "as bokes proceding from godlie men" they "were receiued to be red for the aduancement and furtherance of the knowledge of the historie, & for the instruction of godlie maners: which bokes declare that at all times God had an especial care of his Church and left them not vtterly destitute of teachers and meanes to confirme them in the hope of the promised Messiah, and also witnesse that those calamities that God sent to his Church, were according to his prouidence, who had bothe so threatened by his Prophetes, and so broght it to passe for the destruction of their enemies, and for the tryal of his children."

[36]*Dogmatic Constitution on the Catholic Faith*: chap. 2, "Of Revelation." Vatican II does not go into detail about the Old Testament canon.

[37]Cf. C. Lattey, *The Book of Daniel*, Westminster Version (Dublin, 1948), where the historicity of the protocanonical narratives is defended, whereas the deutero-

sitions taken up in an atmosphere of controversy tend to be maintained as party traditions: there are, for example, some people
even today who, not being well versed in the history or status of
the apocryphal books, think of them as in some sense the per-
quisite of Rome. Thus a reviewer of the New English Bible, criticizing it for including these books, remarked: "Rome can rightly
rejoice that at last her view of the canon of Scripture has displaced that of the Apostolic Church"[38] — as though all the major
Protestant versions of the complete Bible, from Coverdale to the
Revised Standard Version, had not included the Apocrypha as
a matter of course.

THE NEW TESTAMENT CANON

While the Old Testament constituted the church's earliest Bible,
it was the Old Testament read and applied in the light of the
gospel. The gospel — God's final and perfect word to men — was
supremely authoritative, since it was embodied in Christ Himself,
the church's Lord. But for a generation and more there was no
need to appeal to a written record of the gospel: even if from an
early date there were notes or digests of the ministry or teaching
of Jesus, compiled for the use of preachers or teachers, no particular authority attached to such notes or digests. The authority
belonged to the message which they documented, and ultimately
to the Lord whom the message proclaimed. His authority could
not be rated below that of the prophets who foretold His coming:
Clement of Rome, for instance, quotes "the words of the Lord
Jesus" on the same level as the Spirit's utterances through Jeremiah and Hannah.[39]
   The authority of the Lord was exercised by His specially com-
missioned apostles, as may be seen both in those whose base was
Jerusalem and in Paul as he pursued his Gentile mission and
directed his Gentile churches. The Jerusalem decree of Acts 15:29
is an early example of the authority wielded by the Jerusalem
apostles,[40] and a careful reading of Paul's letters indicates that

---

canonical ones "are strange, and while it would be wrong to join in deriding
them, it may be felt wiser not to close the door absolutely to an explanation
which would allow an element of fiction in them" (p. iii).
   [38]I. R. K. Paisley, *The New English Bible — Version or Perversion?* (Belfast, 1961),
p. 3.
   [39]I Clement 13:1f.
   [40]Cf. F. J. A. Hort, *The Christian Ecclesia* (London, 1897), pp. 82f.; C. K. Barrett, "Christianity at Corinth," *BJRL* 46 (1963–64), 269ff.; "Things Sacrificed
to Idols," *NTS* 11 (1964–65), 138ff.

they — or, if not themselves in person, then others in their name — tried to extend their authority over his mission field.[41] Paul, for his part, teaches his converts to recognize in his writings "a command of the Lord" (I Cor. 14:37) and indicates that he lays down one "rule in all the churches" (I Cor. 7:17; cf. 11:16; 14:33b). But in writing to a church outside the area of his own apostolic responsibility he shows the restraint and delicacy that he would have liked his fellow apostles to exhibit in their approach to his churches.[42]

After the apostolic age, however, the recognition of separate spheres of apostolic service disappeared. While in the second century we find Marcion, on the one hand, venerating Paul as the only faithful apostle of Jesus,[43] and the Ebionites, on the other hand, execrating the memory of Paul and exalting the names of Peter and especially James the Just,[44] the church as a whole carried out in practice Paul's own exhortation to recognize that all the apostles and teachers — "whether Paul or Apollos or Cephas" — belonged to them all (I Cor. 3:22). However unhistorical we may judge the claim of the churches of Rome and Corinth to be joint-foundations of Peter and Paul,[45] the *attitude* expressed in such a claim was a sound one. And this attitude finds expression in the New Testament canon, where every document that could colourably be called apostolic found its place in due course.

The gospels, anonymous though they were, were recognized as transcripts of the apostolic witness to Christ and, from an early point in the second century, were brought together, so that they no longer circulated separately in their respective constituencies but as a fourfold collection. It is difficult to say how far advanced this process was in the time of Ignatius, but he clearly had a written gospel to appeal to, and equally clearly he had to contend with more conservative brethren who disapproved of the idea of appealing to any written authority alongside the Old Testament scriptures as interpreted in the church's oral tradition. This is the point of the reference in his Letter to the Philadel-

[41]Cf. II Cor. 10:7ff. (F. F. Bruce, "Paul and Jerusalem," *Tyndale Bulletin* 19 [1968], 3ff. *Corinthians*, Century Bible [London, 1971], *ad loc.*).

[42]Cf. Rom. 1:8ff.; 15:14ff.

[43]Cf. A. Harnack, *Marcion* (Leipzig, 1924); *Neue Studien zu Marcion* (Leipzig, 1923).

[44]Cf. H. J. Schoeps, *Theologie und Geschichte des Judenchristentums* (Tübingen, 1949), p. 120, where Paul is seen as "beyond question" the "enemy" (ἐχθρὸς ἄνθρωπος) of the Ebionite *Epistle of Peter to James*, 2.

[45]Cf. Irenaeus, *Heresies* III.3.1; Dionysius of Corinth, quoted by Eusebius, *Hist. Eccl.* II.25.8.

phians to those people who asserted: "If I do not find it in the
archives [the Old Testament], I do not believe it [if it is con-
tained] in the gospel." To which he replied "It is written" —
"Scripture says" (meaning that the gospel is "scripture"). But
they say, "That is the very point at question" — i.e., is the gospel
"scripture"? And then Ignatius, like many another debater driven
into a corner, takes refuge in rhetoric:

> But my archives are Jesus Christ; the inviolable archives are
> His cross, His death, His resurrection, and the faith which is
> exercised through Him. . . .[46]

Plainly Ignatius regarded Jesus Christ as his "tradition." Within
that tradition everything had a place which bore true witness to
Him — the Old Testament scriptures because they pointed forward to Him, the written gospel because it was the record of His
incarnation and passion, the letters of the apostles because they
were His delegates, and the church's faith and worship because
they had their source in Him. Plainly, too, Ignatius had not
thought his tradition through to first principles, so that he could
give a logical defence of it in every part, including his recognition
of the gospel as "scripture." The earliest recognition of the New
Testament writings was spontaneous and instinctive: the ration-
ale of the canon came later. Hence the history of the canon at its
outset has untidy edges: we cannot give a cut-and-dried account
of its first formation any more than Ignatius or his contemporaries could have done.

The necessity of a canon of written documents as a check on
the corruption of oral tradition was as apparent to many Gnostics
as it was to those who maintained the tradition of the apostolic
churches. Valentinus, according to Tertullian, used the whole
New Testament canon,[47] and the substantial truth of this statement has been confirmed in recent years by the evidence of Valentinian documents found among the Nag Hammadi papyri. The
Gospel of Truth, for example, acknowledges the authority of every
major section of the New Testament except the Pastoral Epistles.[48] It was in their interpretation of the documents, not in their
recognition of them, that the Valentinians were distinguished
from the catholic church.[49]

[46] Ignatius, Philadelphians 8:2.
[47] Tertullian, Prescription against Heretics, 38.
[48] Cf. W. C. van Unnik, "The 'Gospel of Truth' and the New Testament," in
The Jung Codex, ed. F. L. Cross (London, 1955), pp. 81ff., 124.
[49] As in the commentary on John by the Valentinian Heracleon (c. 175), the
earliest commentary on that Gospel, quoted repeatedly by Origen in his commentary on John.

Marcion, for his part, also knew the value of an authoritative written canon and, strong in his cast-iron presuppositions, he promulgated his edition of the *Euangelion* and *Apostolikon* as (in his view) they must originally have been, thus creating a new tradition for his followers. The catholic leaders had an older tradition, but no doubt it was the promulgation of Marcion's canon that stimulated them, and especially the leaders of the Roman church, to define that tradition more precisely than they had thus far felt necessary. Whereas Marcion's canon expressed his exclusive devotion to Paul (Luke the evangelist enjoying special credit because of his association with Paul),[50] the catholic canon was catholic in a further sense, comprising the writings of other apostles or "apostolic men" alongside Paul, and of three other evangelists alongside Luke, and binding the *Euangelion* and *Apostolikon* together with Luke's second volume, henceforth called the Acts of the Apostles, which provided the sequel to the gospel story and the historical context of the apostolic letters, presenting independent evidence for the genuineness of Paul's apostolic claims[51] and for the loyal witness of other apostles whom Marcion had denigrated. Acts was thus, as Harnack aptly put it, the "pivot" of the New Testament.[52]

Justin Martyr attests the use of an informal New Testament canon: he tells how "the memoirs of the apostles," otherwise called "gospels," were read in church in the same way as "the compositions of the prophets"[53] and quotes Old Testament texts together with passages from the writings of the new covenant (especially sayings of Jesus) as though they shared the same authority.[54] If here and there his works contain traces of materials from the pseudonymous Gospels of Peter or Thomas, these are very few in comparison with his use of the fourfold Gospel.

Justin's disciple Tatian is best known for his *Diatessaron* or Harmony of the four Gospels, which provides sufficient evidence

[50]Marcion's *Euangelion* was a revision of the Third Gospel, beginning at Luke 3:1 and going straight on from there to 4:31 so as to exclude all suggestion that the story of Jesus is linked with preceding history or that he came into the world by birth: "In the fifteenth year of Tiberius Caesar Jesus came down to Capernaum, a city of Galilee" (Tertullian, *Against Marcion* IV.7.1).

[51]Cf. Tertullian, *Prescription against Heretics*, 22f.

[52]A. Harnack, *The Origin of the New Testament*, E. T. (London, 1925), pp. 53, 63ff.

[53]Justin, *First Apology* 66:3; 67:3. He refers elsewhere (*Dialogue* 106:3) to the "memoirs" of Peter, meaning either the Gospel of Mark or the pseudonymous Gospel of Peter (see p. 75), the latter of which he seems to quote (from 3:6f.) in *First Apology* 35:6.

[54]E.g., *First Apology* 63:1–8, where Isa. 1:3; Matt. 11:27; Luke 10:16 (or rather something like it) and Exod. 3:6ff. (abridged) are quoted together.

of the separate level on which these four records were placed in
his time. In places Tatian appears to have amplified the fourfold
record by means of the *Gospel according to the Hebrews*, which may
have been a sectarian revision of Matthew but not to an extent
which impairs the fourfold pattern of his Harmony.[55]

For Irenaeus the fourfold Gospel is one of the facts of life, as
axiomatic as the four pillars of the earth or the four winds of
heaven.[56] This shows how thoroughly he and his contemporaries
took it for granted that there were, and could be, only four gospel
writings. Even more thoroughly did they take it for granted that
these four could only be Matthew, Mark, Luke, and John: this
is something which, for them, did not even need to be proved.
By the time of Irenaeus, too, the main contents of the catholic
canon were fixed and accepted throughout the Christian world.
He does not give us a formal list, but it is plain that for him the
fourfold Gospel, Acts, the Pauline corpus, I Peter, I John, and
Revelation were "scripture" (as also were I Clement and The
Shepherd of Hermas).[57]

The earliest catholic list of New Testament books that has
been preserved to us is that in the "Muratorian" canon, which
probably represents the tradition of the Roman church at the
end of the second century.[58] The one surprise in this list is the
omission of I Peter (this omission, in view of the corrupt state of
the text in the only extant copy of the list, could conceivably be
accidental).[59] As it is, the list contains the four Gospels, Acts,
the letters of Paul, Jude, and John,[60] "John's Apocalypse and
Peter's,"[61] with the Wisdom of Solomon.[62] The Shepherd of Her-

---

[55]Cf. A. Baumstark, "Die syrische Übersetzung des Titus von Bostra and das
'Diatessaron'," *Biblica* 16 (1935), 257ff.

[56]Irenaeus, *Heresies* III.11.11.

[57]Irenaeus, *Heresies* III.3.2; IV.34.2.

[58]A convenient edition is that in the series *Kleine Texte* edited by H. Lietzmann:
Das Muratorische Fragment und die Monarchianischen Prologe zu den Evangelien (Berlin,
1933).

[59]T. Zahn thought that some words had fallen out after "John's Apocalypse
and Peter's," and that the original text ran: "John's Apocalypse and Peter's *epistle.
There is also another epistle of Peter*, which some of our people refuse to have read
in church" (*Geschichte des neutestamentlichen Kanons* ii [Erlangen, 1890], p. 142; the
italicized words are supplied by Zahn).

[60]"Two by the aforementioned John," says the list: if this means two in addition to I John, mentioned some lines earlier in connexion with the Gospel of
John, these two will be our II and III John; otherwise we should have to conclude
either that only one of the two shorter letters of John was included, or else that
II and III John were reckoned together as one.

[61]The Apocalypse of Peter has been preserved (cf. *New Testament Apocrypha*,
ed. E. Hennecke, W. Schneemelcher, R. McL. Wilson [ET London, 1965],

mas, edifying as it is, is too recent to be reckoned canonical.[63] The writings of the Valentinians, Marcionites, and Montanists are to be rejected.

As interesting as the contents of the list is the kind of argument put forward for the canonical acceptance of the various books. Luke was Paul's "legal expert," an official who issued decrees and similar documents in accordance with his superior's judgement;[64] thus Luke's writings are made to share Paul's authority. Luke's second volume is inappropriately called "the Acts of *all* the apostles" — possibly by way of anti-Marcionite emphasis but possibly also to make it clear that this was the only genuine book of apostolic Acts. In recent decades the five volumes of "Leucian" Acts had appeared — of Peter, John, Andrew, Thomas, and Paul[65] — and the compiler of our list wishes it to be understood that it is to the canonical Acts, and not to these apocryphal works, that one must go in order to find an authentic record of the apostles' journeyings. Should anyone ask why Luke breaks off his narrative without tracing Paul's career to its end, the answer is that he narrated only those things which took place in his presence.[66] This same insistence on eyewitness testimony — a further token of the author's acquaintance with Roman law — appears in his treatment of the Gospel of John, in which, he maintains, the Evangelist recorded only "what we have seen with our eyes and heard with our ears and our hands have handled" — quoting I John 1:1.

When he comes to deal with the canonicity of Paul's letters, he makes the quite astonishing statement that Paul wrote letters to seven churches in accordance with the pattern set by John, who did the same in the Apocalypse. Presumably the canonicity

---

pp. 663–683); its lurid pictures of the torments of the damned are the source of much medieval imagery, e.g., of their portrayal in Dante's *Inferno*.

[62]We associate Wisdom with the Old Testament Apocrypha rather than with the New Testament, but in date it is closer to the New Testament than to the Old.

[63]Hermas is said to have been the brother of Pius I, bishop of Rome *c.* A.D. 150. He may have been an older brother, as the date of The Shepherd of Hermas is probably nearer the beginning of the second century than the middle.

[64]Cf. A. Ehrhardt, *The Framework of the New Testament Stories* (Manchester, 1964), pp. 16ff.; he deduces from the technical language of Roman law used here that the document must have been composed at Rome, and in Latin, perhaps under Pope Zephyrinus (197–217).

[65]Cf. *New Testament Apocrypha*, ed. E. Hennecke, W. Schneemelcher, R. McL. Wilson, pp. 167–531.

[66]Two events are mentioned as unrelated by Luke for this reason — Paul's departure for Spain and Peter's execution in Rome. It is no accident that both of these are related in the "Acts of Peter."

of John's seven letters depended on his being a prophet, and the authority of Paul's letters was established by analogy with John's.[67] The same implication that prophecy is the main criterion of canonicity appears in his remark about The Shepherd of Hermas. This obviously could not be accepted as an apostolic writing, but its character would have qualified it for inclusion among the prophets, had the prophetic list not been closed long since.

The principal criterion of New Testament canonicity imposed in the early church was not prophetic inspiration but apostolic authorship — or, if not authorship, then authority. In an environment where apostolic tradition counted for so much, the source and norm of that tradition were naturally found in the writings of apostles or of men closely associated with apostles. Mark and Luke, for instance, were known not to be apostles, but their close association with Peter and Paul[68] respectively was emphasized. As for the epistles, however, the tendency was for canonicity to be tied to the ascription of apostolic authorship. The Letter to the Hebrews, for example, was known in the Roman church earlier than anywhere else[69] (so far as our evidence goes), but Rome was one of the last important churches to acknowledge it as canonical, just as Rome was one of the last important churches to ascribe Pauline authorship to it — not out of conviction, but out of an unwillingness to be out of step in this regard with Alexandria and the other great eastern churches.

This unwillingness to be out of step with other churches reminds us that another criterion of canonicity was catholicity. A document which was acknowledged only in one small corner of Christendom was unlikely to win acceptance as canonical; one which was acknowledged over the greater area of Christendom was likely to win still wider acceptance.

Throughout the third and fourth centuries the definition of the New Testament canon continued to become more and more

[67]Cf. K. Stendahl, "The Apocalypse of John and the Epistles of Paul in the Muratorian Fragment," in *Current Issues in New Testament Interpretation*, ed. W. Klassen and G. F. Snyder (New York, 1962), pp. 239ff.

[68]Eusebius mentions some who went so far as to suggest that, when Paul speaks of "my gospel" (Rom. 2:16; 16:25; II Tim. 2:8), he refers to the Gospel of Luke (*Hist. Eccl.* III.4.7).

[69] Clement of Rome (*c.* A.D. 96) knows the letter and quotes it — misinterpreting it in one place (I Clem. 17:1) where he takes those who "went about in skins of sheep and goats" (Heb. 11:37) to be Elijah and Elisha — but he gives no inkling of its authorship nor does he treat it as an apostolic document.

precise until in 367 Athanasius[70] (followed by the Synod of Hippo in 393 and the Third Synod of Carthage in 397) listed as canonical the twenty seven books which have been handed down to us. Until then it was customary to distinguish the (universally) acknowledged books and the disputed books, the spurious books (those laying false claim to apostolic authorship), and the heretical books which were erroneous and utterly to be repudiated. If a disputed book taught apostolic doctrine and was sufficiently ancient, it tended to be given the benefit of the doubt.[71] The authorship of Jude, for example, was uncertain but, as Origen said, it was "full of words of heavenly grace"[72] and so it ultimately gained admission. The Shepherd of Hermas, on the other hand, popular as it was and recommended for reading in church, was *known* to be of post-apostolic origin and so was ruled out on the score of insufficient antiquity.[73]

But, as has already been said, these criteria of canonicity were largely devised to justify a tradition which already existed. Authority precedes canonicity: that is to say, the various writings do not derive their authority from their inclusion in the canon: they were included in the canon because their authenticity was recognized.[74] It is going too far to say, as Oscar Cullmann does, that "among the early Christian writings the books which were to form the future canon *forced themselves on the Church by their intrinsic apostolic authority*, as they do still, because the *Kyrios* Christ speaks in them"[75] — at least, if this is to be taken as a statement of history. "Intrinsic apostolic authority" is a difficult entity to define.

With our longer perspective we can say that the early church, in recognizing the books which make up the New Testament canon as uniquely worthy to stand alongside the sacred scriptures

---

[70]*Thirty-Ninth Festal Letter* (see p. 65). Athanasius includes the *Didache* and The Shepherd of Hermas along with five of the Old Testament apocrypha as read in church but not canonical.

[71]Thus the Gospel of Peter was allowed to be read in the church of Rhossus in Syria, until Serapion, bishop of Antioch, discovered its Docetic tendency and put them on their guard against it (Eusebius, *Hist. Eccl.* VI.12.2ff.).

[72]Origen, *Commentary on Matthew* x. 17 (on Matt. 13:55).

[73]There were also practical considerations which made the contents of the canon better known among the rank and file of Christians; it was important for them to know which books might be appealed to in disputes with heretics and (in the last imperial persecution) which books might be handed over to the police for destruction and which must be guarded at the cost of one's life, if necessary.

[74]Of course their authority came to be recognized in a practical way from their presence in the canon, but this is a *ratio cognoscendi*, not the *ratio essendi*.

[75]O. Cullmann, "The Tradition," in *The Early Church* (London, 1956), p. 91.

of the old covenant, was guided by a wisdom higher than its own. When we think of other early Christian documents more or less contemporary with the latest books of the New Testament — the Epistle of Clement of Rome, the Epistle of Barnabas, The Shepherd of Hermas, the Letters of Ignatius, and the *Didache*, for example — we may be thankful that they did not succeed in gaining admission to the canon, although some of them were on the fringe of it for a considerable time. The question has been raised whether it is legitimate for us to defend the early church's decision about admission and exclusion with arguments quite different from those which were used at the time.[76] But we have no option if we accept the canon: we must defend our acceptance of it with arguments which *we* hold to be valid.

THE REFORMATION AND AFTER

At the time of the Reformation the canon of Scripture, like everything else that was handed down by tradition, was subjected to scrutiny. In many of the traditions handed down through medieval times the Reformers recognized a close kinship to that "tradition of men" with which our Lord found fault because it displaced "the commandment of God."[77] The danger of this tendency, said Calvin, lies in the fact that "whenever holiness is made to consist in anything else than in observing the law of God, men are led to believe that the law may be violated without danger." Then he adds: "Let any man now consider whether this wickedness does not at present abound more among the Papists than it formerly did among the Jews."[78] And in many other places where the Gospels said "Pharisees" the Reformers read "Papists." Yet church tradition was not jettisoned completely by the mainstream Reformers: in doctrine and practice alike they went back beyond the Middle Ages to appeal to the fathers of the early centuries: Calvin himself was no mean patristic scholar and adduces patristic evidence freely and copiously in support of his arguments. But the fathers themselves were subject to the superior authority of Scripture. Calvin himself does not discuss the canon of the Scripture as distinct from its authority, which he defends alike against those who in practice made it subordi-

---

[76]Cf. E. Flesseman-van Leer, "Prinzipien der Sammlung und Ausscheidung bei der Bildung des Kanons," *Zeitschrift für Theologie und Kirche* 61 (1964), 404ff.

[77]Mark 7:8.

[78]*Commentary on a Harmony of the Evangelists*, trans. W. Pringle (Edinburgh, 1845), p. 251.

nate to church tradition and those who rejected it in favour of their private revelations.[79] "Those who are inwardly taught by the Holy Spirit acquiesce implicitly in Scripture. . . . Scripture, carrying its own evidence along with it, deigns not to submit to proofs and arguments, but owes the full conviction with which we ought to receive it to the testimony of the Spirit."[80] He does not explicitly make the inward testimony of the Spirit a criterion of canonicity, but if the question had been directly put to him how he knew (say) that the Hebrew and Aramaic text of Daniel was Scripture whereas the additions in the Greek version were not, he might well have done so. The apostolicity of II Peter is for him secondary,[81] but "it contains nothing unworthy of Peter, and . . . shows throughout the power and grace of the apostolic spirit. . . . Certainly since the majesty of the Spirit of Christ expresses itself in all parts of the epistle, I have a dread of repudiating it, even though I do not recognize in it the genuine language of Peter."[82] This is, in effect, an appeal to the testimony of the Spirit for decision regarding a "disputed" book.[83]

Luther expressed himself more freely, if less systematically. He translated the apocryphal books along with the Hebrew Bible, but gave them the same inferior rank as Jerome did. The same inferior rank, indeed, was given with emphasis to one of the books of the Hebrew Bible: "I hate Esther and II Maccabees so much," he said, "that I wish they did not exist. There is too much Judaism in them and much heathen vice."[84] But within the New Testament also he assigned a lower rank to some books than to others. As is well known, in the list of books prefaced to his German New Testament he attaches serial numbers to the first twenty-three, which he calls elsewhere "the right certain capital books,"[85] and separates off the remaining four — Hebrews, James, Jude, and Revelation — by a space and by the absence of serial numbers. In his prefaces to these books he indicates his reasons

---

[79]*Inst.*, I, 7, 1–9, 3.

[80]Ibid., I, 7, 5.

[81]"I conclude that if the epistle is trustworthy it has come from Peter; not that he wrote it himself, but that one of his disciples composed by his command what the necessity of the times demanded" (*Commentary on Hebrews and I and II Peter*, trans. W. B. Johnston [Edinburgh, 1963], p. 325).

[82]Ibid.

[83]Sebastian Castellio's treatment of Canticles as a secular lovesong (though he included it in his new Latin version of the Bible) was a principal reason for the Genevan ministers' declining to ordain him (*Calvini Opera* xi = CR 39, cols. 674ff.).

[84]*Table Talk*, W.A., 1, p. 208; Cf. *De servo arbitrio*, W.A., 18, p. 666.

[85]Preface to Hebrews, *Die deutsche Bibel*, W.A., 7, p. 345.

for relegating them to what was in essence deuterocanonical status. Hebrews, he reckoned, contained some "wood, straw and hay" along with the "gold, silver and precious stones" which were built into its fabric, and so it could not be placed "on a level with the apostolic epistles."[86] James contradicted the doctrine of justification by faith, and although it pressed home the law of God, it bore no evangelical witness to Christ.[87] Jude, which he (mistakenly, no doubt) regarded as an abstract of II Peter, was "an unnecessary epistle to include among the capital books which ought to lay the foundation of faith"; it was also held against it that it included uncanonical teaching and history (a reference to the Enoch quotation and the dispute about the body of Moses).[88] Revelation "lacks everything that I hold as apostolic or prophetic"[89] — although the sharpness of this judgement, expressed in 1522, was subsequently mitigated.

To a large degree Luther's deuterocanonical books coincide with those which the early church ranked as disputed, but it was not the verdict of the early church that weighed with Luther so much as evangelical content. Therefore he had no difficulty about II Peter or II and III John, although their apostolicity was questioned in the early church. The criterion of canonicity — at least for protocanonicity, for inclusion among the "capital books" — was for Luther "what presses home Christ" (*was Christum treibet*).[90] Not the identity of the writer, but the character of the writing, is what counts. "That which does not teach Christ is not apostolic, even if Peter or Paul taught it. Again, that which does preach Christ is apostolic even if Judas, Annas, Pilate or Herod did it."[91] In this Luther shows himself a true disciple of Paul: "even if we, or an angel from heaven, should preach to you a gospel contrary to that which we preached to you, let him be accursed" (Gal. 1:8).

Luther's criterion is still widely accepted. When Dr. Norman Snaith delivered his Fernley-Hartley Lecture on *The Distinctive Ideas of the Old Testament*, he found that the distinctive ideas were those which were taken up and brought to perfection in the New Testament, not least in the letters of Paul, while "the true development from the Pauline theology is to be found in Luther and

[86]Preface to Hebrews, W.A., 7, pp. 344f.
[87]Preface to James, W.A., 7, p. 387.
[88]Preface to Jude, W.A., 7, p. 387.
[89]Preface to Revelation, W.A., 7, p. 404.
[90]Preface to James, W.A., 7, pp. 384f.
[91]Ibid.

in John Wesley."[92] Some readers might find it a surprising co-
incidence that the finest flowering of the biblical revelation should
be discerned in the tradition of which Dr. Snaith is himself such
a worthy and devoted exponent; but I have no doubt he is right —
although I too may not be entirely unbiased in this regard.

Quite similar is the argument of the late Edward J. Carnell
that, since justification by faith is systematically expounded only
in Romans and Galatians, "therefore, if the church teaches anything that offends the system of Romans and Galatians, it is
cultic"[93] ("cultic" apparently having the sense of "sectarian" as
opposed to "catholic"). Again: "whenever a passage conflicts with
the teaching of Romans and Galatians, either the mind has failed
to grasp its meaning, or the passage falls under the concept of
progressive revelation."[94]

THE CANON IN THE TWENTIETH CENTURY

But we have received the twenty-seven books of the New Testament, and while individual readers or teachers may make distinctions between those among them which are "capital" and
those which are of lower grade, our church tradition has made
no such distinction — since the end of the fourth century. The
statement of Article VI, that these twenty-seven are books "of
whose authority was never any doubt in the Church," is not true
if we press our quest back earlier than that date, but from then
on it represents the general consensus, if we overlook some of the
separated eastern churches. If, however, we are asked today why
we accept these twenty-seven, or why we accept any specific one
of them, do we give our tradition as a sufficient answer or do we
seek an answer more satisfactory to ourselves and to our ques-
tioners?

Some of us, theological students and the like, have studied the
formation of the canon and can give a historical reason of sorts
for our position. But what is the ordinary church member to say,
especially if his church's formularies make no explicit statement
about the canon? A Roman Catholic layman will appeal to the
authority of the church, which has made clear pronouncements
on this subject, but what does the ordinary free churchman say?
Hardly, I suppose, "Because the church say so" — the only church
he knows may be the local church to which he belongs, and it is

[92]N. H. Snaith, *The Distinctive Ideas of the Old Testament* (London, 1944), p. 186.
[93]E. J. Carnell, *The Case for Orthodox Theology* (London, 1961), p. 59.
[94]Ibid., p. 99.

unlikely ever to have made a pronouncement on the canon. Will he say, "Because my pastor says so, and he is a man of such piety and learning — in fact, he is a B.A. (Theol.) of Manchester — that he cannot be wrong"? Perhaps; but what if his pastor voices doubts about the canonicity of Jude or the apostolicity of II Peter? He is then quite likely to say, "My pastor, I fear, is a little unsound; he does not believe the whole Bible — and that is the result of his attending those classes in Biblical Criticism at Manchester University." But how does he know what "the whole Bible" is? Most probably by tradition — sound and reliable tradition, no doubt, but tradition none the less.

I turn now to a body of nineteenth-century origin unsurpassed in its professed adherence to *sola scriptura* and repudiation of the authority of tradition — the Exclusive Brethren — and cite no unlearned church member but their ablest scholar, William Kelly. William Kelly was no mean theologian, but he would have been the last man to acknowledge any debt to "mere" tradition.[95] Yet he "was the staunchest upholder of the entire Nicene and Athanasian doctrine,"[96] and to him the New Testament canon was a *datum*. In his commentary on the Epistles of Peter, for example, he notes the doubts that some had expressed in his day about the authorship of II Peter, but takes a short and sharp line with them.

The Petrine authorship and divine inspiration of II Peter as of I Peter, he says, is apprehended by "any unbiased Christian"[97] — which is a good example of the preemptive strike in theological controversy. He refuses to admit catholic tradition as authority for the genuineness and canonicity of the document, but with equal vigour he rejects the Protestant assertion of private judgement; both alike tend to the deification of man and the dethronement of God. Perhaps he would have allowed the appeal to the inward witness of the Spirit, but he does not explicitly say so. What he does say is more peremptory, and he says it in criticism of Bishop Christopher Wordsworth's argument that, in view of the many pseudepigrapha circulating in Peter's name, it

[95]Except in so far as he was a faithful follower of J. N. Darby. " 'Read Darby!' he used to say, to the last" (*Memories of the Life and Last Days of William Kelly*, ed. H. Wreford [London, 1906], p. 75). C. H. Spurgeon described him as "a man 'who, born for the universe, narrowed his mind' by Darbyism" (*Commenting and Commentaries* [London, 1887], p. 164).

[96]W. B. Neatby, "Mr. William Kelly as a Theologian," *Expositor*, 7th series, 2 (London, 1907), p. 79.

[97]*The Epistles of Peter: The Second Epistle of Peter* (London, 1923), p. 10. The commentaries on I and II Peter in this volume are paginated separately; that on II Peter was left unfinished at his death in 1906.

was the church's duty to suspend judgement on II Peter until adequate proofs of its authenticity were available.[98] "It is *never a duty,*" says Kelly, "even for the simplest Christian, *to doubt Scripture,* but only to believe."[99] True: but how is the simplest Christian to know in the first instance what is Scripture and what is not? Kelly leaves this question unanswered, what is the more surprising in such an able thinker. Again, he may have held that the simplest Christian knows Scripture by the inward witness of the Spirit; but again, he does not explicitly say so. Even so, the Spirit's inward witness may assure me that what I hear or read is the word of God to me: it will hardly give an answer to questions of authorship or date.

It is noteworthy that when it comes to textual criticism or straight exegesis, as distinct from the history of the canon, Kelly can use his private judgement in as sound and uninhibited a manner as any other scholar—though he is always apt, having established the true test of the proper exegesis on a grammatico-historical basis, to turn his weapon round and say that any spiritual and unprejudiced reader can see that this is the right way of it.

To us the canon is something "received"—the books "disputed by some" being handed down with, and carried by, those "acknowledged by all."[100] Any talk of enlarging or contracting it at this time of day is unrealistic. We may toy with the fancy that some discovery of the future, like that of the Qumran or Nag Hammadi texts, may bring to light a lost letter of Paul's—say his "previous" letter to the Corinthians[101]—or a copy of the Gospel of Mark complete with its "lost" ending (supposing that it was not the Evangelist's intention to finish at Mark 16:8). Would there be a move to have such a document added to the canon? It is difficult to see how this could be effected. For one thing, scholars would certainly not be unanimous about its authenticity. For another thing, there is no competent authority, acknowledged throughout Christendom, to decree its addition. Even if we could imagine the Pope, the Ecumenical Patriarch, and the presidents of the World Council of Churches and the International Council of Christian Churches agreeing to recommend the addition, there are some awkward nonconformists who would

---

[98]C. Wordsworth, *The New Testament in the Original Greek*, ii (London, 1862).

[99]Kelly, p. 5.

[100]The terminology is Origen's: the universally acknowledged books are the ἀναντίρρητα or ὁμολογούμενα, while the disputed ones are ἀμφιβαλλόμενα (quoted by Eusebius, *Hist. Eccl.* VI.25).

[101]Cf. I Cor. 5:9.

probably repudiate the idea just because it was recommended by one or all of these. If the analogy of history is relevant, it suggests that the common consensus of Christians over several generations would have to precede any official pronouncement.

Suggestions that the canon might be augmented by the inclusion of other "inspirational" literature, ancient or modern, arise from a failure to appreciate what the canon actually is. It is not an anthology of inspirational literature. The question is not what is to be read in church: when a sermon is read, the congregation is treated to what is usually, in intention at least, inspirational literature, and the same may be said of prayers which are read from the Prayer Book or hymns which are read from the hymn-book. It is a question of getting as near as possible to the source of the Christian faith.

In a lecture delivered at Oxford in 1961 Professor Kurt Aland expressed the view that as the Old Testament canon underwent a *de facto* narrowing as a result of the new covenant established in Christ,[102] so also the New Testament canon "is *in practice* undergoing a narrowing and a shortening," so that we can recognize in the New Testament as in the Old a "canon within the canon."[103] This is a natural attitude on the part of a scholar in the Lutheran tradition; we know how depreciatory is the judgement passed today by many scholars in this tradition on those parts of the New Testament which smack of "primitive catholicism."[104] The "actual living, effective Canon," as distinct from the formal canon, "is constructed according to the method of 'self-understanding.' "[105] But if it is suggested that Christians and churches get together and try to reach agreement on a common effective canon, the difficulty is that the "effective" canon of some groups or individuals differs from that of others. If the inner canon to some consists of Romans and Galatians (with the two Corinthian epistles), to others it consists of the Captivity Epistles, to others of the Synoptic Gospels, to others of the Johannine Gospels and Epistles, and to others (one might be tempted to think) of the Apocalypse.

It would be precarious to try to name any part of Scripture — even the genealogical lists! — in which some believing reader has

---

[102]The reference may be to those parts of the Old Testament directly cited in the New as fulfilled in the gospel.

[103]K. Aland, *The Problem of the New Testament Canon* (London, 1962), pp. 27ff.

[104]E. Käsemann, "Paul and Early Catholicism," *New Testament Questions of Today* (ET London, 1969), pp. 236ff. See critique by H. Küng, *The Structures of the Church* (ET London, 1965), pp. 142ff.

[105]Aland, p. 29.

not heard the word of God addressing him effectively and in context. William Robertson Smith gave as his reason for believing in the Bible as the word of God: "Because the Bible is the only record of the redeeming love of God, because in the Bible alone I find God drawing near to man in Christ Jesus, and declaring to us, in Him, His will for our salvation. And this record I know to be true by the witness of His Spirit in my heart, whereby I am assured that none other than God Himself is able to speak such words to my soul."[106] If he had been asked just where in the Bible he recognized this record and experienced this witness, he would probably not have mentioned every book, but he might well have said that the record of God's love and the witness of the Spirit were so pervasive that they gave character to the Old and New Testament canon as a whole. Other readers might bear the same testimony, but might think of other parts of the Bible than Robertson Smith had in mind. No wonder, then, that Professor Aland speaks of the necessity of questioning one's own actual canon and taking the actual canon of others seriously.[107]

The appeal to the testimony of the Holy Spirit is valid, but it will scarcely enable all to decide the precise limits of the canon. By an act of faith one may identify the New Testament canon as we have received it with the entire *paradosis* of Christ, to which, in Oscar Cullmann's view, all the apostles contribute, each passing on to another that part which he himself received.[108] This may be so, but it cannot be proved. It is better to say of the New Testament books what Hans Lietzmann said of the four Gospels in the early church, that "the reference to their apostolic authority, which can only appear to us as a reminder of sound historical bases, had the deeper meaning that this particular tradition of Jesus — and this alone — had been established and guaranteed by the Holy Spirit working authoritatively in the Church."[109] No doubt within "this particular tradition" diverse strands of tradition — indeed diverse traditions — may be detected, but although critical scholars may emphasize their diversity, the church, both ancient and modern, has been more conscious of their overall unity, in contrast to other interpretations which patently conflict with the New Testament witness but cannot substantiate a comparable claim to apostolic authority.

[106]W. R. Smith, *Answer to the Form of Libel now before the Free Church Presbytery of Aberdeen* (Edinburgh, 1878), p. 21.
[107]Aland, pp. 31f.
[108]O. Cullmann, p. 73.
[109]H. Lietzmann, *The Founding of the Church Universal* (ET London, 1950), p. 97.

In the canon we have the foundation documents or the charter of the Christian faith. For no other document or group of documents from the earliest Christian generations can such a claim be made. (Even the most debatable of the "disputed" books in the New Testament canon has more of the quality of apostolic authority about it than the letters of Clement of Rome and Ignatius of Antioch or The Shepherd of Hermas.) What has been said, however, is not tantamount to shutting the Holy Spirit up in a book or collection of books. Repeatedly, new movements of the Spirit have been launched by a rediscovery of the living power which resides in the canon of Scripture. The New Testament "is not one of the paralysing and enslaving forces of the past, but it is full of eternal and present strength to make strong and to make free."[110]

---

[110]A. Deissmann, *Light from the Ancient East* (ET London, 1927), p. 409.

AUTHORITY:
Doctrine and
Its Development

6 THE BIBLICAL CONCEPT OF REVELATION

DEWEY M. BEEGLE

"The doctrine of inspiration," according to James Orr (1844–1913), "grows out of that of revelation, and can only be made intelligible through the latter."[1] Because of the accuracy of this insight, the most meaningful attempt to understand the cluster of concepts associated with the inspiration of Scripture is to begin with the idea of revelation.

THE PROBLEM OF METHOD

Basic to the theory of modern research is the principle that an investigation of a problem must begin with the data of the primary sources dealing with the issue. This is a valid procedure; therefore our first task is to ascertain the various aspects of revelation as stated in Scripture. The success of this study depends on the degree to which we understand what is being said. We must acknowledge at the outset that there are some limitations in such an investigation because, in spite of our desire to be perfectly objective, each of us brings (often unconsciously) some presuppositions to the task of interpretation. But this need not be a significant defect since careful attention to method can reduce the lack of objectivity to a minimum.

DEDUCTION AND INDUCTION

The human mind is capable of two basic processes of reasoning. One of these is the *deductive* method. It starts with an assumption or generalization from which are deduced details or particulars. The other approach is the *inductive* method. It begins with facts or details from which a generalization or principle is formulated.

The two methods of reasoning are well illustrated by archae-

[1]*Revelation and Inspiration* (Grand Rapids, 1952), p. 197.

From *Dewey M. Beegle*, Scripture, Tradition, and Infallibility, pp. 15–30. Copyright © 1973 by Wm. B. Eerdmans Publishing Company.

ology. In excavating an ancient mound (*tell*) with its many layers of superimposed cities, the primary task is to dig down through these various strata, labeling all the objects and pottery according to the stratum in which they were discovered. When these facts are correlated, the archaeologist observes that the pottery, for example, of a certain stratum has form and features about it that distinguish it from the pottery of other strata. In other words, each stratum tends to have its own type or class of pottery. This process of observation and inductive reasoning from facts to generalization is called "stratigraphy."

On the other hand, when the archaeologist comes across the same type of pottery while excavating another mound, he makes the deduction that the stratum in which the pottery was found dates from the same general period as the similar stratum in the first mound. This deductive reasoning from the generalization of pottery form to certain facts about the pottery is called "typology."

The accurate archaeological results of the last fifty years can be attributed to careful application of both of these methods of reasoning, and it has become increasingly apparent that adequate solutions to complex problems necessitate both induction and deduction. If handled properly, therefore, the two methods are complementary: a valid deduction should result in details that accord with the observable facts, and correct observation and relating of details should lead to a sound generalization.

THE PRIORITY OF INDUCTIVE REASONING

Granting the propriety and necessity of both kinds of reasoning, this does not mean that one is free to begin resolving the problem with whichever method happens to strike his fancy at the moment. The best results are obtained when induction precedes deduction. The history of archaeological activity makes this quite evident. Early attempts at interpreting the data often led to conflicting conclusions because the assumptions of certain archaeologists either distorted their observation of the facts or made it impossible for them to detect some of the pertinent details. Order came out of chaos when priority was given to inductive reasoning, and the same can be said for all other realms of science.

In the early stages of the struggle between science and Christianity, the church in general shied away from the inductive method on the grounds that it was not applicable to the realm of Scripture and theology. Only with the aid of the Holy Spirit, so it was claimed, could one understand the Bible. But this objection failed to see that there are two levels of understanding:

content and experience. True, one cannot fully comprehend the concept of love until one experiences love for another person. Yet it is perfectly possible for a person who has not had this experience to have a great deal of factual knowledge about love by observing lovers and reading books on the subject. Similarly, the secular scholar may not have the faith to believe and experience the claims of the Bible, but if he is sensitive and does not permit his presuppositions to push the evidence aside, he can understand on the level of factual knowledge the content of the declarations. If this were not true, then all preaching to unbelievers would be fruitless. A person without faith in God can understand the essential message of the gospel. The ultimate issue is whether he exercises his will in obedience to the claim of God. It is very important, therefore, to distinguish between knowledge as content and knowledge as experience.

At the level of factual knowledge any intelligent person with proper methods of interpretation and acquaintance with life in the ancient Near East can discern what the Bible is all about. The message is not hidden or esoteric, and there is no need to have the aid of the Holy Spirit in the inductive process. Where that aid is absolutely necessary is in the act of acceptance of the will of God. Without such help there is a rationalization that slides around the confrontation of the claim, or an attempt to postpone a decision, or even an outright refusal to respond positively to the challenge to choose. But the basis of all these reactions is the fact that the will of God is known. As Mark Twain wisely observed, the parts of the Bible that cause the most trouble are those we understand, not those we fail to comprehend.

Another objection to the inductive method has been the tendency in the liberal wing of the church for the historical-grammatical method of biblical interpretation to undercut, rather than support, confidence in the Bible and faith in God. Unfortunately, this condition is still far too prevalent. The failure, however, has not been in the method of interpretation, but in the application of the method. Rather than approaching all the biblical data with empathy, the so-called "scientific mind" has often dismissed a great deal of the evidence with the allegation that such ideas were prescientific and not in accord with reality. The criterion for this judgment has been the interpreter's limited realm of experience. Because the experiences of the biblical characters tended to be outside of his, he could not believe them. Furthermore, this disbelief resulted in a refusal even to try to understand the biblical proclamations.

This one-eyed approach was actually pseudoscientific because the data it did accept were wrenched from their theological contexts. Over and above all else, the Bible is a theological book — it speaks of God and his relation to man. It is a fatal error not to recognize this fact. Accordingly, the proper use of the inductive method demands observation of the theological presuppositions and claims of Scripture along with the data that fit into the so-called scientific category of human, nontheological history. It is recognized that the biblical writers did not set forth their views of revelation with the detail and completeness of systematic theologians, but insofar as they expressed themselves in this regard, their statements are primary data for consideration. Every claim they make for revelation is a relevant fact, and so is every discussion related to the concept of revelation.

By induction, therefore, we do *not* mean an investigation of Scripture to determine whether or not we will believe its message. Some have found Christ in this way, but for the vast majority of Christians the act of faith preceded any systematic attempts to determine the validity and meaning of Scripture. In this study, accordingly, the priority of inductive reasoning means that it is the first method to be employed in the interpretation of the Bible.

Finally, the most conclusive argument in favor of the inductive method is that without it there is no way for Scripture to correct traditions where they have misinterpreted passages in the Bible. The reader who comes to the Bible with the conviction (usually nurtured by his theological tradition) that he has the true understanding of what is being conveyed has made Scripture the prisoner of his own interpretation. The freedom of the Holy Spirit to correct and instruct is possible only when we come to the Bible with an openness that expects to receive new insight for amending and deepening our fellowship with God and his son Jesus Christ. In short, the inductive method (when properly understood and applied) is an honest approach to Scripture that resolves at all costs to let God's written Word speak for itself.

THE TERM "REVELATION" IN THE BIBLE

The specific Old Testament term meaning "to reveal" is the Hebrew verb *galah*. Its root meaning is "to uncover, strip away," and so it signifies the act of opening to view what has been hidden. At times, it refers to the stripping of clothes as a means of humiliation; for example, Isaiah 47:3, "Your nakedness shall be uncovered, and your shame shall be seen." *Galah* appears about twenty-three times in connection with God's manifestation of himself or the communication of his message. In such cases obstacles to perception, hearing, and sight are removed. While under the influence of the Spirit of God, Balaam declares, "The oracle of him who hears the words of God, who sees the vision of Shadday ["the Mountain One," usually translated "the Almighty"], falling yet having his eyes uncovered" (Num. 24:4). In the story of God's call to young Samuel the narrator comments, "Now Samuel did not yet know Yahweh, and the word of Yahweh had not yet been revealed to him" (I Sam. 3:7); but later on he notes, "Yahweh appeared again at Shiloh, for Yahweh revealed himself to Samuel at Shiloh by the word of Yahweh" (I Sam. 3:21).

When God makes a covenant with David and his lineage, David declares, "For you, O Yahweh of hosts, the God of Israel, have uncovered the ear of your servant, saying, 'I will build you a house [or, dynasty]' " (II Sam. 7:27). Isaiah the prophet claimed, "Yahweh of hosts has revealed himself in my ears" (Isa. 22:11), and this explicit affirmation of all the prophets is summed up in the conviction of Amos, "For the Lord Yahweh does nothing without revealing his secret [or, plans] to his servants the prophets" (Amos 3:7).

It is an interesting fact that eight of the twenty-three occurrences of *galah* (in the sense of revelation) appear in the book of Daniel, and seven of these in chapter 2. Here the stress is on the secret interpretation of Nebuchadnezzar's dream, a prediction of "what will be in the latter days" (2:28). After the key to the dream has been made known, the king exclaims to Daniel, "Your God is indeed God of gods and Lord of lords and a revealer of secrets [or, mysteries], for you have been able to reveal this secret" (2:47).

The New Testament equivalent of *galah* is the Greek verb *apokaluptō* ("to uncover, disclose, reveal"), which occurs twenty-six times. After Peter's confession at Caesarea Philippi that Jesus is the Christ, Jesus explains, "Blessed are you, Simon Bar-Jona, for flesh and blood have not revealed this to you, but my Father who is in heaven" (Matt. 16:17).

While the Old Testament has no derivative noun from *galah*, the New Testament has the noun *apokalupsis* ("revelation"), which occurs eighteen times. Concerning the gospel he preaches, Paul affirms, "I did not receive it from man, nor was I taught it. But it came through a revelation of Jesus Christ" (Gal. 1:12). He states that he went up to Jerusalem the second time "by revelation" (Gal. 2:2). In discussing the issue of speaking in tongues Paul informs the Corinthians that his speaking in tongues would mean nothing without an interpretation resulting in "some revelation or knowledge or prophecy or teaching" (I Cor. 14:6). In the church at Corinth, moreover, the various members have "a hymn, a lesson, a revelation, a tongue, or an interpretation" (I Cor. 14:26). "God is not a God of confusion, but of peace," Paul declares; thus in order that there may be genuine edification for all, he urges that they speak "one by one." Accordingly, if a revelation comes to someone seated, then the one who has the floor is to yield to the one with the new insight (I Cor. 14:30).

The New Testament counterpart to Daniel, where revelation is depicted as a forecast of future events, is the Book of Revelation: "The revelation of Jesus Christ, given to him by God in order that he might show his servants what must happen shortly" (1:1).

TERMS AND EXPRESSIONS ASSOCIATED WITH REVELATION

While it is recognized that the terms "to reveal" and "revelation" are relatively sparse, considering the extensive amount of material in the Bible, there are numerous terms and expressions associated with the idea of revelation. As noted earlier, one of these is "secret, mystery." During and after the exile in Babylonia, a number of Jews despaired of expecting God's redemptive activity in the normal course of history. For them the only hope was the culmination of the age, when God would fulfil his promises to his people and restore justice and peace. Although "secret" (Hebrew, *sod*) in Amos 3:7 seems to refer to God's redemptive plans in the course of history, the concept came increasingly to signify the hidden purpose of God concerning the last days, and so in Daniel 2 the "secret" (Aramaic *raz*) is a prediction of what God will do at the end of the age.

In the New Testament the term *musterion* (from which the English word "mystery" derives) occurs twenty-seven or twenty-eight times. In answering the disciples' question "Why do you speak to them in parables?" Jesus remarks, "It has been given to you to know the secrets [mysteries] of the kingdom of heaven" (Matt. 13:11). Paul speaks of his gospel as being "the revelation of the mystery which was kept secret for long ages" (Rom. 16:25). This secret (mystery), made known by the Spirit, is Paul's insight that "the Gentiles are fellow heirs [with the Jews], members of the same body, and sharers of the promise in Christ Jesus" (Eph. 3:6). The "mystery of the faith" (I Tim. 3:9) and "mystery of our religion" (3:16) clearly refer to the apostolic teaching about Christ as the newly revealed content of faith.

Another way of expressing the idea of revelation was the verb "to manifest, show oneself" (Greek, *phaneroō*) and its related noun "manifestation." Jesus was God "manifested in the flesh" (I Tim. 3:16), "made manifest at the end of the times" (I Pet. 1:20). In I John 1:2 the author declares, "The life was made manifest and we saw it." The various gifts of the Christians at Corinth were "the manifestation of the Spirit" (I Cor. 12:7). During the years in the wilderness God made himself known to the Israelites by means of a cloud (Hebrew *anan*, Exod. 40:38). The more original meaning of the term was "manifestation," and so the cloud was thought of as "the manifestation of Yahweh."

Yet another term associated with revelation is "glory." A cloud, as "the glory of Yahweh," appeared in the wilderness (Exod. 16:10). Also it settled on Mt. Sinai (Exod. 24:16). Yahweh spoke of his plagues on the Egyptians as being "my glory and my signs" (Num. 14:22). Thus God's acts in behalf of his people were signs of his glory. According to the psalmist, "The heavens declare the glory of God" (Ps. 19:1). In his vision in the temple Isaiah heard the seraphim chanting, "Holy, holy, holy is Yahweh of hosts. The whole earth is full of his glory" (Isa. 6:3). The theme of Yahweh's glory appears many times in the Old Testament, and it carries over as a dominant idea in the New Testament: "So the Word became flesh and dwelt among us, full of grace and truth. We have seen his glory, glory befitting the Father's only son" (John 1:14).

In Psalm 29:2 the psalmist exhorts, "Ascribe to Yahweh the glory of his name." It was a well-known tradition among the Israelites that the name "Yahweh," most likely meaning "He causes [all things] to be," was made known to Moses by revelation at the burning bush (Exod. 3:15). In another context God says to Moses, "I appeared to Abraham, to Isaac, and to Jacob as El Shadday [God Almighty], but by my name Yahweh I did not make myself known to them" (Exod. 6:3). In the ancient Near East a name was thought to express the character of the person bearing it. From the times of Moses, therefore, "Yahweh" became the personal designation for the creative, sovereign God of Israel. From this name developed the idea of God's universal control. "It is he who sits enthroned on the vaulted roof of the earth whose inhabitants are like grasshoppers. He stretches out the skies like a curtain and spreads them like a tent to dwell in. He brings princes to nothing, and makes the earth's rulers as nothing" (Isa. 40:22–23). "Have you not known, have you not heard? Yahweh is the everlasting God, the Creator of the limits of the earth. He neither faints nor grows weary. His understanding is unsearchable" (Isa. 40:28).

Even the names of God's servants and their children could convey God's message and point to his glory. Isaiah (meaning "Yahweh is salvation") and his sons Shear-jashub ("A remnant shall return") and Maher-shalal-hash-baz ("The spoil speeds, the plunder hastens") were walking sermons because of their names. Accordingly, Isaiah could say, "I and the children whom Yahweh has given me are signs and portents in Israel" (Isa. 8:18).

Luke 8:20 informs us that Jesus, on meeting the Gerasene demoniac, asked him, "What is your name?" He replied, "Legion," because many demons had entered him. Jesus, praying to God, says, "I have manifested your name to the men you have given me out of the world" (John 17:6). He could do this because, as he claimed to Philip, he had a unique relationship with God: "He who has seen me has seen the Father" (John 14:9). In speaking about God's judgment Joel states, "All who call upon the name of Yahweh shall be delivered [saved]" (2:32), and Paul quotes the passage in Romans 10:13. In numerous other passages "the name" is associated with God's communication of himself.

One of the most commonly used terms in expressing the concept of revelation is the verb "to know" (Hebrew, *yada*, Greek, *ginōskō*). Throughout the Bible it is a comprehensive word including both experiential and factual knowledge. On being confronted by Moses, Pharaoh retorts, "Who is Yahweh, that I should obey him and let Israel go? I do not know Yahweh" (Exod. 5:2). From that moment the showdown struggle between Pharaoh and Moses becomes Yahweh's school for instructing both the Israelites and the Egyptians. Yahweh promises, "I will take you for my people, and I will be your God. You shall know that I am Yahweh, your God" (Exod. 6:7). Moreover, Yahweh declares, "The Egyptians shall know that I am Yahweh when I extend my hand [power] over Egypt and bring out the Israelites from among them" (Exod. 7:5).

The experience of knowing another person always results in some factual knowledge whether the participants formulate it explicitly or not. A favorite expression of the prophets for designating this content of experience is "the word of Yahweh": "Hear the word of Yahweh, you rulers of Sodom! Listen to the teaching [Hebrew, *torah*] of our God, you people of Gomorrah!" (Isa. 1:10). *Torah*, often translated "law" in the older versions, has the broader meaning of "teaching, instruction": "For instruction comes from Zion, and the word of Yahweh out of Jerusalem" (Isa. 2:3). The eternal authority of God's revelation is affirmed in Isaiah 40:8, "The grass withers, the flower fades, but the word of our God endures forever." In his desire to experience God's revelation, one of the psalmists implores, "Make your ways known to me, O Yahweh. Teach me your paths" (Ps. 25:4).

There are a number of other terms associated with the concept of revelation. Beyond the nouns noted above ("revelation, word, teaching, name, glory, prediction, wisdom, manifestation, and path or way"), there are numerous biblical examples where the following nouns are used to express the idea of revelation: "commandment, announcement, proclamation, promise, knowledge, counsel, truth, tradition, testimony, covenant, appearance, and light." Over and above the verbs "to reveal, prophesy, foretell, speak, and know," there are examples of the verbs "to appear, lead (guide), open, shine, bear witness, promise, and proclaim." The fact that so many terms and expressions are used to describe the biblical idea of revelation is an indication of both the complexity of the concept and the tenacity with which it was held throughout the various periods of biblical history. The author of the Book of Hebrews was certainly correct when he claimed that God had spoken "in many and various ways" (1:1).

CHANNELS OF REVELATION

God employed many different channels, as well as ways, in communicating his message. A classic passage is Jeremiah 18:18: "Come, let us plot against Jeremiah because instruction shall not perish from the priest, nor counsel from the wise, nor the word from the prophet." In a similar vein Ezekiel 7:26 notes, "They seek a vision from the prophet, but instruction perishes from the priest, and counsel from the elders." These verses indicate that by late seventh century B.C. the traditional concept of God's revelation was threefold: (1) the prophet with "the word" and "visions"; (2) the priest with "instruction" concerning God's teaching or law; and (3) the wise man or elder with "counsel."

Concerning the regular prophet God states, "I, Yahweh, make myself known to him in a vision, I speak with him in a dream" (Num. 12:6). Yahweh even "put a word" in the mouth of Balaam, the Syrian seer (Num. 23:5). Moses, however, was a special kind of prophet, and when Aaron and Miriam challenged his authority Yahweh said, "With him I speak clearly, mouth to mouth" (Num. 14:8). In the intimate call of Jeremiah, Yahweh touches his mouth, explaining, "I have put my words in your mouth" (Jer. 1:9). Time and again the prophets claim, "The word of Yahweh came to me," or "Thus says Yahweh." They have an absolute conviction that their messages come from Yahweh.

The priests also claimed that the regulations concerning the ritual and cult were given by God (Lev. 1:1). In addition to his sacrificial duties the priest was to instruct the people (Deut. 33:10; II Chr. 17:8–9). In crucial situations the chief priest was to ascertain the will of God by the "Urim and Thummim" (Num. 27:21; Deut. 33:8; I Sam. 28:6). Moreover, the levitical priests, along with the judges, held court at times by interpreting the case law and passing sentence (Deut. 17:8–9). In some degree all of these functions of the priest involve God's special guidance.

While the Israelite wise man or elder seldom claims that his insights come directly from Yahweh, it is implicit that God does reveal himself in the practical affairs of life. This basic assumption is made explicit in Proverbs 2:6: "For Yahweh gives wisdom. Knowledge and understanding come from his mouth." It is felt that the experience of the covenant relationship with Yahweh adds a depth of insight not plumbed in the wisdom of neighboring cultures: "Awe of Yahweh is the beginning of knowledge [wisdom]" (Prov. 1:7; 9:10).

Whereas the most prominent channel of revelation in the Old Testament was the prophet, his New Testament counterpart was the apostle. It was quite natural that those persons specially called and trained by Jesus would exercise the greatest authority in the church. According to Paul, the priority of roles performed by members of the church was this: apostles, prophets, teachers, miracle-workers, healers, helpers, administrators, and speakers in tongues (I Cor. 12:28). Although there is a difference in rank, the first three roles pertain to the teaching ministry and each is considered as a channel of revelation.

Judaism defined the close of the Hebrew canon as the time when the spirit of prophecy ceased to function. The moving of the Spirit of God in the early church reinstated the role of the prophet. Some prophets from Jerusalem visited Antioch and "one of them named Agabus stood up and predicted by the Spirit that there would be a great famine over all the world. This took place in the days of Claudius" (Acts 11:28). Apparently the same Agabus came down from Judea to the home of Philip the evangelist in Caesarea, where Paul was staying. After tying Paul's hands and feet with Paul's own belt, he predicted in the name of the Holy Spirit that the Jews in Jerusalem would arrest Paul and turn him over to the Gentiles (Acts 21:11).

This role of short-range prediction picked up one of the facets of the classical Old Testament prophets. About 735 B.C. Isaiah assured Ahaz that before the child Immanuel would know how to distinguish good from evil, the territory of Rezin, king of Damascus, and Pekah, king of Israel, would be devastated (Isa. 7:16). Within three years Tiglath-pileser III overran Syria and the northern part of Israel, thus bringing to pass the prediction of Isaiah. In the struggle to authenticate his word against that of the false prophet Hananiah, Jeremiah predicted that Hananiah would die within a year (Jer. 28:16), and his word came true in two months (Jer. 28:1, 17).

The role of the teacher in the New Testament is not spelled out in detail, but in all likelihood it was similar to the teaching ministry of the priests. He probably instructed church members about the Old Testament and its role in preparing for Jesus Christ. Most certainly he taught the apostolic tradition about Jesus, and quite possibly he had a share in interpreting the gospel and making it relevant to the local conditions of the church in question.

THE RANGE AND MEANS OF REVELATION

In some cases the channel of revelation is not conscious of any rational effort on his part and the message is attributed completely to Yahweh. At the burning bush, for example, Yahweh communicated his message directly to Moses (Exod. 3:2– 17). In one tradition Moses is credited with writing the Decalogue on the tablets of stone (Exod. 34:28), but another tradition claims that the tablets were "written with the finger of God" (Exod. 31:18). Moses undoubtedly inscribed the tablets, but the tradition that God wrote them is valid in the sense that Moses was conscious of such help in formulating the Ten Commandments that he felt God's finger had guided him.

But in the attempt to live by the Decalogue, the stipulations of the covenant, there arose the need for interpretations and setting of guidelines. When situations required further information about God's will, Moses resorted to the tent of meeting, and there Yahweh spoke to him "face to face, as a man speaks to his friend" (Exod. 33:11). In due time these decisions grew into a collection of case law. At the renewal of the covenant at Shechem this corpus was updated by Joshua in order to make the Ten Commandments more applicable to the situation in Canaan (Josh. 24:25– 26). This process continued in the period of the judges and carried over into the monarchy.

The later prophets, like their great predecessor Moses, often felt that their messages came directly from Yahweh. At times, however, the insights were triggered by events and objects of everyday life. Out of the despair and tragedy of his marriage, Hosea was given an insight into Yahweh's covenant love for his people Israel. Amos saw a mason building a wall with a plumb line and received Yahweh's word, "I am setting a plumb line in the midst of my people Israel" (Amos 7:8). A "boiling pot" being poured toward the south was the occasion for Yahweh's message to Jeremiah that evil would come over the people from the north (Jer. 1:14). While visiting the potter's house, Jeremiah learned of Yahweh's intent concerning Israel (Jer. 18:3– 11). A basket of good figs in front of the temple became a symbol of the exiles to Babylonia, while the basket of bad figs characterized those who stayed on in Judah or would go to Egypt (Jer. 24:1– 10).

After the destruction of the temple in 587/6 B.C., the idea of God's immanence was dealt a severe blow. More and more, God was envisioned as remote and otherworldly. In this excessive stress on transcendence the chasm between God and man became so great that some of the postexilic prophets believed that God communicated his message by means of heavenly messengers. Zechariah, for example, refers constantly to "the messenger [angel] who talked with me" (Zech. 1:1, 13, 14, 19; 2:3, etc.).

As noted above, the insights of the wise seldom claim to be the direct words of Yahweh, and yet the experience of living in covenant relationship with Yahweh is basic to receiving words of counsel. Thus even the understanding gained from the practical aspects of life is credited ultimately to the help of Yahweh.

THE BIBLICAL CONCEPT OF REVELATION

In discussing the idea of revelation James Barr states, "In the Bible, however, the usage of the terms which roughly correspond to 'revelation' is both limited and specialized. . . . Thus there is little basis in the Bible for the use of 'revelation' as a general term for man's source of knowledge of God, or for all real communication from God to man."[2] His conclusion is possible because of his limited definition of revelation: "Previously I did not know God, but now (since this incident or speech) he is known or revealed to me."[3] "It is the absence of this kind of approach," according to Barr, "which makes the revelational model doubtful for application to the Old Testament; and, we may add, to the New Testament also, for even the coming of Christ does not pro-

[2]*Old and New in Interpretation* (New York, 1966), p. 88.
[3]Ibid., p. 82.

duce the kind of statement which I have just cited. The coming
of Christ, like the Old Testament incidents, is a further (and
amazing) act of one who is known; it is not a first disclosure of
one who is not known."[4]

On the other hand, Barr admits that "it is not easy to develop
a different term which will say what used to be said by 'revelation' "; therefore he does not "strictly avoid the use of 'revelation,' " but he treats it in a loose way as an equivalent of communication.[5]

"My argument," Barr declares, "is not against the word 'revelation', but against the way in which the use of this word has
grouped together a number of different things in a way that does
not suit them and so distorts them."[6] Yet this is precisely the
problem posed by the biblical evidence. The solution is not to
discount the data by an arbitrary definition of revelation. Rather,
the inductive method demands that we analyze and distinguish
as carefully as we can the various ways by which, according to
the biblical writers, God made himself known and communicated
his message to man. Admittedly, there are the difficulties of evaluation of the claims and of classification of the various levels of
revelation. For the moment, however, it is absolutely clear that
practically all theological insights in Scripture are attributed to
God or his Spirit. The claim is explicit in the case of the prophets,
where the message is perceived directly by means of their ears,
eyes, and lips, or delivered to them by messengers, and it is
implicit in wisdom where the insight comes in the context of a
life in covenant relation with Yahweh.

[4]Ibid.
[5]Ibid., p. 86.
[6]Ibid.

7 THE BIBLE

DONALD G. MILLER

The problem of biblical authority is a part of the larger problem of *any* authority today. The question of biblical authority rests on the question of the authority of God. If there is a God, and humans are creatures made to find the meaning of their lives in dependence on Him, then God is authoritative over humanity. The nature of God, however, makes His highest authority spiritual in character, and this spiritual authority is so radically self-authenticating that the penitent, believing person can respond only in glad acceptance and worship. For a person to respond in this way, that person must discover who God is through the divine being's self-revelation as Holy Seeking Love. Through what means has God made Himself known? Among the options of human reason, human experience, the church, and the Bible, the latter is best seen as the locus of this self-revelation. I would like now to pursue further the question of the authority of the Bible in its function as the vehicle of God's self-revelation.

Why is the Bible necessary to the soul's fellowship with God? Because here and nowhere else do we have the record of the historic process whereby God made Himself known to humans. The Bible is the record of the special stream of holy history which ran through ancient history as a whole as the Gulf Stream runs through the ocean. Here God was at work making Himself known in a special way through a special series of events. Of course, God was at work in all of history. He was Lord of Egypt and Babylon as well as of Israel. But His Lordship was not recognized outside Israel as it was within it. His providential works were over all people, but His *saving* deeds were done in Israel — at the Exodus and in all the ups and downs of Israel's history through

---

From Donald G. Miller, The Authority of the Bible, *pp. 28–46.* Copyright© 1972 by William B. Eerdmans Publishing Company.

nearly 2,000 years. Not that salvation was limited to Israel. It was for all nations. But all nations would have to know of it through what God had done for Israel. As God said through the great prophet of the exile: "Turn to me and be saved, all the ends of the earth! For I am God, and there is no other" (Isa. 45:22). But how were they to look unto Him? Through what He had done "for the sake of my servant Jacob, and Israel my chosen" (Isa. 45:4). When His preparatory work through Israel had been completed, "when the time had fully come, God sent forth his Son" (Gal. 4:4). This Son was sent to Israel, "for salvation is from the Jews" (John 4:22). But these same Jews were to be "witnesses" of "all that Jesus began to do and teach" in the days of His flesh to "the end of the earth" (Acts 1:1, 8). God's holy seeking love is therefore known through the special series of events which took place in the narrow stream of Israel's history from Abraham to Jesus Christ. Since these events are recorded in the Bible, and nowhere else, the Bible becomes forever the source and norm of the Christian faith. The heart of the faith is this story through which we know God and through which we make our response to Him. If we lost the Bible, we would lose the story. And if we lost the story, the Christian faith would be at an end.

This is expressed with great force by H. H. Farmer, who insisted that since Christianity is at heart an absolutely "unique, decisive . . . final, completely adequate, wholly indispensable" event, it could never have been discovered by human reflection, for reflection cannot produce an event. "An event can only establish itself—by happening! . . . And it can only become generally known . . . by the story being told."[1] Dr. Farmer illustrates his point by proposing that we imagine the Hindu religion obliterated from the mind of man—not one Hindu left, not one copy of Hindu sacred writings, not one record in extant history that there ever was such a thing as Hinduism. Given this situation, it is conceivable that Hinduism could arise again, within five years, or fifty years, or five hundred years. For Hinduism is basically a way of thinking, a way of looking at life. If men thought this way once, it is conceivable that other men could think this same way at a later time. But imagine Christianity obliterated—not one living Christian, not one copy of the Christian Scriptures, not one mention in extant history that Christianity had ever existed. Given this situation, it is inconceivable that Christianity could ever arise again. For Christianity basi-

---

[1] *The Servant of the Word* (New York, 1942), pp. 18f.

cally is a story, the story of God's special dealings in history from Abraham to Jesus Christ. It is to this story that Christians respond in faith, love, and obedience, and this story is found only in the Bible. The Bible is indispensable. Christianity is a historic religion. It is a "given." It comes to us. We are free to accept it, but not to remake or modify it. Since it comes to us through the Bible, the Bible is therefore authoritative as the only record of the saving events by which the Christian faith was brought into being. Karl Barth wrote:

> Even the smallest, strangest, simplest or obscurest among the biblical witnesses has an incomparable advantage over even the most pious, scholarly and sagacious latter-day theologian. From his special point of view and in his special fashion, the witness has thought, spoken and written about the revelatory Word and act in direct confrontation with it. All subsequent theology, as well as the whole of the community that comes after the event, will never find itself in the same immediate confrontation.[2]

But did not the church produce the Bible? If so, would not the church which produced the Bible be authoritative over it? At least two things must be said about this. First, it is true that the church existed before the Bible and that the books of the Bible were collected and preserved by the church. In reality, however, the church did not bring the Bible into being, nor did the Bible bring the church into being. It was the *message* of the Bible, the *gospel*, which produced both the church and the Bible. The content of the Bible was a *gospel* before it was a book. This is clearly borne out in the Westminster Confession of Faith, where we read: ". . . It pleased the Lord, at sundry times, and in divers manners, to reveal himself, and to declare . . . his will unto his church; and *afterwards* . . . to commit the same wholly unto writing" (italics mine; I:1). It is the declaration of God's will in historic events "at sundry times, and in divers manners" that constitutes the gospel. *Afterwards* it was made a matter of record. The gospel antedates the record of it. The record is authoritative, therefore, not because the church produced it but because it is the record of that gospel which produced the church, and which continues to nourish her life. As Luther put it, "The church is the daughter born of the Word, not the mother of the Word."[3]

The second thing to be said is this: For the church to select certain books as authoritative and to bind them together into a Bible was not to give those books authority. It is one thing to

---

[2] *Evangelical Theology* (London, 1965), p. 34.
[3] *Werke*, W.A., V, p. 23.

bestow authority, it is another to *recognize* it. For the church to recognize the authority of the gospel in the books which she chose as her Bible does not place the church above these books. In fact, in developing a canon of Scripture at all, the early church demonstrated that she was fully aware that she herself was not authoritative. Had she assumed herself to be authoritative, she would not have raised over herself a particular group of books as the norm by which she and the church of the future would be judged.

In declaring the books of the Bible authoritative over her life, the church was but witnessing to the historic nature of her faith and the uniqueness of the saving events by which she was brought into being and by which she was to be forever nurtured. If revelation were merely ideas, it is conceivable that persons might get better or more refined ideas through the discipline and experience of the years. The works of Augustine, or Aquinas, or Luther, or Calvin might be added to the biblical record. But, as H. Scott Holland has said, ". . . The whole body of spiritual experience dates from an original experience which cannot but possess the authority which belongs to it through being, by its very nature, unique. . . . Blessed indeed are they that have not seen, and yet have believed. . . . But they can only arrive at this blessing through the witness of those who believed because they saw. They have no other means of acquiring it."[4] It was the apostolic generation, and they alone, who could say to us: "It was there from the beginning; we have heard it; we have seen it with our own eyes; we looked upon it, and felt it with our own hands; and it is of this we tell. . . . What we have seen and heard we declare to you, so that you and we together may share in a common life" (I John 1:1, 3). We can receive our faith only from those who "touched and handled."

The strongest witness to this is the attitude toward the Bible held by those great Christian spirits whose writings would be added to it were it not unique. Augustine is certainly one of these, and he once wrote to St. Jerome, "Dear brother, I hope that you do not expect your books to be regarded as equal to those of the apostles and prophets. God forbid that you should desire such a thing."[5] Of his own works he said: ". . . Do not follow my writing as you do Holy Scripture. Instead, whatever you find in Holy Scripture that you would not have believed before, believe

---

[4]*Creeds and Critics* (London, 1918), p. 187.
[5]Quoted by Luther, *Selected Writings of Martin Luther, 1529–1546*, ed. Theodore G. Tappert (Philadelphia, 1967), p. 243.

without doubt. But in my writings you should regard nothing as certain that you were uncertain about before, unless I have proved its truth."[6] St. Bernard once compared the Scriptures to a spring and the writings of later Fathers to a brook which flowed from it. He insisted that only a fool would drink from the brook when he could drink from the spring, and that the function of the brook is to lead one to the spring. The value of later Christian writers, then, if they have any worth, is to lead back to the Bible. Luther once said that he "would be ashamed to death"[7] if anybody ever regarded his books as equal to those of the apostles and prophets. In fact, he resisted for long any attempt to publish a collection of his works:

> I wish all my books were extinct, so that only the sacred books in the Bible would be diligently read. . . . For all other writing is to lead the way into and point toward the Scriptures, . . . in order that each person may drink of the fresh spring himself, as all those fathers who wanted to accomplish something good had to do. . . . Therefore it behooves us to let the prophets and apostles stand at the professor's lectern, while we, down below at their feet, listen to what they say. It is not they who must hear what we say.[8]

James Denney put the matter well when he said, "There has been no interpretation of the revelation made in Jesus which has done more than try to grasp the breadth and depth of apostolic teaching; and the perennial impulse which Scripture and Scripture alone communicates to spiritual life and spiritual thought is always sealing its pre-eminence anew."[9] The Bible stands, and always shall, as the unique record of the unique and unrepeatable deeds by which the church came into being, and from which her life, till the end of the world, will be nurtured and judged.

But how must we approach this book so that its inherent, self-authenticating, spiritual authority may grip us and command us? How do we get beyond mere theory to the point where the Bible's authority begins to function in our lives? A complete answer to this is beyond our comprehension. There is a mystery about the authority of the Bible over the human spirit, as profound as the mystery of God. As we have said, if the Bible has any inherent authority it is because it is the vehicle of God's authority. And who can define the mystery of the approach of God to the human

[6] Ibid., p. 217.
[7] Ibid., p. 218.
[8] *Selected Writings, 1517–1520*, ed. Theodore G. Tappert (Philadelphia, 1967), pp. 6, 8.
[9] *Studies in Theology* (London, 1895), p. 226.

soul? His is an authority which defies "our ability to localize or define and which by the same token is beyond our control, but whose presence is as sure as the rising of the sun."[10]

Insofar as we can think our way into this problem at all, we can establish, it seems to me, two major aspects. One has to do with the Bible, the other has to do with ourselves. One is objective, the other subjective. The problem is how to approach the Bible so that we may hear God's voice speaking to us through it. The Bible is the medium through which God speaks. We are the listeners. In order to allow the Bible to perform its proper function, we must know something about the medium and we must also know how to listen. Let us look first at the Bible as the medium of God's voice.

It is well to point out initially that our concern with the Bible should be more with its function than with itself. That is, the God to whom it bears witness should be central in our interest rather than the instrument through which that witness comes. The worth of the Scriptures is determined by their power to convey the voice of God. It is not the Bible which speaks, but God who speaks through the Bible. Our whole attention in studying the Bible, therefore, should be given to listening for the voice of God through it.

The function of a light bulb, for example, is to be the medium of producing light. The bulb is not the light, yet you do not have the light without the bulb. Its value to us, however, does not lie in looking at the bulb itself, nor even in understanding its nature. Its value is that light comes through it, enabling us to see in the darkness. Likewise, the value of a lens in a telescope is that it enables us to see the stars.

The Bible is the instrument through which God speaks, the means by which His light is cast upon life, the lens through which we see "him who is invisible." If we turn our attention to the Bible itself rather than to the voice, the light, and the God from whom they come, we should be putting the Bible in the place of God, and thus turning it into an idol. Even if the instrument should in places seem to us to be faulty, and to distort the voice of God in some measure, still its excellence lies in its power to convey to us, even in distorted fashion, the authentic voice of God. There are those who prefer to hear the voice of Alma Gluck through the imperfect recordings made in her time, than to hear the voices of most modern singers through the vastly superior

---

[10]Frederick W. Schroeder, *Preaching the Word with Authority* (Philadelphia, 1954), p. 117.

recordings of today. These people are convinced that her voice, even when distorted, had a superb quality that is unmatched by most other voices heard clearly. And if her voice is to be heard today, it must be heard through these imperfect recordings. So it is with the voice of God. It is better to hear His voice, though faintly and amid scratches and other extraneous sounds, than to hear any other voice. And if we are to hear it, we must listen for it through the Bible, which is the only available record of His speaking "to our fathers by the prophets" and His final word "to us by a Son" (Heb. 1:1, 2).

The second thing to say about the Bible is that we should listen through it only for that which it is designed to speak. The Bible exists to tell us—what we can find out in no other way—about God, about ourselves, and about the interrelations between God and us. In other words, the Bible is a *religious* book, and should be asked to yield answers to nothing but religious questions. It is interesting how unselfconscious the Bible writers seem to be about their own writing. The Bible seldom speaks of itself or of its role in human life. But when it does, it seems to speak solely about its dynamic function in making God known, in revealing man to himself, and in repairing the broken relationships between the two.

The classic passage in this regard is II Timothy 3:15, 16. There the writer speaks of a twofold function of the Scriptures. First, they "are able to instruct you for salvation through faith in Christ Jesus." Second, they are "profitable for teaching, for reproof, for correction, and for training in righteousness, that the man of God may be complete, equipped for every good work." Here we see that the Scriptures are "able," or as the New English Bible puts it, they "have power," to lead people into a saving knowledge of God in Christ, and that they then continue to function by leading the Christian to a mature understanding of the truth and by leading one in a life of good works.

These functions are stated in other places as well. In Romans 16:25, 26 Paul says that "the prophetic writings," that is, the Old Testament, were the bearers of the "mystery" of salvation designed "to bring about obedience to the faith." In the same letter he says that the Scriptures function by producing "hope" in the believer (15:4). Twice in Acts Paul is described as using the Scriptures to show that "Jesus . . . is the Christ" (17:3; 18:28). In the Fourth Gospel, Jesus says that the Scriptures "bear witness to [Him]" (5:39). Luke tells us that the risen Lord, "beginning with Moses and all the prophets . . . interpreted to them in all the scriptures the things concerning himself" (Luke 24:27). There seems to be a unanimous witness, in the few places where the Scriptures speak of their own function, that they exist to proclaim the gospel and lead people to Christ, and that they are to be judged solely by their power to do this.

Luther grasped this clearly when he said that the New Testament was "but a public preaching and proclamation of Christ, set forth through the sayings of the Old Testament and fulfilled through Christ. . . . Here you will find the swaddling cloths and the manger in which Christ lies, and to which the angel points the shepherds. Simple and lowly are these swaddling cloths, but dear is the treasure, Christ, who lies in them."[11]

The Westminster Confession supports Luther at this point when it describes the function of Scripture as giving "that knowledge of God, and of his will, which is necessary unto salvation" (I, 1). It further describes the Scriptures as giving "the whole counsel of God, concerning all things necessary for his own glory, man's salvation, faith, and life" (I, 6).

The Scriptures themselves, then, and these guides to its understanding, suggest that we are making proper use of the Bible only when we are asking it questions about God, His will, His glory, and human salvation, faith, and life.

How often the Bible is misused by being used for other ends. I was once told by a man that the dimensions of Noah's ark are the perfect dimensions for boat building, implying that the art of boat building was a matter of divine revelation. I know nothing about the proper dimensions of boats, but if my friend's judgment is true, I should attribute it to the fact that either Noah, or whoever wrote down the story, was a skilled builder of boats rather than that the dimensions were given by divine inspiration. What a needless struggle was set up in the days of Galileo by turning the Bible into a book of astronomy; and in the days of Darwin, by turning it into a book of biological science. In matters of science, ask the scientist. In matters of religion, ask the Bible. It is a sure guide about that — and nothing else. It may have accompanying historical and geographical information, but these are of value in showing where and when God did His saving work for humanity. They are incidental to their religious significance. The Bible is time-conditioned and limited in other spheres, often reflecting the naive scientific world view of its time and filled with much that is the accompaniment of the Word of God rather than a witness to God. There is much in the Bible, particularly in the early strands of the Old Testament, that must be

---

[11]Luther, *Selected Writings, 1529–1546*, p. 376.

judged by the gospel and Christ. It must not be confused with
the gospel and the will of Christ. There is much that is frame
rather than painting. There is much that is scaffolding rather
than building. There is much that is dark background rather
than shining light. Luther put this boldly when he said, "The
pure Scripture must be separated from their dregs and filth;
which it has ever been my aim to do, that the divine truths may
be looked upon in one light, and the trifles of these men in another."[12] Let us not, therefore, stumble over such idle and futile
questions as where Cain got his wife, whether the six days of
creation in Genesis were twenty-four-hour days, and whether
Noah's flood covered the whole earth or just the Mesopotamian
area, the answer to which is quite irrelevant to God's will to save
us in Christ and our need to respond to His saving action in faith
and obedience.

A third thing that must be kept in mind about the Bible is
that it is language *and* literature. As language, it must be read
in the light of what its original words meant, not what we think
they meant or what we should like them to have meant. And as
literature it must be interpreted at each particular place in accord
with the type of literature with which we are dealing. We cannot
interpret poetry as prose, drama as history, parable as detailed
theological writing, apocalyptic as literal. This means that language and literature must be taken seriously. Luther said: "Although the gospel came and still comes to us through the Holy
Spirit alone, we cannot deny that it came through the medium
of languages, was spread abroad by that means, and must be
preserved by the same means."[13] He added that it was a great
"sin and loss that we do not study languages. . . ."[14] He added
later: "I would surely have never flushed a covey if the languages
had not helped me and given me a sure and certain knowledge
of Scripture."[15] Luther also took into account the various literary
forms of the Bible, recognizing that details of dramatic form were
to be understood as such and not made the basis of theological
interpretation, and refusing to interpret the Bible allegorically
unless he was dealing with allegory. Any of us can go far toward
examining the type of literature embodied in any particular passage; where we do not have access to the original languages, we
can examine several translations in English and compare them,
and seek help in other works about the exact meaning of words.

[12]Quoted by George W. Richards, *Beyond Fundamentalism and Modernism* (New
York, 1934), p. 168.
[13]Luther, *Selected Writings*, *1523–1526*, pp. 50f.
[14]Ibid., p. 56.
[15]Ibid., p. 58.

One further thing about the Bible itself, and that is that we should deal with it in its broad sweep, not merely in snippets. It is well known that isolated sentences, taken out of context, can be twisted to almost any purpose. It is well known, too, that the Bible itself has differences of emphasis in various places which, if taken alone, would be either partial truth or perverted truth. These need the wholeness and balance of the "harmonious opposites" to be found in other passages of Scripture. Here again the Westminster Confession offers wise counsel: "The infallible rule of interpretation of Scripture is the Scripture itself; and therefore, when there is a question about the true and full sense of any scripture (which is not manifold, but one), it may be searched and known by other places that speak more clearly" (I, 9). The truth, then, is not merely the partial truth of any one word of Scripture, but the truth to be drawn from the whole sweep of the biblical drama, culminating in Jesus Christ.

Now we come to the more subjective side of the question — to the reader, the listener for the voice of God through Scripture. Even though a voice should echo loudly through the forest, there is no hearing if all within earshot are deaf. Communication involves hearing as well as speaking. Jesus sensed this when several times He said to His listeners, "Take heed then how you hear" (Luke 8:18). God speaks. How do we hear?

The first suggestion I would make is that if God speaks through the Bible, we should listen for His voice *there*. We can only hear where He has chosen to speak. I may have preferred Him to speak elsewhere, but if the Bible is where He has spoken, that is where I must listen. We should not, therefore, despair of hearing the voice of God through the Scriptures until we have exposed ourselves to them directly and faithfully in order that they may do their work in our lives. But how few do any regular or systematic reading or study of the Bible!

Some years ago, the late D. T. Niles of Ceylon was on shipboard. When, in conversation with him, a group of young people discovered that he was a minister, they immediately began to attack the Christian faith. He said that he had not been in the confrontation long before it became apparent that the most vocal one in the group was totally ignorant of the Christianity he was supposedly rejecting. After a while, Dr. Niles forced him to admit that he had never so much as read even one of the Gospels. Dr. Niles then told the group that they could carry the discussion no further until they sufficiently informed themselves about what they were denouncing to carry on an intelligent interchange of thought. This situation is perhaps more typical than we suppose. The Bible is a best seller. It is not a best read book.

And even those of us who would like to understand its meaning are more inclined to read books about the Bible than to read the Bible itself. Now consulting secondary sources may be worthy, for the Bible is a difficult book. We need to help each other understand it, and there are those whose training or whose deep and long experience with the Scriptures gives them eyes to see what we may miss. The study of responsible word books, commentaries, and devotional literature, then, may be extremely helpful in enabling us to hear the voice of God through the Bible. While Luther and Calvin put the Bible into the language of the people, they also wrote commentaries to try to help the people understand it. We have already seen, however, that Luther's aim in writing books was to throw such light on the Bible that people would finally leave his books and go back to the Bible itself.

There is no way to mediate the throb of any great book save through the book itself. Emile Cammaerts tells of spending a summer reading through Dante's *Divine Comedy* with his mother. He writes: "I remember the armchair in which she sat in a shady corner of our small garden, her keen pale face framed in a halo of thin red hair, and the impatience she showed when I struggled too long over the notes of various commentators who did not always agree: 'Oh! Leave your notes alone,' she exclaimed, 'can't you *hear?*' "[16] She wanted him to listen not to what others said about Dante, but to Dante himself. A minister friend has told me how he used to hate Calvin, whom he knew only through his interpreters. One day he decided that it was unfair for him to judge Calvin at second-hand; he would read him directly. After a careful study of the great theologian himself, he came out with a profound admiration for his work and a permanent mark on his own life and ministry.

How much better off would we be if we had the patience and the determination to come to the Bible directly, to listen for the voice of God there. As we have already said, there is nothing wrong with using helps to Bible study. They are necessary. But either before using these helps, or after, or both, we owe it to ourselves and to the Bible to sit before it with all our powers of heart and mind alert, listening for the voice of God to our spirits. It might be surprising what would happen through this process. Then we might join the friends of the Samaritan woman who said, "It is no longer because of what you said that we believe,

---

[16]*The Flower of Grass* (New York, 1945), p. 94.

for we have heard him ourselves; and we know that this is in truth the Saviour of the world" (John 4:42).

During the Hitler regime in Germany, Dietrich Bonhoeffer, who was later martyred, conducted an illegal Preachers' Seminary for some months. One who participated in it tells that after the "external shock" of the barren surroundings and bleak existence was overcome, they experienced an "inner shock":

> In the mornings, there was half an hour of silent meditation on one biblical text in Luther's translation; the same text for a week. We were not allowed to consult the original text, a dictionary or other books during this period. . . . What we experienced, however, at least at the beginning, was emptiness in ourselves and in the texts, where knowledge and answers had been promised to us. . . . The time of meditation . . . did not grow into a time of revelation; the text did not speak to us, and if it did, it was in our own voice.

Bonhoeffer kept them at it, however, although he finally permitted them "to meditate together, and not in silence, once or twice a week."[17] After long periods of this discipline, the Word began to break through. The writer says:

> We had not known what it means that the word preaches itself. . . . Only through long times of waiting and quiet did we learn that the text "may be our master." Half an hour of concentration: it is amazing what comes into your head during that time. . . . For many of us that half hour remained a burden to the end. But it taught all of us that the biblical word is more than a "subject" which can be handled *ad libitum* [just as one wishes].[18]

Maybe God would speak to us in the Scriptures if we should put ourselves within hearing distance.

Another, and exceedingly important, requisite to hearing God's voice in Scripture is a humble spirit that is willing to acknowledge its own inadequacy of mind and heart, that is willing to be taught, that is willing to confess through prayer that it is only with the help of the Holy Spirit that the Bible may become the vehicle of the voice of God. As the Westminster Confession says, ". . . Our full persuasion and assurance of the infallible truth and divine authority [of Holy Scripture] is from the inward work of the Holy Spirit, bearing witness by and with the Word in our hearts" (I, 5). Are we willing to grant this, to allow that natively we

---

[17]Wolf-Dieter Zimmermann, "Finkenwalde," in *I Knew Dietrich Bonhoeffer*, eds. Wolf-Dieter Zimmermann and Ronald Gregor Smith, trans. Käthe Gregor Smith (New York, 1966), p. 107.
[18]Ibid.

cannot hear the voice of God; that He must open our ears to His Word; that only by the action of His Spirit, shattering all our self-sufficiency and pride, can we have converse with Him?

The critical study of the Bible raises a thousand problems for the modern mind. These are often used as excuses for not trusting the Scriptures, as though our difficulties with them were mainly intellectual. One wonders whether our problems are not more deeply rooted in our pride and hardness of heart. Jesus once said to His disciples when they failed to understand Him, "Do you not yet perceive or understand? Are your hearts hardened?" (Mark 8:17). And the writer to the Hebrews pleaded, "Today, when you hear his voice, do not harden your hearts" (3:15). Do not our difficulties with the Bible spring more from a self-centered, humanistic world view which has little or no place for God than from our intellectual difficulties? In the words of P. T. Forsyth, "It is the wills of men, and not their views, that are the great obstacle to the Gospel."[19] Or as George W. Richards put it, "The offense of the gospel is not against the intellect but against the heart of man."[20] E. C. Blackman has said: ". . . The common assumption is that there is no source of authority outside the stream of history itself and the sum total of human experience. The issue is between humanism in all its varieties . . . and the transcendentalism of Christian faith, with its assurance that there is light from on high for man's darkness, and its warning that man's authority is not in himself, but in God."[21]

> The angels keep their ancient places —
> Turn but a stone and start a wing!
> 'Tis ye, 'tis your estrangèd faces,
> That miss the many-splendored thing.[22]

What is needed most is not the criticism that is demanded of the mind — though that has its worth — but the criticism which moves in the realm of redemption. Are we willing to allow God to redeem us in His Son? If so, then the Bible would speak to our redeemed souls with authority. Again as P. T. Forsyth put it, "The most present and real fact of our Christian faith is the fact accessible to faith alone. It is the fact that Christ has brought us God and destroyed our guilt. You do not yet know the inner Christ who are but His lovers or friends. You need to have been His patients and to owe Him your life. That is Christianity."[23]

[19]*Positive Preaching and the Modern Mind* (Cincinnati, 1907), p. 288.
[20]Richards, p. 178.
[21]*Biblical Interpretation* (Philadelphia, 1957), p. 49.
[22]Francis Thompson, "The Kingdom of God."
[23]Forsyth, p. 277.

One of the strange passages in the New Testament casts its light at this point. In the final conflict between Jesus and His enemies at the close of His life, He was asked: "By what authority are you doing these things, or who gave you this authority to do them?" (Mark 11:28). Jesus made a strange reply: "I will ask you a question; answer me, and I will tell you by what authority I do these things. Was the baptism of John from heaven or from men? Answer me." When, after some deliberation with each other, they replied, "We do not know," Jesus then said: "Neither will I tell you by what authority I do these things" (Mark 11:29— 33). Unless we think that our Lord was playing a clever word game with them, engaging in merely a "skillful maneuver" to best them in an argument, this strange passage suggests that there is some vital connection between the authority of Jesus and the authority of John. This is to be seen at one level in the fact that the voice of prophecy had been silenced in Israel for three or four centuries. Its reappearance in John the Baptist was in itself, according to their own tradition, one of the signs of the approach of the Messianic Age. Furthermore, John had borne direct witness to Jesus as the Coming One. If John's testimony were authentic, belief in his message would have pointed to Jesus as the Messiah.

There is a deeper element here, however. What was the baptism of John? It was "a baptism of repentance for the forgiveness of sins" (Mark 1:4). It insisted that humanity is in the wrong with God; that in itself humanity has no power to bring about its own fulfillment; that the whole prophetic movement climaxed in John had held out hopes that humankind could not achieve and had set ideals which there was no human dynamic adequate to fulfil. As H. Scott Holland has put it so profoundly, the "crucial discovery" made by John the Baptist

> was the nature of the limit set on the upward movement of humanity. That movement went so far; achieved so much; was full of such heroic possibilities; suggested, promised, fostered such high hopes. Yet, out of itself, it could not attain to its own proper crown and culmination. It worked up towards a fulfilment which was beyond its own powers. . . . Man is not, himself, in possession of that which should complete his manhood. He waits for something more—for an entry, for an arrival. There is that which comes from beyond, from afar. It enters in upon him, it takes possession, it lifts, it quickens, it transfigures, it fulfils. . . . He is most himself when he is most surrendered to this other.[24]

24Holland, pp. 107ff.

The problem, then, is this: "Has man power to deliver himself? Can he wrestle himself away out of his sin, by development from within? If he can, then the Baptist made a mistake; he falsified experience."[25] If, however, he was right, then John's prophetic authority confronts us with a decision. Are we willing to admit our own sin, failure, and need? Does our inner nature yearn for a fulfillment which we ourselves have no power to achieve? Is this yearning to remain forever unanswered? Or, is there One who comes to us with a redemptive love which is more than a match for our yearning, with a consummation of meaning that forever brands Him as authoritative, as the One whose authority rests in the fact that He "has brought God's life to me"? In other words, am I willing first to accept the authority of John — the demand for "repentance for the forgiveness of sins" — which, if accepted, leads directly to Jesus Christ as the Forgiver of those sins, whose authority then needs no explanation or defense — only glad acceptance and surrender?

We come back, then, to where we began. The problem of biblical authority is the problem of the authority of God over humanity. And since God has chosen to make Himself known to us in His Son, the problem of biblical authority must ultimately be answered by facing the question put by Jesus to His disciples: "But who do you say that I am?" (Mark 8:29). This is brought to a focus in another passage from P. T. Forsyth. After granting that we need historical criticism, that literary criticism has its rights, that psychological criticism is worthy, he says:

> But allowing for all such things, the question remains dogmatic, was He, is He, what Christian faith essentially believed? Did these convictions, of His and of the Church, correspond to reality? Was He, is He, in God what He thought He was and what He was held to be? When the first Church worshiped Him with God's name, and set Him on God's throne, were they a new race of idolaters? Was His influence so poor in quality that it could not protect from that? He thought Himself redeemer; did He really redeem? Did God redeem in Him? Was God the real actor in His saving action? These are the questions; and in all such questions, criticism is *ultra vires* [beyond its power]. These things are settled in another and higher court. ... The soundest criticism is the criticism by a believing Church, daily living on the Grace of the Cross and the venture of faith. ... The real criticism ... is not our criticism of Christ, but Christ's criticism of us, His saving judgment of us.[26]

[25]Ibid., p. 112.
[26]Forsyth, pp. 278ff.

It was facing such questions as these which led Forsyth to say, "I was turned from a Christian to a believer, from a lover of love to an object of grace."[27]

Are we, or are we willing to be, believers and objects of grace? If so, we shall find Christ in the Scriptures, and He will be the touchstone of their authority for us. Then we shall understand what Sir Walter Scott meant when, as he lay dying, he said to his son-in-law, Lockhart, "Bring me the book." "What book?" asked Lockhart. "*The* book," said Sir Walter; "the Bible; there is but one."[28]

[27] Ibid., pp. 282f.
[28] Quoted by F. W. Farrar, *The Bible, Its Meaning and Supremacy* (New York, 1899), p. 278.

8 THE PRIMACY OF SCRIPTURE

DONALD G. BLOESCH

Every word of God proves true. . . . Do not add to his words, lest he rebuke you, and you be found a liar.

Proverbs 30:5, 6

Did not our hearts burn within us while he talked to us on the road, while he opened to us the Scriptures?

Luke 24:32

All scripture is given by inspiration of God, and is profitable for doctrine, for reproof, for correction, for instruction in righteousness. . . .

II Timothy 3:16

Who does not know that the Holy canonical Scripture is contained within definite limits and that it has precedence over all letters of subsequent bishops, so that it is altogether impossible to doubt or question the truth or adequacy of what is written in it?

Augustine

It is impossible for me to recant unless I am proved to be wrong by the testimony of Scripture. My conscience is bound to the Word of God.

Martin Luther

The whole counsel of God, concerning all things necessary for his own glory, man's salvation, faith and life, is either expressly set down in Scripture, or by good and necessary consequence may be deduced from Scripture: unto which nothing at any time is to be added, whether by new revelations of the Spirit, or traditions of men.

Westminster Confession I, 6

"The Primacy of Scripture" (pp. 51-87) *in* Essentials of Evangelical Theology, *Volume One:* God, Authority, & Salvation *by Donald G. Bloesch. Copyright © 1978 by Donald G. Bloesch. Reprinted by permission of Harper & Row, Publishers, Inc.*

ITS DIVINE AUTHORITY

Evangelical theology appeals to the authority of Scripture because it sees Scripture as the written Word of God. The precise relationship between divine revelation and the human writings which comprise the canonical Scripture has been and still is a subject of debate in both evangelical Protestant and Roman Catholic circles, but there is no gainsaying the fact that Scripture is given a crucial role in the determining of doctrine because of its divine authority.

Scripture cannot be rightly understood unless we take into consideration that it has a dual authorship. It is not only a human witness to divine revelation, but it is at the same time God's witness to himself. The Bible is not partly the Word of God and partly the word of man: it is in its entirety the very Word of God and the very word of man. If we contend as do many liberals that the Bible is fundamentally a human account of a particular people's experiences of God or the product of a heightened religious consciousness, that it only leads us to divine truth, then we have an ebionitic view of Scripture.[1] On the other hand if we affirm, as do many within the camp of orthodoxy and fundamentalism, that the Bible is predominantly a divine book and that the human element is only a mask or outward aspect of the divine, then we have a docetic view of Scripture. Some would even say that the Bible is an exact reproduction of the thoughts of God, but this denies its real humanity as well as its historicity.

While it is important to underscore the inseparability of the biblical text and divine revelation, one must not make the mistake of equating them. In Bavinck's view: "Scripture is . . . not the revelation itself, but the description, the record, from which the revelation can be known."[2] "It should . . . be remembered," Barth declares, that the biblical writings as such are "not the Revelation" but instead "the witness to the Revelation, and this is expressed in human terms. . . ."[3] Berkouwer replies to those evangelicals who object to describing Scripture as a human witness:

> Calling Scripture a human witness . . . does not at all mean a separation of Scripture and revelation, but rather an honoring of

[1]The terms *docetic* and *ebionite* are derived from heresies in the early church relating to the person of Christ. The docetists did not give full weight to the humanity of Christ and emphasized only the divinity, whereas the ebionites in their stress on the humanity lost sight of his essential divinity.

[2]H. Bavinck, *Our Reasonable Faith* (Grand Rapids, 1956), p. 95.

[3]Karl Barth, *The Preaching of the Gospel*, trans. B. E. Hooke (Philadelphia, 1963), p. 64.

integral Scripture. The witness is indeed directed to that which
is witnessed to. It is not a relativizing of Scripture, but the ac-
knowledgment of its meaning, intention, and function when it
witnesses *of* Christ and therefore as God's Word is distinguished
from him.[4]

Yet we must go on to affirm that Scripture is more than a
human witness to revelation: it is revelation itself mediated
through human words. It is not in and of itself divine revelation,
but when illumined by the Spirit it becomes revelation to the
believer. At the same time it could not become revelation unless
it already embodied revelation, unless it were included within
the event of revelation. Scripture is not simply a "pointer to revelation" (as Brunner has asserted), but by the action of the Spirit
it is a veritable bearer of revelation, a vehicle or "conduit of
divine truth" (C. Henry).

While in his earlier writings Barth sometimes gives the impression of calling into question the revelational status of Scripture,
he becomes more consciously orthodox in his *Church Dogmatics* I.
Continuing to maintain the distinctiveness of the scriptural witness from revelation, he is also insistent on its unity with revelation "in so far as revelation is the basis, object and content of
this word."[5]

> As the Word of God in the sign of this prophetic-apostolic word
> of man Holy Scripture is like the unity of God and man in Jesus
> Christ. It is neither divine only nor human only. Nor is it a mix-
> ture of the two nor a *tertium quid* between them. But in its own
> way and degree it is very God and very man, i.e., a witness of
> revelation which itself belongs to revelation, and historically a
> very human literary document.[6]

While we must resist the temptation to posit a direct identity
between Scripture and revelation (since this could lead to bib-
liolatry), we do affirm an indirect identity in that by the work of
the Holy Spirit the very human words of the prophets and apos-

[4]G. C. Berkouwer, *Holy Scripture*, trans. Jack Rogers (Grand Rapids, 1975),
pp. 165–166.
[5]Karl Barth, *Church Dogmatics*, ed. G. W. Bromiley and T. F. Torrance (Edinburgh, 1956), I/2, 463.
[6]Ibid., p. 501. It should be noted that in his *Church Dogmatics* I and II Barth
reflects a neo-Calvinist sacramentalism by which Scripture, sermon, and sacraments are seen as means of grace having a human form but a divine content. In
his later writings Barth tends to return to his earlier position of speaking of Jesus
Christ as the one Word of God and the Bible (as well as the sermon and rites of
the church) as only a human witness to this Word. See especially *Church Dogmatics*,
trans. G. W. Bromiley (Edinburgh, 1961), IV/3, 3–165. He here is inclined to
underplay the sacramental character of Scripture as both divine and human.

tles are conjoined with the Word spoken by God to them. God's Word is consequently not the Bible in and by itself but the correlation of Scripture and Spirit (Barth). The revelation comes to us in the veiled form of the language of Zion, but at the same time it is not known except in and through this language. It can be seen that the most appropriate symbol of the Word of God is not the Bible as a closed book but the cross of Christ shining through the pages of the open Bible.

While Barth was unable to maintain his understanding of the three-fold unity of the Word of God as revealed, written, and proclaimed (because of his stress on the transcendence of the Word over the words), in his emphasis on the revealing work of the Spirit he is closer to the intention of the Reformers than is modern fundamentalism in this regard.[7] The Reformers too spoke of the necessity for the unity of the Holy Spirit and the biblical word, and only this unity is the divine criterion for faith. Luther declared: "Thus Scripture is a book, to which there belongeth not only reading but also the right Expositor and Revealer, to wit, the Holy Spirit. Where He openeth not Scripture, it is not understood."[8] Just as the Bible only makes sense when illuminated by the Spirit, so the Spirit only gives sense in and through the biblical witness. "Do not seek the Spirit through solitude or through prayer," Luther said, "but read Scripture. When a man feels that what he is reading is pleasing to him, let him give thanks; for these are the first fruits of the Spirit."[9] In Calvin's view the truth of Scripture cannot be discerned as the Word of God apart from "the sealing of the Spirit" which imparts to the conscience of believers "such certainty as to remove all doubts."[10] As he saw it, the work of the Spirit is not to supplement or supersede the heavenly doctrine in Scripture but to authenticate it and to bring it home to our hearts.

The mainstream of historic evangelicalism has also perceived the indispensable role of the Holy Spirit in bringing us the veritable Word of God, though a rationalistic strand in modern

[7]It is a mistake to aver, as do David Kelsey and Carl Henry, that Barth sees the authority of the Bible in purely functional terms. It is more proper to say that he views biblical authority in relational terms—in the light of its divine center, the cross and resurrection of Christ. In this position the authority, infallibility, and power of the Scriptures to convict and save lie not in what they are in themselves but in their incommensurable relationship to Jesus Christ.

[8]*Sermons on Luke 24:13 f.* Quoted in Barth, *Church Dogmatics* I/2, 508.

[9]*Luther's Works*, Vol. 29, ed. Jaroslav Pelikan (St. Louis, 1968), p. 83.

[10]John Calvin, *Commentary on Galatians 1:12, 13, Corpus Reformatorum, Calv. 50*, p. 177.

evangelicalism has obscured this truth. Jonathan Edwards's position is described as follows: "God's Word is really *God's* Word when it is accompanied by the Spirit dwelling in the human heart; when unaccompanied by the Spirit it is simply another natural, human word."[11] Packer rightly observes that "the Holy Spirit is . . . the one who, in a mystery for which the Incarnation provides the only analogy, caused the verbal witness of man to God and of God to himself to coincide."[12] Carl Henry, seeking to do justice to the written word, underlines the unity of Spirit and Scripture: "The rule of the Spirit does not remove man from the will of God objectively revealed in the Bible, and emancipate him to moral self-sufficiency. The Spirit rules in and through the written word, which he has inspired."[13]

It should be recognized that God's Word is not only revealed in the Scripture by the Spirit but also concealed by human finitude and sin. With the Reformers and the neo-Reformation theology of Barth and Brunner, and against the Christian rationalism of the Enlightenment and its modern representatives including Pannenberg and Langdon Gilkey, we hold that the revelation in Scripture is not open to general reasonableness but is disclosed only to the ears and eyes of faith. It is as if light shone through biblical characters on a stained glass window in a cathedral. The light is objectively shining but because of our blinded eyes we cannot make out the images on the window. It is only when the Spirit opens our eyes from within that we can perceive the message on the window and receive it into our hearts. The truth of revelation is objectively given in biblical history, but revelation also encompasses the interior work of the Holy Spirit by which this truth is gratefully acknowledged and received (cf. Eph. 1:17, 18; Gal. 1:12).[14]

---

[11]Conrad Cherry, *The Theology of Jonathan Edwards* (Garden City, N.Y., 1966), p. 48.

[12]James Packer, "Taking Stock in Theology" in *Evangelicals Today*, ed. John C. King (London, 1973, pp. 15–30), p. 21.

[13]Carl Henry, *Personal Christian Ethics* (Grand Rapids, 1957), p. 360.

[14]Our position is in accord with the biblical understanding of revelation where it is depicted primarily, though not exclusively, in dynamic terms. Albrecht Oepke declares: "Revelation is not understood in terms of a fixed historical or eschatological objectivism." The making known of what God reveals "is itself part of the act of revelation." And again: "Revelation is not a material possession which we have in black and white. It is a divine act, the unveiling of what is hidden." *Theological Dictionary of the New Testament*, Vol. 3, ed. Gerhard Kittel, trans. G. W. Bromiley (Grand Rapids, 1965), pp. 581, 583. For an informative discussion of the meaning of revelation as this relates to various biblical words, see C. F. D.

We affirm that Scripture is not only a human witness and medium of divine revelation but also a divinely inspired witness and medium. In II Tim. 3:16 we read: "All scripture is inspired by God and profitable for teaching, for reproof, for correction, and for training in righteousness . . ." (cf. I Cor. 2:13; II Pet. 1:21). With Warfield we hold this to mean that all Scripture is breathed out by God, is a product of the creative activity of the Spirit of God. It must not be taken to mean (as in Protestant liberalism) that the writers were simply assisted and illumined by the Spirit: they were so guided by the Spirit that what was actually written had the very sanction of God himself.

While revelation refers to the action by which God discloses himself and the truth of his Gospel to his church, inspiration refers to the divine election and guidance of the biblical prophets for the express purpose of ensuring the trustworthiness and efficacy of their witness through the ages (cf. Isa. 30:8; Hab. 2:2). God's Spirit was operative upon both the writers and their writings, and he continues to be present in their testimony throughout the history of the church, preserving it from corruption. By the gift of inspiration the biblical writings are made the repository of divine truth as well as the unique channel of divine revelation.

Inspiration, which pertains basically to the verbal witness of the prophets and apostles and which is completed, is to be distinguished from illumination, which denotes the ongoing action of the Spirit in awakening men and women in every age to the truth of what is given in Scripture. In our view inspiration is both conceptual and verbal, since it signifies that the Spirit was active both in shaping the thoughts and imagination of the biblical writers and also in guiding them in their actual writing. We read that the Spirit of the Lord came upon the prophet *and* his words (Isa. 59:21; cf. Exod. 31:18; II Sam. 23:2; Prov. 30:5, 6; Isa. 49:2; Jer. 1:9; I Cor. 2:13). Verbal inspiration must not be confused with perfect accuracy or mechanical dictation. Warfield explains inspiration as the *concursus* of divine and human activity.[15] The divine activity does not supersede the human but works

---

Moule, "Revelation" in *Interpreter's Dictionary of the Bible*, Vol. 4 (New York, 1962), pp. 54– 58; and Dewey M. Beegle, *Scripture, Tradition and Infallibility* (Grand Rapids, 1973), pp. 15– 52. Both these authors recognize that revelation includes the communication of conceptual knowledge as well as communion and confrontation with God, but Beegle is better in holding objective and subjective dimensions of revelation in balance.

[15]Benjamin Warfield, *The Inspiration and Authority of the Bible,* ed. Samuel G. Craig. Introduction by Cornelius Van Til (Philadelphia, 1948), pp. 158, 162. For a balanced appraisal of Warfield's doctrine of inspiration see David H. Kelsey,

confluently with the human so that the Scriptures are the joint product of both God and man. The writers are not to be thought of as simply the pens of the Holy Spirit (as a number of seventeenth-century divines taught) but as partners with the Spirit so that the end product can be attributed to coauthorship.

We also affirm the plenary inspiration of Scripture, meaning that Scripture in its totality is inspired. The words of both prophets and apostles are deemed authoritative (II Pet. 3:2), and the New Testament letters are called Scripture along with the Old Testament (II Pet. 3:15, 16; I Tim. 5:18). This does not mean, however, that all Scripture has equal value. We oppose the so-called "flat view" of Scripture which does not consider levels of revelation and the fulfillment of revelation in Jesus Christ. All of Scripture is binding upon the church, all of Scripture is a product of the Holy Spirit, but not all Scripture attests equally to the incarnation and atoning work of Jesus Christ, to the Gospel of reconciliation and redemption, which is the formal norm of Scripture.[16] Luther relegated some books in the Bible to the level of Law, whereas other books give a forthright and potent testimony to the message of salvation, the center and apex of Scripture.

In contradistinction to both Barth and Forsyth, we hold that the doctrine of inspiration is preeminently concerned with the written product and not just with the writers and readers of Scripture. Yet we share with these men a dynamic view of both revelation and inspiration. The will and purpose of God have been fully and adequately revealed in Jesus Christ for all time and, therefore, revelation in this sense is final and complete. Since the original witness to this revelation is also complete, inspiration too is something that is finished.[17] In another sense, however, revelation continues in that people in every age must be awakened to the significance of the Christ-event for their lives. But continuing revelation does not signify a new revelation, simply the clarification and illumination of what has already been disclosed definitively and conclusively in the sacred Scripture.

Against a certain Marcionite tendency in modern liberalism

The Uses of Scripture in Recent Theology (Philadelphia, 1975), pp. 17–24. For Kelsey, Scripture is authoritative only in a functional sense.

[16]We are here using *formal* in the Aristotelian sense which denotes *goal* or *criterion*.

[17]Inspiration, like revelation, can be conceived of as continuing in a qualified sense, but the meaning is that the Spirit is constantly acting to safeguard the original witness from corruption. Just as we can distinguish between original and dependent revelation, so we can distinguish between original inspiration and the providential preservation of the Spirit in assuring these writings as the divinely appointed channel of revelation.

and existentialist theology, we affirm that the revelation of Jesus Christ is present in the Old Testament as well as the New. The Old Testament was not simply a preparation for the New Testament, but the Gospel was already anticipated in the Old Testament though not in final or definitive form. This is why Calvin could preach a series of sermons on the Gospel according to Isaiah. Jesus Christ, in his preexistent state, was present to the patriarchs and prophets of Old Testament history, though his full identity was hidden from them. They looked forward to the fulfillment of time *(kairos)* when Jesus Christ would be incarnate in human form, but they were nevertheless in continuity with Christ. In this sense it can be said that the church had its beginnings in the ancient history of the Hebrews.

The divine authority of Scripture was seriously undermined by the rise of higher criticism, and while not discounting the solid gains that were made, we must not ignore the damage that was also caused by many of the critics who were heavily influenced by an evolutionary philosophy of history.[18] When the Old Testament is seen as the climax of a continuing cultural and religious development, or when revelation is believed to be contingent on the level of man's spiritual maturity, then the very meaning of revelation as supernatural intervention into earthly history is subverted. Historical criticism has enabled us to recapture the humanity of Scripture, but we must not lose sight of its divinity if we are to recover the Bible as an authoritative guide for the church of today.

SCRIPTURAL PRIMACY

A conflict that had already emerged in biblical times concerns the relation between the written Scriptures and the rabbinical and ecclesiastical traditions. Jesus himself made the Scriptures the ruling norm.[19] The Pharisees on the other hand added their

---

[18]Julius Wellhausen in the later nineteenth century formulated a philosophy of Israel's history which traced this history in terms of religious evolution with the prophets and exile being the high point. Elizabeth Achtemeier caustically comments: "In this view everything that was earliest in Israel's history was automatically labeled as primitive and put at the bottom of the scale of development as having minimal worth." See her *The Old Testament and the Proclamation of the Gospel* (Philadelphia, 1973), p. 28.

[19]It should be recognized that Jesus' ultimate criterion was not Scripture by itself but the Scripture and the Spirit together. He said that the Sadducees erred because they knew "neither the scriptures nor the power of God" (Mark 12:24; cf. John 5:39, 40; 14:15–17).

traditions to the Scriptures while the Sadducees subtracted the supernatural from Scripture. Jesus accused the Pharisees of making the Word of God void (Mark 7:13; Matt. 15.6) and reprimanded the Sadducees for being ignorant of it (Mark 12:18–27).

For the most part both the patristic fathers and the medieval theologians before the fourteenth century taught that the Bible is the unique and sole source of revelation.[20] To be sure, it was generally assumed that the Scriptures need to be supplemented and interpreted by the church tradition. In the Eastern church it was believed that the *Philokalia,* an anthology of patristic texts on prayer, clarifies and illumines what the Bible holds in secret and which cannot be easily grasped by our limited understanding. Yet the traditions of men cannot add anything new to what is already contained in the Scriptures, either explicitly or implicitly. The priority of Scripture over tradition was clearly enunciated by Thomas Aquinas: "Arguments from Scripture are used properly and carry necessity in matters of faith; arguments from other doctors of the Church are proper, but carry only probability; for our faith is based on the revelation given to the apostles and prophets who wrote the canonical books of the Scriptures and not on revelation that could have been made to other doctors."[21]

In the fourteenth and fifteenth centuries, with the rise of nominalism and the flowering of mysticism, an appeal was made not only to Scripture but also to mystical experience and the church tradition. Roman Catholic theologians came to speak of a parallel source of truth — the oral tradition which continues in the history of the church. According to Gabriel Biel, Scripture and tradition should be held in equal esteem. Heiko Oberman contends that this was also the view of the Council of Trent, though some contemporary Catholic theologians are of the mind that Trent made no decision on this matter.[22] In late medieval theology it

[20]See George Tavard, *Holy Writ or Holy Church* (New York, 1959), pp. 22f.

[21]Thomas Aquinas, *Summa Theologica* I, 1, 8.

[22]See Heiko Oberman, *The Harvest of Medieval Theology* (Grand Rapids, 1967), pp. 406f. Also see his "The Tridentine Decree on Justification in the Light of Late Medieval Theology" in Robert W. Funk, ed., *Journal for Theology and Church,* Vol. 3 (New York, 1967), pp. 28–54.

R. J. Geiselmann argues that Trent really did not have anything to say about the relationship between Scripture and tradition. He says that Trent did not mean to teach a theory of two sources of revelation. The final report of Trent read: "Scripture *and* tradition"; the original reading was "partly Scripture . . . partly tradition." See Geiselmann, *Die Heilige Schrift und die Tradition* (Freiburg, 1962).

was also assumed that the church authenticates Scripture and
therefore has a certain primacy over Scripture. In the words of
Duns Scotus: "The books of the holy canon are not to be believed
except insofar as one must first believe the church which approves and authorizes those books and their content."[23]

Many Catholic scholars today (including Karl Rahner, Hans
Küng, Yves Congar, and George Tavard) speak of only one source
of revelation, sacred Scripture. While contending, however, that
all the truth of salvation is contained in Scripture, they affirm
that the teaching office of the church gives the authoritative interpretation of Scripture. Yet although the church tradition interprets the truth of revelation, it does not create this truth. Congar
goes so far as to declare, "Scripture has an absolute sovereignty."[24]

Against the prevailing view in their time that church tradition
is on a par with Scripture, the Reformers resolutely maintained
that there is only one source of revelation, Holy Scripture. Scripture, moreover, contains not only the revealed, divine truth but
the *whole* revealed truth. For the Reformers the church is under
the Word but does not authenticate or authorize it. "The church
of God," said Luther, "has no power to establish any article of
faith, and it neither has established nor ever will establish any
article of faith, and it neither has established nor ever will establish one."[25] Augustine had declared: "I should not believe the
gospel except as moved by the authority of the Catholic Church."[26]
Calvin explains that when this remark is seen in its proper context it is clearly understood that Augustine was not maintaining
that Scripture is authenticated by the church but only that Scripture has its most potent appeal when reverence is given to the
church as well.[27] Luther also seeks to interpret Augustine's statement in an evangelical sense; but in the "papist" sense, he says,

---

Lennerz argues against Geiselmann that the alteration did not represent a
material revision of the original report. But many Catholic scholars including
Karl Rahner and Hans Küng are now speaking of only one source of revelation,
sacred Scripture.

For an illuminating account of the recent discussion in Catholic theology see
G. C. Berkouwer, *The Second Vatican Council and the New Catholicism,* trans. Lewis B.
Smedes (Grand Rapids, 1965), pp. 89f.

[23]Quoted in Lev Shestov, *Athens and Jerusalem,* trans. Bernard Martin (Athens,
Ohio, 1966), p. 298.

[24]Yves Congar, *La Tradition et les traditions,* II (Paris, 1963), p. 176.

[25]Luther, *Werke,* W. A., 30/II, 420.

[26]Augustine, "St. Augustin: The Writings Against the Manichaeans and Against
the Donatists" in *A Select Library of the Nicene and Post-Nicene Fathers,* Vol. 4, ed.
Philip Schaff (Grand Rapids, 1956), p. 131.

[27]John Calvin, *Institutes of the Christian Religion,* ed. John T. McNeill, trans.
Ford Lewis Battles (Philadelphia, 1960), I, 7, 3, pp. 76–78.

it is "false and un-Christian. Everyone must believe only because it is the word of God, and because he is convinced in his heart that it is true."[28]

Luther gave poignant expression to the newly emerging consensus of the Reformation when he referred to the Word as the judge and creator of the church. At one place he pointed to Scripture as the light and the church tradition as the lantern. He spoke approvingly of Bernard of Clairvaux who said that he would rather drink from the spring itself (the Scriptures) than from the brook (the fathers of the church). For Luther and other Reformers, as well as for Bernard, the brook is helpful mainly in leading us back to the spring.

The Reformers intended not to denigrate the church, but to make clear that the church must be a servant of the Word, not its master. They were even willing to affirm that the true church, the church which subordinates itself to the Word, is infallible, though this infallibility is derivative and relative. Zwingli declared that the true church "depends and rests only upon the word and will of God. . . . That Church cannot err. . . . That is the right Church, the spotless bride of Jesus Christ governed and refreshed by the Spirit of God."[29] And as Luther put it, "The church cannot err for the Word of God which it teaches cannot err."[30]

Against their Catholic opponents the Reformers contended that Scripture authenticates itself and interprets itself. It gains its credence neither from the church nor from reason but from the One to whom it testifies and who is himself its living center, Jesus Christ.[31] By the power of his Spirit it is able to impress upon the minds of its readers and hearers the trustworthiness of its doctrine and the urgency of its message (cf. Luke 24:32; II Tim. 3:15, 16). It is not Scripture in and of itself but Scripture ruled and imbued by the Spirit of God that convicts people of their sins and convinces them of the truth.

The Reformers also staunchly affirmed the perspicuity of Scripture, its inherent clarity. They meant by this that its basic message is clear even to the unsophisticated layman, and therefore every person can go to the Bible directly to search and find

[28]*Luther's Works*, Vol. 35, ed. E. Theodore Bachman (Philadelphia, 1960), p. 151.
[29]S. M. Jackson, ed., *Selected Works of Huldreich Zwingli* (Philadelphia, 1901), pp. 85–86.
[30]Luther, *Werke*, W. A., 51, 518.
[31]The Christocentric orientation of the Reformation doctrine of Scripture is ably delineated in J. K. S. Reid, *The Authority of Scripture* (New York, 1957), pp. 29–72.

the truth. The doctrinal mysteries need to be expounded by theologians so that one can perceive them rightly, but everything necessary for salvation is plainly attested in the Scriptures. The language in certain parts of Scripture will also prove difficult to the layman, but God's truth shines through even obscure terminology. Luther maintained that the clearness of Scripture is twofold: the one kind is external, referring to the objective testimony in Scripture, and the other internal, referring to the illumination of the Spirit.

> If you speak of the *internal* clearness, no man understands a single iota in the Scriptures by the natural powers of his own mind, unless he have the Spirit of God; all have obscure hearts. The Holy Spirit is required for the understanding of the whole of Scripture and of all its parts. If you allude to the *external* clearness, there is nothing left obscure and ambiguous, but all things brought to light by the Word are perfectly clear.[32]

In neo-Protestantism the consciousness of the ecclesial community again came to take precedence over the Scriptures. For Schleiermacher the Holy Scripture as the witness to Christ is subject to the judgment of "the corporate spirit." It is the result of faith, not the basis of faith. Culture came to be seen as a source or norm of theology in addition to Scripture.

Modern neo-Catholicism reflects a similar orientation. Karl Rahner, for example, refers to the church's "awareness of faith" as "a theological supreme court."[33] Avery Dulles holds that the living magisterium is endowed with authority from Christ to interpret rightly the Word for the community.[34] In some neo-Catholic circles reference is made to the infallibility of the people of God, which takes precedence over the infallibility of the Word.

Against both Roman Catholicism and neo-Protestantism dialectical theology vigorously asserted the primacy of Scripture over the church as well as over religious experience. Karl Barth declared, "Scripture is in the hands but not in the power of the Church."[35] It was his conviction that

> the Church is most faithful to its tradition, and realises its unity with the Church of every age, when, linked but not tied by its past, it today searches the Scriptures and orientates its life by

[32]In Heinrich Schmid, ed., *Doctrinal Theology of the Evangelical Lutheran Church*, 3d ed. rev. (Minneapolis, 1961), p. 73.
[33]In L. Bruce Van Voorst, "Follow-up on the Küng-Rahner Feud," *The Christian Century* (Aug. 25, 1971, pp. 997–1000), p. 999.
[34]Avery Dulles, *Models of the Church* (Garden City, N.Y., 1974), p. 81.
[35]Barth, *Church Dogmatics* I/2, 682.

them as though this had to happen today for the first time. And, on the other hand, it sickens and dies when it is enslaved by its past instead of being disciplined by the new beginning which it must always make in the Scriptures.[36]

Dietrich Bonhoeffer, who shared with Barth a dynamic view of revelation, also subordinated the church to the criterion of the divine Word in Scripture:

> The Word of God seeks a *Church* to take unto itself. It has its being *in* the Church. It enters the Church by its own self-initiated movement. It is wrong to suppose that there is so to speak a Word on the one hand and a Church on the other, and that it is the task of the preacher to take that Word into his hands and move it so as to bring it into the Church and apply it to the Church's needs. On the contrary, the Word moves of its own accord, and all the preacher has to do is to assist that movement and try to put no obstacles in its path.[37]

In identifying ourselves with the theology of crisis over neo-Protestantism and Roman Catholicism we do not mean to deprecate the role of the church or deny the movement of the Holy Spirit in the church. Yet while Scripture is inspired by the Spirit, the church is assisted by the Spirit (Max Thurian). The role of the Spirit is to awaken the church to the truth contained in the Scriptures and then to empower the church to proclaim this truth. With the Reformers and the dialectical theologians, we contend that Scripture when illumined by the Spirit authenticates itself. The church simply recognizes the truth that Scripture upholds and then applies this truth to the world.

Our position is that the Spirit both indwells the church and judges the church by the Word. The Word functions normatively over the church as the Sword of the Spirit. With Berkouwer we have definite reservations concerning the contention of Roman Catholic scholars that the Spirit is the church's immanent life principle, since this seems to deny the transcending, judging role of the Spirit. An American Benedictine Kilian McDonnell reflects Reformation motifs when he declares, "The Word always calls the church and constitutes it. And having constituted it, warns, judges, purifies, strengthens, nourishes, edifies it."[38]

Evangelical theology holds that Scripture has primacy not

---

[36]Barth, *Church Dogmatics* II/2, 647.

[37]Dietrich Bonhoeffer, *The Cost of Discipleship*, rev. and unabridged ed., trans. R. H. Fuller (London, 1959), p. 225.

[38]Kilian McDonnell, *John Calvin, the Church, and the Eucharist* (Princeton, N.J., 1967), p. 358.

only over the church but also over religious experience. The Word, said Luther, must be believed "against all sight and feeling and understanding." The Word must indeed be experienced, but this is the experience of faith itself, which transcends the reach of man's perception as well as the power of man's conception. Moreover, the experience of faith is forever critical of itself as an experience and always points beyond itself to the Word. Luther averred that our theology is certain because "it snatches us away from ourselves and places us outside ourselves, so that we do not depend on our own strength, conscience, experience, person, or works. . . ."[39]

This brings us to the perennial misconception that Reformation theology elevates the individual conscience as the ultimate authority. In the words of Forsyth: "The Reformation . . . stood not for the supremacy of conscience, but for the rescue of the conscience by the supremacy of Christ in it."[40] Luther averred that his conscience was bound to the Word of God, and this is why he could not go against conscience. In evangelical theology the authority for faith is nothing in us but something within history (Forsyth). It is the voice of the living God speaking to us in the sacred history mirrored in the Scriptures. This voice to be sure also speaks to us in our conscience, but its basis and origin are beyond man's conscience and imagination. Conscience, like experience, can be a trustworthy guide only when it is anchored in the divine revelation given in Holy Scripture.

In addition we affirm the primacy of Scripture over dreams, signs, and wonders. Also to be included in this connection are proofs and evidences of the faith. In the Book of Deuteronomy we read that a prophet or dreamer of dreams who gives a sign that comes to pass must not be listened to if what he says contradicts the word of God (13:1– 5). Forsyth gives a timely warning on seeking after proofs and empirical evidences for faith:

> They are tests of nature and not of faith, tests of feeling rather than insight, tests of empirical experience instead of soul experience, of success rather than of devotion. We withhold full committal till we have tested things in life. We make no inspired venture of faith, but we put Christ on His mettle to see if He is effective in thought or practice. We turn pragmatists and trust Christ because He works; which may come suspiciously near to

[39]Martin Luther, *Luther's Works,* Vol. 26, ed. Jaroslav Pelikan (St. Louis, 1963), p. 387.
[40]P. T. Forsyth, *The Gospel and Authority,* ed. Marvin Anderson (Minneapolis, 1971), p. 172.

trusting Him because it spiritually pays and enhances our spiritual egoism.[41]

Signs and wonders have a place in the life of faith, but they are to be seen not as the basis for faith but as illuminations of the truth of faith for those who already believe (cf. Rom. 15:19; II Cor. 12:11–13; Heb. 2:4). We are not to seek after signs or put God to the test, but we should be open to the signs which he is already working for his people. The most authentic signs are those that form part of the message of faith itself, such as the resurrection of Jesus Christ from the grave. In this light we can understand these words of our Lord: "This generation is an evil generation; it seeks a sign, but no sign shall be given to it except the sign of Jonah" (Luke 11:29).

Likewise we must resist any claim to a new revelation, one that completes or even supersedes Scripture and does not merely illumine or clarify Scripture. Various cults and sects have arisen in the modern age which in effect deny Scripture as the original and fundamental vehicle of divine revelation, the sole and unique source of saving truth. We can here mention Mormonism, Christian Science, Anglo-Israelism, the Unification Church of Sun Myung Moon, the Church of the Living Word, Bahaism, and to a lesser degree Seventh Day Adventism and the Community of True Inspiration.[42] Against these new religions we affirm with Luther: "No one is bound to believe more than what is based on Scripture."[43] We also concur with Watchman Nee's timely word of wisdom: "All the revelation today is but the light regained from the word of the past."[44]

Again, we must assert the primacy of Scripture over culture. Too often in the past theologians have drawn upon the creative thought of their culture as well as the Bible in constructing their theology. Although Albrecht Ritschl believed that theology should derive its content from the New Testament and from no other source, he in fact unwittingly accepted the guiding principles of the then current philosophy (Kantianism) including the conflict of man with nature and the need to gain mastery over nature. Schleiermacher, in his *Speeches on Religion,* upheld not the biblical Christ, the divine Savior from sin, but a cultural Christ, the

[41]P. T. Forsyth, *The Principle of Authority* (London, 1952), p. 335.

[42]Though some of these groups uphold the infallibility of Scripture, they regard continuing revelation through the gift of prophecy as on a par with Scripture if not superseding Scripture.

[43]*Luther's Works,* Vol. 32, ed. George W. Forell (Philadelphia, 1958), p. 96.

[44]Watchman Nee, *The Ministry of God's Word* (New York, 1971), p. 67.

principle of mediation between infinite and finite. Karl Barth on the contrary was strident in his criticisms of what he termed culture-Protestantism and contended that the basic content of our faith must be derived from Scripture alone *(sola Scriptura)*. For him culture is not a norm or source for theology but the field in which theology functions and addresses itself.

In concluding this section on Scriptural primacy, we must bear in mind that the ultimate, final authority is not Scripture but the living God himself as we find him in Jesus Christ. Jesus Christ and the message about him constitute the material norm for our faith just as the Bible is the formal norm. The Bible is authoritative because it points beyond itself to the absolute authority, the living and transcendent Word of God. Against both fundamentalism and the old Catholicism we do not conceive of the authority of Christian faith in heteronomous terms. Our authority is not an external standard that impresses itself upon the soul, but a Word from God that enters into the depths of the soul and creates its own response. As Forsyth put it:

> The authority in theology is not external to the matter it works in. It is spiritual. It is inherent in the fontal fact, and connate to the soul. It belongs to the revelation as such, and not to any voucher which the revelation created, like a book or a church. It is an authority objective to us in its source, but subjective in its nature and appeal.[45]

We must go on to affirm, however, that the absolute authority of faith, the living Christ himself, has so bound himself to the historical attestation concerning his self-revelation, namely, the sacred Scripture, that the latter necessarily participates in the authority of its Lord. The Bible must be distinguished from its ground and goal, but it cannot be separated from them. This is why Forsyth could also say: *"The Bible is not merely a record of the revelation; it is part of the revelation.* It is not a quarry for the historian, but a fountain for the soul."[46]

Jesus Christ is the one who speaks, the message of the Bible is the word that he speaks within history, and the church is the mouth through which he speaks. Just as the church is subordinated to the Bible, so the Bible in turn is subordinated to Jesus Christ, who embodies the mind and counsel of God. To put it another way, the church is the phonograph by which we hear the

---

[45] P. T. Forsyth, *The Principle of Authority*, p. 396.
[46] P. T. Forsyth, *The Gospel and Authority*, p. 25.

voice of Christ on the record, the Scriptures.[47] To carry the illustration further, it is the Holy Spirit who sets the phonograph in motion. The authority of the Bible is operative within the context of the church by the action of the Spirit. Where these analogies fall down is that Christ is free to speak his Word in a slightly different way for every age and culture, though he remains faithful to the Word that he uttered once for all in the history of the biblical revelation.

Forsyth points to this higher criterion within the Bible, the canon within the canon, when he says: "The gospel of God's historic act of grace is the infallible power and authority over both church and Bible. It produced them both. They both exist for its sake, and must be construed in its service."[48] The ruling criterion of the Gospel, however, must not be construed as referring only to particular sections of Scripture, but it is either implicit or explicit in the whole of Scripture.

The authority and infallibility of the Bible as well as of the church are derivative, having their basis in Christ and his Gospel. We must listen to the dictates of the Bible and also to the counsel of the universal church because they have their ultimate sanction in God himself. When these authorities seem to disagree, this means that we have not really made contact with the real Word of Scripture or the true head of the church, who are one and the same. We must subject the discordant voices that we hear to Christ's self-witness within the Scriptures, thereby bringing a transcendent norm to bear upon the point of contention. Yet this transcendent norm is not within our possession: to hear the voice of the living Christ is a miracle of grace which we can hope and pray for but cannot take for granted.[49]

INFALLIBILITY AND INERRANCY

Evangelical theology affirms both the infallibility and inerrancy of Scripture, but these terms must be qualified in the light not so much of modern historical research but of Scripture's own judgment concerning itself. The biblical authors did not claim to

[47] Another pertinent illustration is the church as the lamp, the Bible as the light bulb, and Christ as the light. The light comes to us only through the vehicles of the light bulb and lamp, but apart from the light these have little value.

[48] P. T. Forsyth, *The Gospel and Authority*, p. 17.

[49] It should be borne in mind that the voice of the living Christ cannot be divorced from either the Scriptures or the church. This voice is none other than the Word of God in the Scriptures which speaks to and through the church in every age.

possess a synoptic or absolute perspective concerning the truth that they attested and proclaimed. The Psalmist declared, "Such knowledge is too wonderful for me; it is high, I cannot attain it" (Ps. 139:6). And again: "Teach me, Lord, the meaning of your laws" (Ps. 119:33). Job testified: "Therefore I have uttered what I did not understand, things too wonderful for me, which I did not know" (Job 42:3; cf. Dan. 12:8). Peter describes the prophets as seeking and striving to understand what the Spirit of the Messiah was teaching them (I Pet. 1:10, 11). Some prophecies, moreover, undergo revision in the Scriptures. Jesus, for example, assures us that John the Baptist is the object of the prophecy of Malachi (in Mal. 4:5) even though he referred explicitly to Elijah (Matt. 11:10).[50] Paul is careful not to equate his own opinions on marriage with the mind of God, though he claims to have the Spirit of Christ (I Cor. 7:12, 25, 40).

We must also bear in mind that the prophets and apostles were men of their times though the message that they attested transcended their age and every age. The enlightened biblical Christian will not shrink from asserting that there are culturally conditioned ideas as well as historically conditioned language in the Bible. Both Luther and Calvin recognized that in the hermeneutical task a distinction must always be made between the inward content and the outward form of the Bible. Calvin, in his attempt to reconcile historical and cultural elements in the Bible with its divine inspiration, referred to the accommodation of the Holy Spirit. As he saw it the Holy Spirit accommodated himself to the thought-forms and language of the people of that age in order to impress upon them the heavenly doctrine which speaks to every age. Calvin was here anticipated by Origen and Augustine, who also acknowledged the condescension of the Spirit to our human ways of communicating and understanding. The Puritan William Gouge perceived the possibility of error if we concern ourselves only with the words as such and not with the Word: "This Word is properly and truly the right sense and meaning of the Scriptures; for except that be found out, in many words there may seem to be matter of falsehood."[51]

The Lausanne Covenant gives this potent witness: "We affirm the divine inspiration, truthfulness and authority of both Old and New Testament Scriptures in their entirety as the only written

---

[50]This is not to be construed as an error, however, since Malachi is in all probability referring to a spiritual Elijah. Here, as in many other places, it is more proper to speak of "difficulties" rather than "errors" in Scripture.

[51]William Gouge, *The Whole-armour of God* (1616), p. 308. Quoted in Gerald R. Cragg, *Freedom and Authority* (Philadelphia, 1975), p. 142.

word of God, without error in all that it affirms, and the only infallible rule of faith and practice."[52] We can heartily assent to this statement but with the proviso that the infallible truth of Scripture is not something self-evident. The doctrine or message of Scripture, which alone is infallible and inerrant, is hidden in the historical and cultural witness of the biblical writers. They did not err in what they proclaimed, but this does not mean that they were faultless in their recording of historical data or in their world view, which is now outdated. The Scriptures are entirely trustworthy in what they purport to give us, but this trustworthiness is a property not simply of the letter of the Bible but of the Spirit, the primary author of the Scripture. Apart from the work of the Spirit, the inherent, transcendent truth of the Scripture cannot be perceived. This is why our ultimate criterion is not the Scripture in and of itself but the Word and the Spirit, the Scripture illumined by the Spirit.

The Reformers were very emphatic that Scripture does not err, but we must ask in what sense. Luther declared, "But everyone, indeed, knows that at times they [the fathers] have erred, as men will; therefore, I am ready to trust them only when they give me evidence for their opinions from Scripture, which has never erred."[53] At the same time he can make a statement like this: "When one often reads [in the Bible] that great numbers of people were slain — for example, eighty thousand — I believe that hardly one thousand were actually killed. What is meant is the whole people."[54] He said of the Book of Job that though he tended to regard it as real history, he did not believe that everything happened just as reported and that some ingenious, pious and learned man added to the story characters and circumstances.[55] As is well-known, he was exceedingly critical of the emphasis on works in the Epistle of James, though he was not willing to bar this book from the canon.[56] The various authors of both Testaments, he said, built not solely with "gold, silver, and precious stones" but also with "wood, hay, and stubble."[57]

[52]See John R. W. Stott, *The Lausanne Covenant: An Exposition and Commentary* (Minneapolis, 1975), p. 10.

[53]*Luther's Works*, Vol. 32, p. 11.

[54]*Luther's Works*, Vol. 54, ed. and trans. Theodore G. Tappert (Philadelphia, 1967), p. 452.

[55]Ibid., pp. 79, 80.

[56]He also cast doubt upon the value of Esther and Revelation.

[57]In Willem Jan Kooiman, *Luther and the Bible*, trans. John Schmidt (Philadelphia, 1961), p. 227. For Kooiman's discussion of Luther's view of the inspiration and inerrancy of Scripture, see pp. 225–239. Also cf. J. K. S. Reid, *The Authority of Scripture*, pp. 56–72.

Moreover, he freely acknowledged that there was failure as well as success in prophetic prediction. There is little doubt that Luther's ultimate authority was the Word enlightened by the Spirit and not simply the *graphē* or writing of Scripture: "I care not if thou bring a thousand places of the Scripture for the righteousness of works against the righteousness of faith, and cry out never so much that the Scripture is against me. I have the Author and Lord of the Scripture with me, and on whose side I will rather stand than believe thee."[58] He steadfastly declared, "When our opponents interpret the scriptures against Christ, we are prepared to hold fast to Christ against scripture."[59]

Calvin, too, upheld biblical infallibility and inerrancy without falling into the delusion that this means that everything that the Bible says must be taken at face value. He felt remarkably free to exercise critical judgment when dealing with textual problems. He tells us, for example, that Jeremiah's name somehow crept into Matthew 27:9 "by mistake," and no reference is made to the autographs as a way out of this difficulty. Again, he was prone to doubt the Petrine authorship of II Peter despite its claim to be written by the apostle Peter; at the same time he firmly held to the inspiration and canonicity of this epistle. While referring to the Bible as "the certain and unerring rule," he clearly meant by this the rule for faith. He contended that the biblical writers when referring to matters of science might well be speaking "in mere accommodation to mistaken, though generally received opinion."[60] He warned that we must not expect to learn natural science (specifically astronomy) from Genesis 1, which is composed in popular phenomenal language. Calvin was committed to a high view of the Scriptures, even regarding them as the oracles of God, but this did not prevent him from examining the text critically.

Many latter-day evangelical Christians have felt the need to extend the meaning of inerrancy to cover purely historical and scientific matters, even where the treatment of these in the Bible does not bear upon the message of faith.[61] It is no longer suffi-

---

[58] Martin Luther, *A Commentary on St. Paul's Epistle to the Galatians*, ed. Philip Watson (London, 1953), p. 260.

[59] Luther, *Werke*, W. A., 39/I, 47.

[60] John Calvin, *Commentary on the Book of Psalms*, Vol. II, 58:4, trans. James Anderson (Edinburgh, 1846), p. 372.

[61] We do not dispute the fact that notions of total or absolute inerrancy have appeared in the church from the first centuries onward, but these ideas were not given systematic formulation until the rise of evangelical orthodoxy and fundamentalism. See Jack Rogers, ed., *Biblical Authority* (Waco, Tex., 1977), pp. 15–46.

cient to declare that Scripture is the infallible standard for faith and practice: it is now regarded as *totally* inerrant.[62] A view of error is entertained that demands literal, exact, mathematical precision, something the Bible cannot provide. The extrabiblical criterion of scientific exactitude is imposed on the Scriptures, and certainty is thereby made to rest on objective, external evidence rather than on the internal witness of the Holy Spirit (as with the Reformers). Such persons mistakenly believe that this approach insures the canons of orthodoxy whereas in reality it is a suicidal position that rests the case for Christianity on the shifting sands of scientific and historical research. The discovery of one discrepancy in Scripture can then discredit the entire Christian witness. The defenders of total or absolute inerrancy are quick to assert that they uphold only the inerrancy of the autographs, which are nonexistent, thus allowing for the possibility of copying errors in Scripture.

This position has been increasingly questioned in recent years in the light of the advances in textual and historical criticism as well as the new understanding of revelation.[63] In addition, the

---

[62]Recent works that tend to give support to the doctrine of total inerrancy are John Warwick Montgomery, ed., *God's Inerrant Word* (Minneapolis, 1974), and Harold Lindsell, *The Battle for the Bible* (Grand Rapids, 1976). One reviewer has these critical comments on the first book: "The authors . . . are right about the Bible being a perfect book but are wrong in the way they define perfection. They demand that we must have a Bible that is perfectly accurate in all matters of religion, morals, history, geography, arithmetic, astronomy, biology. They are defining *perfect* the way a mathematician or scientist would define it; they are not defining *perfect* the way the cross of Jesus Christ defines it." Robert H. Smith in *Lutheran Forum* (May 1975), p. 38. In our opinion these remarks do not apply to the essays by Packer and Pinnock, but the book as a whole creates this overall impression.

Harold Lindsell's book is an informative historical survey on how denial of biblical infallibility and inerrancy finally leads to apostasy (though not all of his examples stand up under scrutiny). In our estimation Lindsell would have strengthened his case for the truthfulness of the biblical witness had he distinguished between the inerrancy of Scripture in its teaching authority and in its historical preciseness in the reporting of events. Lindsell does show that the Bible is amazingly accurate and that many of its alleged historical errors have no basis in actuality. Yet one should keep in mind that amazing accuracy, even in the areas of history and science, is not the same as perfect accuracy. The inerrancy of Scripture must not be made to rest upon consistency in detail or scientific exactness — norms which are derived from scientific empiricism; instead it should be based upon the faithfulness of God to communicate his word to his appointed spokesmen and to preserve their testimony as the vehicle for his continual revelation to his children.

[63]See Dewey M. Beegle, *Scripture, Tradition and Infallibility* (Grand Rapids, 1973); Stephen T. Davis, *The Debate About the Bible* (Philadelphia, 1977); and Richard J. Coleman, "Reconsidering 'Limited Inerrancy,' " *Journal of the Evan-*

rise of pseudo-Christian cults that champion biblical inerrancy has been a source of embarrassment to those who contend that this doctrine is the foundation stone and practical guarantee of orthodoxy.[64] Because of the ambiguity related to the word "inerrancy," Clark Pinnock has proposed that "we ought to suspend it from the list of preferred terminology for stating the evangelical doctrine of Scripture, and let it appear only in the midst of the working out of details."[65]

We are not willing to abandon the doctrine of inerrancy, but we must take the Scripture's own understanding of this concept instead of imposing on Scripture a view of inerrancy drawn from modern empirical philosophy and science. Berkouwer perceptively reminds us that inerrancy in the biblical sense means unswerving fidelity to the truth, a trustworthy and enduring witness to the truth of divine revelation.[66] It connotes not impeccability, but indeceivability, which means being free from lying and fraud. He warns us that we must not identify the precision of journalistic reporting with the trustworthiness of the Gospel records. The man of faith must not be surprised by what Abraham Kuyper has termed "innocent inaccuracies" in Scripture.[67] The Scrip-

---

gelical Theological Society 17:4 (Fall 1974), 207–214. Coleman says: "To impose upon all Christians the deduction that plenary inspiration automatically guarantees total inerrancy is unwarranted. The gift of inspiration was granted not to insure the infallibility of every word and thought, though it did accomplish this in particular instances, but to secure a written Word that would forever be the singular instrument by which man learns and is confronted by God's will" (p. 213).

[64]Cults or sectarian movements that hold to biblical inerrancy are the Jehovah's Witnesses, the Christadelphians, the Mormons, and the Unitarian (Oneness) Pentecostals. Seventh-Day Adventism, which has a sectarian as well as an evangelical bent, also contends for biblical inerrancy. The Christadelphians in England occasionally hold public forums in defense of biblical inerrancy.

[65]Pinnock sees several disadvantages in the use of the term "inerrancy": "First, inerrancy does not describe the Bible we actually use. It is so strict a term that it can refer only to the lost autographs. Second, because it points to a text we do not have, it fails to assert forcibly the authority of the text we do have. Third, by its very nature, inerrancy directs attention to small difficulties in the text rather than to the infallible truth of its intended proclamation. Finally, it has become the slogan of a given party and thus serves to exacerbate conflict and ill-feeling." Pinnock prefers the recent statement of the International Fellowship of Evangelical Students: "Scripture is entirely trustworthy in the sense that its message conveys the true knowledge of God and his works, especially the way of salvation." See Clark Pinnock, "Inspiration and Authority: A Truce Proposal" in *The Other Side* (May–June 1976, pp. 61–65), p. 65. Also see Clark Pinnock, "Three Views of the Bible in Contemporary Theology" in Jack Rogers, ed., *Biblical Authority*, pp. 47–73.

[66]Berkouwer, *Holy Scripture*, pp. 240ff.

[67]Ibid., p. 245.

tures do not lie in their witness to the heavenly truth which God revealed to the prophets and apostles, not only the truth of salvation but also the truth of creation; yet this does not mean that everything reported in the Scriptures is factually accurate in the modern historical sense.[68] Nor does such a judgment detract in the slightest from the full inspiration of the Scriptures. As we have seen, it is possible and necessary to affirm that the Spirit accommodated the truth of the Gospel to the mind-set and language of the writers. They were both children of their times and prophets to their times, since they were witnesses and bearers of a transcendent truth. As Paul averred, "we have this treasure in earthen vessels, to show that the transcendent power belongs to God and not to us" (II Cor. 4:7).

We should also bear in mind that not only the historical and cultural perspective of the biblical writers was limited but also their theological and ethical ideas. It is only when their testimony is related to and refined by the self-revelation of Jesus Christ that it has the force of infallible authority. The Law of God is both fulfilled in and transcended by the Gospel, and this means that it is properly understood only in the light of the Gospel. Any text when taken out of its proper context and when divorced from the culminating revelation in the Bible becomes susceptible to error. In the light of its inspired meaning, however — the meaning which the Spirit gives it in its relationship to the incarnation and self-revelation of Jesus Christ — it is inerrant and infallible.

Both sides in the fundamentalist-modernist controversy were mistaken. The fundamentalists rigorously maintained that Scripture contains no discrepancy or flaw as modern science would understand this. The modernists, on the other hand, appealed to eternal religious and moral insights that are contained in Scripture but that are available to people of every age and culture. The truthfulness and reliability of Scripture can only be properly measured in the light of its own criterion, the Gospel of the cross, embodied in Jesus Christ, and attested to in both the Old and New Testaments.

We are not persuaded that the idea of infallibility or inerrancy

[68]Francis Schaeffer, despite his adherence to biblical inerrancy in the narrow sense, recognizes that the genealogies in Scripture do not have perfect historical accuracy. "The Bible," he says, "does not invite us to use the genealogies in Scripture as a chronology." In his *No Final Conflict* (Downers Grove, Ill., 1975), p. 40.

should be replaced by indefectibility, as Hans Küng urges.[69] *Indefectibility* means abiding or remaining in the truth despite errors even in doctrinal matters. This seems to call into question the absolute normativeness of Scripture in the church's understanding of the truth of revelation. With the Reformation we wish to maintain that the heavenly doctrine of Scripture is infallible but that this doctrine can only be discerned by the eyes of faith. In the last analysis it is the consensus of faith and not historical science that can and must decide on the inerrancy and credibility of Scripture. We cannot affirm with some of our evangelical brethren that an unbiased investigation will disclose that the Bible does not err. Only an investigation made by faith and to faith will disclose that the Scriptures are indeed the infallible and inerrant Word of God. While faith alone can grasp the significance of Scripture, this very faith is dependent on Scripture for its reality and sustenance.

The Bible contains a fallible element in the sense that it reflects the cultural limitations of the writers. But it is not mistaken in what it purports to teach, namely, God's will and purpose for the world.[70] There are no errors or contradictions in its substance and heart. It bears the imprint of human frailty, but it also carries the truth and power of divine infallibility. It is entirely trustworthy in every area of which it claims to be trustworthy. We vigorously dissent from the position of Rosemary Ruether that

[69]Küng, it should be noted, believes that *indefectibility* stands in basic continuity with the original meaning of *infallibility (infallibilitas)*, which is dependability or trustworthiness rather than "immaculateness" or "faultlessness" *(Fehlerlosigkeit)*. Küng's remarks relate primarily to ecclesiastical authority, but they also have bearing upon his understanding of Scriptural authority. The problem with Küng is that he creates the impression that the infallible truth of the Gospel can be conveyed through erroneous propositions, whereas we hold that the biblical propositions come to have an infallible character when they are illumined by the Spirit and thereby seen in their rightful context. Because the whole course of the origin, collecting, and transmission of the word is under the guidance and disposition of the Spirit, the biblical writings participate in the infallibility of the One whom they attest. While human propositions in themselves are always ambiguous, through the action of the Spirit they can genuinely reflect and communicate infallible truth. Küng maintains that the Scriptures do not possess any inherent propositional inerrancy, since only God is unconditionally and a priori free from error. While we are in basic agreement with him, this must not be taken to mean that the truth in the Bible is purely external to its composition and not also internal. The truth inheres not in the biblical proposition in and of itself but in the proposition in its relationship to Jesus Christ. See Hans Küng, *Infallible? An Inquiry,* trans. Edward Quinn (Garden City, N.Y., 1971), pp. 139ff., 181ff.

[70]We maintain that the authentic teaching of the Bible concerning man and the cosmos is as binding as its teaching on salvation and morals.

Scripture is basically "an unreliable witness."[71] Nor can we go along with Hanson who seeks to substitute the uniqueness and sufficiency of Scripture for its inspiration and infallibility.[72] The Scriptures are infallible because their primary author is God himself, and their primary content is Jesus Christ and his salvation (cf. John 5:46, 47; II Tim. 3:15). Yet we have the infallible, perfect Word of the living God enclosed and veiled in the time-bound, imperfect words of sinful men. As Abraham Kuyper averred, "The 'shadows' remain humanly imperfect, far beneath their ideal content. The 'spoken words,' however much aglow with the Holy Ghost, remain bound to the limitations of our language, disturbed as it is by anomalies."[73] The divine content, of course, cannot be separated from its human form and is available to us only in its human form. It is only when people of faith are given spiritual discernment that they can perceive the priceless treasure of God's holy Word in the earthen vessel of the human word.

This must not be taken to mean (as in liberal theology) that the Scriptures are a mixture of truth and error and that it is human reason that therefore decides what can be believed. Because of the superintendence of the Holy Spirit we have in the Bible an accurate portrayal of the will and purpose of God. Yet we reverently acknowledge that the biblical writings are not uniform in their witness to Christ and that the kernel of the Gospel is always to a certain degree hidden in the husk of culturally conditioned concepts and imagery.[74] Only reflection done in faith can grasp what is of abiding significance and what is marginal and peripheral.

It is inadmissible to treat the Bible as though it were a source book of revealed truths that can be drawn out of Scripture by deductive or inductive logic. The truth of the Bible can only be known as the Spirit makes it known in the event of revelation, yet even here there is no direct perception of truth but only a submission and reception which are adequate for salvation but

[71]Rosemary Ruether, "Sexuality and Transcendence" in *The Christian Century*, 92:8 (March 1975), 230.

[72]See R. P. C. Hanson, *The Attractiveness of God* (Richmond, 1973), p. 22.

[73]Abraham Kuyper, *Principles of Sacred Theology*, trans. J. Hendrik De Vries (Grand Rapids, 1954), p. 479.

[74]The husk, which here represents the cultural garment that encloses the kernel (the gospel), only becomes error when it is confused with the kernel. Though the husk is the servant form of the truth and not the truth itself, it is not superfluous but indeed indispensable for coming to know the truth.

not for comprehension. The truth in the Bible is enveloped in mystery and therefore can only be dimly perceived (I Cor. 13:9, 12). Indeed mystery and revelation often seem to go together (cf. Mark 13:11; I Cor. 2:7; Rom. 16:25). This does not mean that the Word of God is basically unknowable but that it cannot be known exhaustively and that it remains mysterious even to faithful reason (Rom. 11:33). Mystery does not connote obfuscation but an illumination that eludes rational assimilation. "Though transcending logic in the sense of going beyond it," Macquarrie observes, "mystery is neither absurd nor opaque. It has its own translucency."[75] God is truly revealed even as he comes to us in a form that signifies his veiling (Barth). With Pascal we can say that there is in the self-revelation of God as we find it in Scripture "sufficient clearness to enlighten the elect, and sufficient obscurity to humble them."[76]

While it is important to recognize the element of mystery in revelation, we must stay clear of the opposite error of denying the element of rationality. This is the temptation in mysticism and existentialism. What is revealed is not simply a spiritual presence but a rational message. Revelation is both a *dandum* (event) and a *datum* (objectively given truth), and the two cannot be separated. Yet this truth, because it can only be apprehended in part and because it disrupts and challenges the natural inclination of reason, can never be assimilated into a rational or logical system. The central tenet of Christianity—God becoming man in Jesus Christ—will always remain (at least in this life) a paradox to human reason and indeed can only be grasped by the inwardness of faith (Kierkegaard). At the same time faith also seeks understanding, as Augustine and Anselm forcefully remind us; and there can be at least a certain measure of understanding because the object of faith is not a mystical void or infinite abyss wholly beyond the rational, but the historical embodiment of true rationality, the very wisdom of God (I Cor. 1:24).[77]

---

[75]John Macquarrie, *Thinking About God* (New York, 1975), p. 42.

[76]*Pascal's Pensées and Provincial Letters*, trans. W. F. Trotter and Thomas M'Crie (New York, 1941), p. 189.

[77]Neither God nor Christ is exclusively or exhaustively rational, however, and it is well to pay heed to the reminder of Rudolf Otto in his *The Idea of the Holy* that God also has a nonrational side—dynamic will and energy, which Otto calls "the numinous." God's nonrational energy and majesty are integrally related to his reason, but they are not wholly subordinate or ancillary to his reason. God wills the Good not simply because he thinks the Good but because he is the Good. Yet he is more than the Good: he is the "Holy" which includes as well as transcends the Good as an ethical category.

THE HERMENEUTICAL TASK

This brings us to the hermeneutical task, the problem of interpretation. If the infallibility of the Bible were self-evident, if the divine truth of Scripture were directly accessible, then the hermeneutical task would be quite easy, but for better or worse it is much more complicated.

We must first recognize that the Bible is not principally a source book of data on Israel's history (as Wellhausen alleges) but a witness to divine revelation, a witness that points beyond itself to a supernatural reality. This means that in order for us to come to a true understanding of the basic content of the Bible, our inward eyes must be opened to the divine message to which the texts attest. But this is no longer a matter of historical analysis and research but of spiritual discernment. The divine truth of the Bible can only be known by a miracle of divine grace.

Nonetheless, the believer who truly seeks for the spiritual meaning of the biblical texts can prepare himself for the divine-human encounter which comes to one through wrestling with the text. He can amass historical knowledge through a scientific examination of the text, knowledge which can help him to appreciate the context in which the revelation was given, though the encounter with this revelation is not necessarily contingent on such knowledge.

We see the hermeneutical task in a series of stages. First, one must come to the Bible with an open heart and a searching mind. This presupposes that the seeker is a believer, one who has already been grasped by the spiritual reality to which the Bible attests. We agree with Barth that one must approach sacred Scripture without any overt presuppositions or at least with a critical attitude towards one's presuppositions. We affirm this against Tillich who has declared that one must "read the Bible with eyes opened by existentialist analysis."[78] We also oppose Bultmann who contends that one must come to the Bible with a preunderstanding concerning the meaning of human existence. Going on to the second stage one must now examine the text critically, and this means using the tools of literary and historical criticism. He must seek to ascertain what the writer actually intended. He must try to discern the cultural matrix in which the text was written *(Sitz im Leben)*.

Yet one must not be content with historical-grammatical exegesis, but must proceed to theological exegesis, which means

[78]Quoted in Hans Zahrnt, *The Question of God* (New York, 1970), p. 308.

seeing the text in the light of its theological context, relating the text to the central message of Holy Scripture. He must now subject his own preconceptions to the scrutiny of Scripture itself. He must listen to the voice of the living Christ within Scripture. Historical criticism must give way to spiritual discernment, which must ultimately be given to the critic by the divine author of Scripture (cf. Luke 24:45). The text is no longer the interpreted object but now the dynamic interpreter (Bengel).

Finally, the interpreter must relate the text, now understood in the light of Scripture itself, to the cultural situation of his time. He must translate the theological meaning of the text into the language and thought forms of modern man so that his hearers are presented with a coherent and intelligible message.

Yet though the theological exegete can make the message of faith intelligible, only the Holy Spirit can make it credible and knowable. The illumination of the Spirit is necessary not only for the interpreter but also for the hearer if a real translation of meaning is to take place.

Historical criticism is not to be disregarded, but it has a secondary or ancillary role. It can enable us to understand the cultural and historical background of the text, but it cannot uncover the spiritual significance of the text, the meaning that was in the mind of the Holy Spirit and that was at least in part grasped by the biblical authors. Karl Barth has these pertinent words on this subject:

> Historical criticism has led to a better understanding of the Scriptures than was possible in the past, for those situations which show the historical and secular aspects of the Bible have also something to teach us. . . . However, in course of time, historical criticism has assumed exaggerated importance, so that there is a tendency to identify the real meaning of Scripture with its historical significance.[79]

There has been much resistance to historical criticism in conservative evangelical circles. According to E. J. Young: "A man may practice the principles of criticism or he may be a believer in evangelical Christianity. One thing, however, is clear: if he is consistent, he cannot possibly espouse both."[80] George Eldon Ladd, on the other hand, has shown that higher criticism, including form criticism, can be helpful in the exegesis and expo-

---

[79]Barth, *The Preaching of the Gospel*, p. 61.
[80]E. J. Young, *Thy Word is Truth* (Grand Rapids, 1957), p. 219. Cf. Gerhard Maier, *The End of the Historical-Critical Method*, trans. Edwin Leverenz and Rudolph Nordern (St. Louis, 1977).

sition of the biblical text.[81] What has made many evangelicals understandably suspicious of historical criticism is that it has too often been associated with a naturalistic philosophy or world view that denies a priori the very possibility of supernatural intervention into human history. Brevard Childs has warned against using the principles of criticism with liberal presuppositions.[82]

It is necessary to understand that historical criticism in the sense of historical-literary investigation can only take us so far, and then we must go on to what Forsyth calls "the highest criticism," seeing every text in the light of the Gospel, the theological center of the Bible. We must move from the analytic criticism of the scientific historian to the synthetic criticism of the theologian if the full intent of the text is to be comprehended. For a true understanding we must bring to the text "the mind of Christ" (I Cor. 2:16).

When the Reformers contended that Scripture interprets itself, they meant that the inner meaning of the text must be revealed to the interpreter of Scripture, who must then formulate it as best he can. Karl Barth has put it this way:

> The door of the Bible texts can be opened only from within. It is another thing whether we wait at this door or leave it for other doors, whether we want to enter and knock or sit idly facing it. The existence of the biblical texts summons us to persistence in waiting and knocking.[83]

Luther, too, saw that human reason cannot penetrate the spiritual significance of the biblical text: "Those who presume to grasp Holy Scripture and the Law of God with their own intellect and to understand them by their own effort are exceedingly in error."[84] Instead of bringing our own understanding to the reading of Scripture, he warned, we "ought to come bringing nothing, but seeking to carry away thoughts from the Scriptures."[85]

To be sure, the interpreter of Scripture must do all within his power to ascertain the spiritual and theological significance of the text in question, but in the process he must be open to the guidance and illumination of the Spirit. He should have not only a critical but also a prayerful attitude born of the recognition that the matter of the text is the property only of Jesus Christ.

---

[81]See George Eldon Ladd, *The New Testament and Criticism*, 2d printing (Grand Rapids, 1971).

[82]See Brevard Childs, *Biblical Theology in Crisis* (Philadelphia, 1970), pp. 94, 102.

[83]Barth, *Church Dogmatics* I/2, 533.

[84]*Luther's Works*, Vol. 29, p. 186.

[85]Luther, *A Commentary on St. Paul's Epistle to the Galatians*, p. 465.

Barth observes: "The Holy Scriptures will interpret themselves in spite of all our human limitations. . . . The Bible unfolds to us as we are met, guided, drawn on, and made to grow by the grace of God."[86]

We must take care, of course, not to read our own thoughts and imagination into the text in question. Our aim should be to discover as best we can what was in the mind of the writer, that is to say, the original or literal sense. If the writer intended to convey a figurative meaning, then we must by no means interpret the text literalistically. At the same time we wish to discover what was in the mind of the Holy Spirit, and not simply the mind of the writer, and what the Holy Spirit would have us hear today in and through this text. This is not pneumatic exegesis, which ignores or devalues the meaning of the written word, but theological exegesis which tries to relate the original meaning to the central message of Scripture. In theological exegesis the original meaning is both fulfilled and transcended in that the biblical writer only partially grasped what the Spirit was teaching him to see (I Pet. 1:10, 11). There is definitely a place for typological exegesis so long as events and insights in the Old Testament are related to the self-revelation of Jesus Christ and not to events that are only on the margin of biblical history or even outside its scope. What the Reformers objected to in the exegetical methods of the fathers and medieval scholastics was that the literal or original sense was too often bypassed in favor of a purely subjective or mystical interpretation. We cannot remain with the natural or literal sense, but this must be our point of departure, the basis on which we make our synthetic judgments.

This is not to imply that one must consciously go through these various stages in hermeneutics before one can hear God's Word in the Bible. The simplest believer who comes to the Bible emptied of his own understanding and truly seeking the will of God for his life will discover what the Bible is really saying more quickly than an exegete trained in the latest biblical scholarship who nevertheless tenaciously clings to his own preconceptions. There is no doubt that the tools of historical criticism and research can be most helpful in understanding the linguistic history and cultural and religious background of any given text. They can enable one to see the text in a broader perspective. Yet it is not simply a knowledge of the cultural and historical setting of the text that is the goal of true Bible study; our preeminent concern is to uncover the intention of the text, but this is only pos-

---

[86]Karl Barth, *The Word of God and the Word of Man*, trans. Douglas Horton (New York, 1957), p. 34.

sible when one has moved beyond criticism to a state of receptivity in which one is open to the guidance and direction of the Holy Spirit.

MISCONCEPTIONS IN
MODERN EVANGELICALISM

With the rise of scholastic orthodoxy in the two centuries following the Reformation, the Bible became increasingly identified with divine revelation itself, and inspiration came to be interpreted in terms of mechanical dictation. M. Flacius in the sixteenth century resisted this trend and sought to maintain a dynamic view of both revelation and inspiration.[87] It was asserted by many Protestant scholastics that the Scriptures not only do not err but cannot err. "No error, even in unimportant matters," said Calovius, "no defect of memory, not to say untruth, can have any place in all the Holy Scriptures."[88] Barth makes this trenchant observation:

> The Bible was now grounded upon itself apart from the mystery of Christ and the Holy Ghost. It became a "paper Pope," and unlike the living Pope in Rome it was wholly given up into the hands of its interpreters. It was no longer a free and spiritual force, but an instrument of human power.[89]

In modern fundamentalism, which signifies a synthesis of the old orthodoxy and evangelical pietism, the humanity of the Bible is virtually denied or ignored and the truth of the Bible is held to be directly accessible to human reason. Criswell reflects this docetic view of Scripture: "For this Volume is the writing of the Living God. Each sentence was dictated by God's Holy Spirit. . . . Everywhere in the Bible we find God speaking. It is God's voice, not man's."[90] Gordon Clark speaks of the Bible as a verbal revelation, thereby unwittingly calling into question the dual authorship of Scripture. Both Clark and John Warwick Montgomery refer to the univocal language of Scripture concerning God, which contravenes the position of most theological luminaries of the past who held that human language concerning God is either

[87]J. K. S. Reid, *The Authority of Scripture*, pp. 89ff.

[88]Heinrich Schmid, ed., *The Doctrinal Theology of the Evangelical Lutheran Church*, p. 49.

[89]Barth, *Church Dogmatics* I/2, 525.

[90]W. A. Criswell, *Why I Preach That the Bible is Literally True* (Nashville, 1969), p. 68.

metaphorical or at the most analogical.[91] This is to say, such language points beyond itself to a supernatural reality that transcends the compass of man's cognitive faculties (I Cor. 2:7ff.; Eph. 3:19). We take issue with Clark in his assertion that man's statements concerning God are to be taken literally or that man's logic and knowledge are identical with God's.[92] Through the gift of faith there can be a partial correspondence between man's knowledge and God's but not an equation, since God remains hidden *(deus absconditus)* even in his revelation.

It is well to note that Benjamin Warfield, who from our standpoint can be faulted for underplaying the human element in the Bible, never made the mistake of denying this side of Scripture. He candidly recognized its dual authorship and acknowledged that "inspiration is not the most fundamental of Christian doctrines, nor even the first thing we prove about the Scriptures."[93] He was careful not to make all Christian doctrines rest upon the single doctrine of biblical inerrancy, but he had absolute confidence in the trustworthiness of the biblical writers "as teachers of doctrine."[94] Both Warfield and Hodge conceded that the biblical writers were at times "dependent for their information upon sources and methods in themselves fallible, their personal knowledge and judgment were in many matters hesitating and defective or even wrong."[95]

---

[91]For Clark's reservations on the use of analogy in theology see Ronald Nash, ed., *The Philosophy of Gordon Clark* (Philadelphia, 1968), pp. 77–79. According to Ronald Nash, Clark does not rule out analogical language altogether in reference to God but is insistent that every analogy must contain some univocal meaning; in a personal letter to this author dated Feb. 17, 1977. Note that Henry follows Clark in holding to univocal predication in our language about God. See Carl Henry's *God, Revelation and Authority,* Vol. II (Waco, Tex., 1976), p. 115. In our view the analogical knowledge of God derived from faith is real knowledge but nonetheless incomplete.

[92]Nash, pp. 57ff., 406, 407.

[93]Benjamin B. Warfield, "The Real Problem of Inspiration" in *The Living God: Readings in Christian Theology,* ed. Millard J. Erickson (Grand Rapids, 1973, pp. 277–291), p. 279.

[94]Ibid. On the significance of the article by A. A. Hodge and Warfield in which they extend the meaning of inerrancy to cover other matters as well, see Bernard Ramm's discussion in Jack Rogers, ed., *Biblical Authority,* pp. 109ff.

[95]Cited in Richard J. Coleman, "Biblical Inerrancy: Are We Going Anywhere?" *Theology Today* 31:4 (Jan. 1975, pp. 295–303), 299. This contrasts with the position of many of the church fathers, e.g., Irenaeus, who believed that the writers of Scripture "were filled with perfect knowledge on every subject." See Irenaeus, *Heresies,* III, 1. Cf. III, 22. For a cogent exposition of the views of the church fathers on this matter see George Duncan Barry, *The Inspiration and Authority of Holy Scripture, A Study in the Literature of the First Five Centuries* (New York, 1919).

Our main difference from Warfield is that while he affirms the Bible as a divine product through the instrumentality of men, he is reluctant and often unwilling to affirm the other side of the paradox — that the Bible is at the same time an incontestably human witness to divine truth, a witness that ipso facto bears the marks of historical conditioning. While we grant that in one sense the Bible is the revelation of God to man, this revelation is in the form of human witness and is, therefore, to a degree hidden from sight and understanding. Warfield refers to the "inscripturation" of the divine Word in Scripture, and we too can speak in this fashion, though this must not be taken to mean that the words of the Bible are now divine words but rather that the eternal divine Word is given in and through these very human words, which to be sure have been elected or inspired by the Spirit of God.[96]

The bane of much of modern evangelicalism is rationalism which presupposes that the Word of God is directly available to human reason. It is fashionable to refer to the biblical revelation as propositional, and in one sense this is true in that the divine revelation is communicated through verbal concepts and models. It signifies that revelation has a noetic as well as a personal dimension, that it is conceptual as well as experiential.[97] Revelation includes both the events of divine self-disclosure in biblical history and their prophetic and apostolic interpretation. At the same time we must not infer that the propositional statements in the Bible are themselves revealed, since this makes the Bible the same kind of book as the Koran which purports to be exclusively divine. It also seems to imply a transubstantiation of the human

[96]Warfield can speak of the biblical words as the "immediate words of God." Warfield, *The Inspiration and Authority of the Bible,* p. 149.

[97]We can also assert that revelation is cognitive but only in a qualified sense. It is capable of being apprehended not by man's natural faculties as such but by the spiritual eyes of faith. Faith is knowledge as well as trust, but its object transcends the empirical and humanly rational: it concerns the "secret and hidden wisdom of God" (I Cor. 2:7; cf. Isa. 55:8: Dan. 2:22). This wisdom can enter into the humanly rational but nevertheless remains distinct from all general wisdom. Once illumined by the Spirit, human reason plays a formative role in faith's quest for understanding, but even then the central mysteries of the faith defy rational comprehension and can be expressed only in symbolic and paradoxical language. Our position here differs from that of Carl Henry who affirms with Pannenberg that revelation can be grasped by the "normal powers of human apprehension" requiring "no special work of the Spirit." Henry, *God, Revelation and Authority,* Vol. II, p. 309; cf. Vol. I, p. 229. We concur with Henry in his espousal of a supernatural world view and his contention that revelation includes ontological as well as personal truth.

word into the divine word.[98] The Bible is not directly the revelation of God but indirectly in that God's Word comes to us
through the mode of human instrumentality.[99]

Revelation is better spoken of as polydimensional rather than
propositional in the strict sense, in that it connotes the event of
God speaking as well as the truth of what is spoken: this truth,
moreover, takes various linguistic forms including the propositional.[100] Objective intelligible truth is revealed (though not exhaustively),[101] but the formulation in the Bible is one step removed
from this truth even while standing in continuity with it. The
truth of revelation can be apprehended through the medium of
the human language which attests it but only by the action of
the Spirit. Those who reduce the content of revelation to declar-
ative statements in the Bible overlook the elements of mystery,
transcendence, and dynamism in revelation.

Karl Barth warns against this rationalistic approach to
Scripture:

> The irremediable danger of consulting Holy Scripture apart
> from the centre, and in such a way that the question of Jesus
> Christ ceases to be the controlling and comprehensive question
> and simply becomes one amongst others, consists primarily in the
> fact that . . . Scripture is thought of and used as though the mes-
> sage of revelation . . . could be extracted from it in the same way
> as the message of other truth or reality can be extracted from
> other sources of knowledge. . . .[102]

[98]Ray S. Anderson skirts the opposite danger when he speaks of a kenosis of
the Word becoming Scripture analogous to the kenosis of the Word becoming
man in Jesus Christ. If the kenotic theory is carried too far, this means that the
divine Word is transmuted into the human word of Scripture and is thereby
emptied of its divine content. In our view the human words of Scripture are taken
up into or united with the divine Word, but the divine Word does not literally
change into the human word. The two natures of the Bible are inseparable but
must not be confused. See Ray S. Anderson, *Historical Transcendence and the Reality
of God* (Grand Rapids, 1975), pp. 212ff.

[99]God speaks to us indirectly when we hear the good news from his appointed
spokesmen, but he also speaks directly when he conjoins his Word with their
word by his Spirit. Scripture is not immediate revelation, but revelation is mediated through Scripture as the Holy Spirit acts upon it.

[100]Cf. Bernard Ramm, *Special Revelation and the Word of God* (Grand Rapids,
1961), pp. 154ff. Ramm contends that the term *propositional revelation*, while having
some validity, is basically an "unhappy one" because "it fails to do justice to the
literary, historical, and poetic elements of special revelation" (p. 155).

[101]Revelation is primarily personal and only secondarily conceptual, since its
principal object is Jesus Christ himself. Nonetheless, Christ not only makes himself known and sheds his love abroad in our hearts; he also tells us who he is and
why he has come.

[102]Barth, *Church Dogmatics* IV/1, 368.

Another earmark of Christian rationalism is the attempt to prove the credibility of Scripture by arguments and evidences. The fascination of many evangelicals with the current effort to unearth Noah's Ark is a reflection of a rationalistic temper. Calvin was amazingly forthright in his condemnation of rationalistic apologetics: "Scripture, carrying its own evidence along with it, deigns not to submit to proofs and arguments, but owes the full conviction with which we ought to receive it to the testimony of the Spirit."[103] And again: "Therefore Scripture will ultimately suffice for a saving knowledge of God only when its certainty is founded upon the inward persuasion of the Holy Spirit. . . . Those who wish to prove to unbelievers that Scripture is the Word of God are acting foolishly, for only by faith can this be known."[104]

Helmut Thielicke claims that an apologetics which seeks "to show a historical symmetry between prophecy and fulfillment, or to use historical miracles as a ground of faith, or to argue . . . that the resurrection of Christ is the best-attested event in all antiquity" actually destroys faith by giving it a foundation in something that is generally valid. It takes away the wonder of the salvation event and reduces faith to a purely "practical obedience in which I actively confess demonstrable supernatural facts."[105] It creates the illusion that "God's action is restricted to purely historical facts when in reality it also embraces illumination by the Holy Spirit, i.e., the granting of access to these facts, the opening of the eyes and ears, and the overcoming of hardness of heart."[106]

Like Barth, Thielicke warns against positing a direct identity between divine revelation and the scriptural writing. We must avoid the "confusion of the Word of God with an aggregate of letters and sounds. Naturally the Word does take the form of letters and sounds. But these are only a medium. They are only a mode of manifestation which helps it to be perceived. Its true

---

[103]John Calvin, *Institutes of the Christian Religion*, trans. Henry Beveridge (Edinburgh, 1845), I, 7, 5.

[104]Calvin, *Institutes*, I, 8, 13. Cf. Voetius: "As there is no objective certainty about the authority of Scripture, save as infused and imbued by God the Author of Scripture, so we have no subjective certainty of it, no formal concept of the authority of Scripture, except from God's illuminating and convincing inwardly through the Holy Spirit." In Heinrich Heppe, ed., *Reformed Dogmatics*, trans. G. T. Thomson (London, 1950), p. 25.

[105]Helmut Thielicke, *The Evangelical Faith*, Vol. I, trans. and ed. Geoffrey W. Bromiley (Grand Rapids, 1974), pp. 269, 270.

[106]Ibid., p. 270.

essence lies in what it says, from whom it comes, and to whom it is directed."[107]

One must remember that the basis of faith is not the trustworthiness of the manuscripts (though this is to be gratefully acknowledged) but the saving act of God in Jesus Christ and the inward testimony of his Spirit. The historical events of the Bible, which are accessible to sense perception, are the occasion but not the foundation of faith. The disciples knew Jesus according to the flesh, but they did not perceive his Messianic identity until they were granted illumination by the Spirit (Matt. 16:17; Luke 24:31). With Calvin we contend that in order to attain the knowledge of God "the human mind must exceed and rise above itself."[108] The Bible is a means through which God unveils himself, but he unveils himself only to the eyes of faith, not to natural reason (cf. Ps. 119:18).

In fundamentalism and much of the older orthodoxy the Bible offers no surprises. Too often it is used to support a dogmatic system — whether this be Lutheranism, Calvinism, Arminianism, or some other ism — instead of being treated as a vehicle of the Holy Spirit who uproots our man-made systems and confounds the vanity of our reason. We must remember that the Word of God is not fettered (II Tim. 2:9). It leaps and runs and is not even bound to the means of grace — the Bible, the sermon, the sacraments — though we are so bound. We need to recover the biblical concepts of the freedom of the Word and the unpredictability of the Word. We should remember with the Puritan father John Robinson that "the Lord has more light and truth yet to break forth out of his holy Word."

In his noted work on the Lutheran Confessions Edmund Schlink maintains that authentic orthodoxy posits a higher criterion than Scripture, namely, the Gospel. "This intense concern with the Gospel," he declares, "suggests that the Gospel is the norm in Scripture and Scripture is the norm for the sake of the Gospel."[109] Yet we must also avoid the error present in some neo-orthodox circles of separating the Gospel from the Law and treating only the Gospel as the Word of God. While acknowledging the priority of the Gospel over the Law, we must avoid a simple Gospel reductionism and a love monism, both of which

[107]Ibid., p. 181. Thielicke's position is here in accord with such luminaries of Protestant Orthodoxy as Flacius, Voetius, and Gerhard.
[108]Calvin, *Institutes of the Christian Religion,* trans. John Allen, 7th ed. (Philadelphia, 1936), III, 2, 14.
[109]Edmund Schlink, *Theology of the Lutheran Confessions* (Philadelphia, 1961), p. 6.

disregard complementary truths and insights that are also testified to in Scripture.

Evangelical theology in its most authentic sense will indeed be a theology of the Word of God. We assert this against Rahner's call for reconceptualization and Bultmann's call for demythologization. As theologians we are bound to the concepts of Scripture as well as to its mythical imagery. Though we are constrained to put the message of faith in new forms and imagery, we must always return to what Barth terms "the language of Canaan" and the "language of Zion." Barth warns that it is "nonobligatory, uncommissioned, and perilous" to use words that are "at a distance from the vocabulary of Scripture."[110] Where the church "does not venture to confess in its own language, it usually does not confess at all."[111] Even Tillich, who sought to translate the language of the Bible into contemporary categories, confessed that no term or concept could take the place of the biblical term *sin,* which contains nuances of meaning that *alienation* and *estrangement,* for example, simply do not encompass.

At the same time evangelical theology will be a theology under the Word of God. Our theological systems as well as our confessions of faith must forever be reexamined and purified in the light of the Word of God. An authentic evangelical theology will be a theology forever in the process of reformation *(semper reformanda).* It will acknowledge that God is still free to remold and purify his church through his holy Word which, in its role as an instrument of the Spirit, remains in every age a thoroughly sound and relevant standard and guide.

[110]Barth, *Church Dogmatics* I/1, 396, 397.
[111]Karl Barth, *Dogmatics in Outline,* trans. G. T. Thomson (New York, 1954), p. 31.

9 THE TESTIMONY OF THE SPIRIT
G. C. BERKOUWER

There has always been great interest in our confession of the testimony of the Holy Spirit regarding belief in Scripture. This shows that belief in Scripture was not considered an irrational, isolated response, but rather a commitment that had a connection with the Holy Spirit and with a divine witness. On the other hand, it points out that this belief was not viewed as a rational insight — an intellectual acceptance of the trustworthiness of Scripture within an impersonal relationship to it — which in a true Christian faith was merely accompanied by a trust in a personal God. On the contrary, this kind of dualism was emphatically rejected. It was realized that faith in the sense of "faith *in*" was a personal relationship of trust in another person;[1] but the intent was never to see belief in Scripture as something impersonal or objective.

Remarkably, during the Reformation, theologians did not merely relate the witness of the Spirit to man's filial relationship to God, but they also related it to his belief in Scripture. This happened in a time when frequent isolated and fragmentary references to the Spirit were being made — a fact the Reformers (Luther as well as Calvin) always viewed as the danger of what has usually been called "spiritualism."[2] Despite running the risk of being associated with this movement, which in some ways minimized the written Word as something "external," the Reformers did not hesitate to mention the name of the Holy Spirit

---

[1] See Herman Bavinck, *Gereformeerde Dogmatiek*, Vol. 1, 4th ed. (Kampen, 1928-30), p. 539, on belief *in* Christ and "believing Scripture."

[2] We cannot justly speak of Luther's "spiritualism" (because of his extensive discussion of the essence and the work of the Spirit) as does K. G. Steck, *Luther und die Schwärmer* (Zurich, 1955), p. 12. To use this word to contradict R. Prenter, *Spiritus Creator* (ET, 1953), who speaks of Luther's "antispiritualism," is confusing the issue.

From G. C. Berkouwer, Holy Scripture, *trans. Jack B. Rogers (Studies in Dogmatics series), pp. 39-66. Copyright © 1975 by William B. Eerdmans Publishing Company.*

at the decisive juncture of faith and its certainty. Later theologians pointed out the problems inherent in this confession, accusing the Reformers of intending to point out the objectivity of the witness of Scripture as the witness of the Spirit and then still accepting a witness of the Spirit in the heart. Did not such a "doubling" of the witness indicate the Reformers' inability to solve the problem of certainty? Was not this "objectivity" (trustworthiness and self-authentication) unsatisfactory to them, so that they felt the need for a *testimonium internum?* On this basis, Strauss considered this confession "the Achilles' heel of the Protestant system."[3] Obviously his meaning is that for Protestantism the ultimate authority no longer resided in the "objective" revelation itself, but in the human heart, feeling, or experience, or at least in the subjectivity of an "internal" revelation.

It is, of course, very important to determine whether this pneumatological confession of the Reformers does indeed contain a possible unconscious opening that can admit the subjectivism of the doctrine that the inner light is the true light of revelation. These are the problems that arise repeatedly in the many discussions of the witness of the Holy Spirit. The Reformed churches have never issued a further declaration concerning the *testimonium Spiritus Sancti*, but theologians have asked whether this confession evidences an inner contradiction or rather a deep and responsible perspective.

The Reformation confession of the *testimonium Spiritus Sancti* must be considered against the background of the controversial situation at that time: Rome's very strong emphasis upon the authority of the church, in which the *testimonium ecclesiae* played an important part in the attainment of certainty. Were not the believers after all taken by the hand and safely guided by the church in their personal lives as well as in their contact with the gospel? A reflection upon this question is found in Article V of the Belgic Confession, which says that we accept without any doubt all that is written in the holy and canonical books, "not so much because the Church receives and approves them as such, but more especially because the Holy Ghost witnesses in our hearts that they are from God." There is something striking about the wording here. The contrast is not one of "not . . . but" (as might have been expected on the basis of the controversy with

[3]D. F. Strauss, *Die christliche Glaubenslehre in ihrer geschichtlichen Entwicklung und im Kampfe mit der modernen Wissenschaft*, Vol. I (Tübingen and Stuttgart, 1840-41), p. 136. Cf. O. Weber, *Foundations of Dogmatics*, Vol. I (ET Grand Rapids, 1981), p. 243; Bavinck, *GD*, I, 554, 569; K. Barth, *Church Dogmatics* (ET Edinburgh, 1956), I/2, 598.

Rome), but rather one of "not so much . . . but more especially."
No doubt the reason for this is that the composers of the confession did not wish to give the impression that the church and its
testimony in the life of faith and subjection to Holy Scripture are
entirely without significance. What the confession does say is that
the authority of the church can never be the ultimate and final
ground of belief in Scripture. This echoes Calvin, who calls the
belief that Scripture is important only to the extent conceded to
it by the suffrage of the church a pernicious error. Furthermore,
according to Calvin, to say that the amount of reverence due
Holy Scripture depends on the determination of the church is an
insult to the Holy Spirit (*Inst.*, I, vii, 1).

Yet Calvin does not wish to deny the importance of the church,
and in this connection he cites Augustine's often quoted statement: "I would not believe the gospel, except as moved by the
authority of the Catholic Church" (*Inst.*, I, vii, 3). Calvin's interpretation of this statement is that a person who does not yet have
faith can embrace the gospel only through the authority of the
church,[4] but not that faith in Scripture finds its ultimate explanation in the authority of the church. The real and ultimate
explanation is, according to Augustine, that our spirit is not enlightened by men but by the Spirit of God himself. For Calvin,
too, the authority of the church is the introduction "through
which we are prepared for belief in the gospel"; but we are fully
convinced only in a higher way — by the hidden witness of the
Spirit (*Inst.*, I, vii, 5).

Only God himself is a sufficient witness to himself. The Word
of God finds no acceptance until it is sealed by the inward witness
of the Spirit, and the heart finds its rest in Scripture only through
this inward teaching. Scripture is not subject to human argumentation and proof, and Scripture's own assuring power is higher
and stronger than all human judgment. No matter how large a
role the church may play in the genetic process[5] of ascertaining,
ultimately no one can accept Scripture *because* the church testifies
that it is God's Word. The moving of the church as *praedicatrix
evangelii*[6] is not the ultimate explanation of faith in Scripture.

---

[4] A. Kuyper, *Principles of Sacred Theology*, rpt. (Grand Rapids, 1954), p. 555,
where he discusses this statement of Augustine and speaks of "the link of the
Church." Moreover, according to Kuyper, the word "gospel" in this statement
(*evangelio non crederem*) has been incorrectly understood as the *Sacra Scriptura inspirata*.

[5] Obviously, this gentle aspect, this *coming* to certainty, cannot be separated
from the question regarding the foundation of faith, but the differentiation does
not therefore lose its significance.

[6] Kuyper, p. 555.

This conviction is also expressed in other Reformed confessions, which always speak of the convincing power of the Holy Spirit in connection with belief in Scripture.[7] The inevitable question of what is meant by the *testimonium Spiritus Sancti* arises at this point. Is it a separate, mystical, and supernatural witness of the Spirit, and therefore called a hidden operation? Is this witness the voice of God — the real revelation — in contrast to the revelation of Scripture, which in itself is insufficient? Were this so, it would be justifiable to speak of a separate pneumatic characteristic that assures us of the divine origin and quality of Holy Scripture and contains a confirmation of Scripture as a book. This pneumatic aspect could explain why one person accepts Scripture and another does not. If one were to take the words of Article V (*Belgic Confession*) — "the Spirit testifies in our hearts that they come from God" — out of context, he might indeed arrive at such a conclusion and interpret the confession to mean that there is a separate witness of the Spirit — in the sense of some form of spiritualism. But it has been constantly, and correctly, pointed out that in the context of the Reformation this simply could not have been the intention of Article V, since the confession of the *testimonium* is never contrasted with that of Holy Scripture or its authority and self-authentication. In any case, there is no formal confirmation or voice that whispers something to us about the origin or quality of Scripture. Preiss points out that only later did theologians begin to speak more and more formally and abstractly about the convincing *testimonium*, "as if there were such a thing as a formal authority of an abstract Word of God apart from its content." By speaking thus, the *testimonium* was reduced to an "abstract and artificial matter."[8]

Whenever the words "abstract" and "formal" appear frequently in the discussion, what is meant is that Scripture is received as writing, as a book of divine quality, while its content and message as such are thereby not taken into account from the outset. We are touching here on a very important point of the doctrine of

---

[7]Cf. The French Confession of Faith (1559), Art. IV (in P. Schaff, *The Creeds of Christendom*, Vol. III, 4th ed. [New York, 1919], p. 361); Scots Confession (1560), Art. XIX (Schaff, p. 464); Helvetic Confession (1562), which says that it is not *ex hominibus* (Schaff, p. 237); Westminster Confession (1647), which says, ". . . our full persuasion . . . is from the inward work of the Holy Spirit" (Schaff, p. 603); Waldensian Confession (1655), which says, ". . . not only from the testimony of the Church, but more especially . . ." and then lists the truth of the teaching contained in Scripture and "the operation of the Holy Spirit" (Schaff, pp. 759f.). The Waldensian also states that the Spirit makes us "receive with reverence the testimony which the Church on that point renders us" (p. 760).
[8]Th. Preiss, *Das innere Zeugnis des Heiligen Geistes* (Zurich, 1947), pp. 14–15.

Scripture, which also forms the background of many discussions. Bavinck's criticism that Calvin and other Reformed theologians "related the *testimonium Spiritus Sancti* much too one-sidedly to the authority of Scripture"[9] is itself a dogmatic-historical assertion; but, whether his criticism is historically correct or not, he is undoubtedly dealing with the same central problem. His own view concerning the *testimonium* becomes apparent here: "It seemed that this doctrine had no other context than the subjective assurance that Scripture was the Word of God." As a result, the *testimonium* became something separate: "It was isolated from the life of faith and seemed to imply an extraordinary revelation, about which Michaelis was honest enough to declare that he had never experienced it."[10]

After criticizing this "one-sidedness," Bavinck goes on to say that Scripture itself speaks quite differently, and that the testimony of the Spirit is not a dream or a vision or "a voice from heaven." What does Bavinck mean by his rather strong objection to isolating the *testimonium* from the life of faith?[11] Obviously, it is inevitable that such an isolation will determine the nature of the *testimonium*. Bavinck points out that the witness of the Spirit "gives no assurance regarding the objective truths of salvation apart from connection with the condition of the religious subject," because it first of all has a bearing on a person's sonship.[12] It is only thus that the Spirit brings us to a believing subjection to Holy Scripture, uniting us "in the same measure and power to it as to the person of Christ."[13] Seen in this way, the correlation between Scripture and faith loses all its foreboding formality. Thus, Bavinck obviously wished to answer Strauss's charge that the doctrine regarding the *testimonium* was Protestantism's great weakness, for to Bavinck it is the very cornerstone of the Christian confession, the crown and victory of the truth.[14]

Bavinck places the *testimonium* fully in the dynamic context of the entire life of faith. It is so intertwined with that life that, according to him, "our belief in Scripture decreases and increases together with our trust in Christ."[15] He adds that the *testimonium*

---

[9] *GD*, I, 563.

[10] Ibid., pp. 563ff. Michaelis' statement also appears on p. 554.

[11] R. Preus, *The Inspiration of Scripture* (Edinburgh, 1955), p. 115. Preus accuses the Lutherans of the same thing. They viewed the *testimonium* "almost exclusively in reference to the authority of Scripture." Cf. also "a one-sided emphasis on the witness of the Spirit in respect to Scripture."

[12] *GD*, I, 564.

[13] Ibid., p. 567.

[14] Ibid., pp. 554, 569–70. Bavinck mentions Strauss's criticism twice.

[15] Ibid., p. 569.

is not always equally strong, and hence it is no *a priori* confirmation that always remains the same because of its origin in the Holy Spirit. This also implies, concerning the nature of the testimony, that it does not supply direct certainty regarding the authenticity, canonicity, or even the inspiration of Holy Scripture; nor regarding the historical, chronological, and geographical data "as such"; nor regarding the facts of salvation as *nuda facta*;[16] nor, finally, regarding the closedness of the canon, as if it were possible to solve the problems regarding canonicity with an appeal to the witness of the Spirit.[17] Instead, it is inseparably connected with faith and salvation in Christ. In this way Bavinck tried to avoid any formalization and isolation of the doctrine, as well as every form of dualism between belief in Scripture and faith in Christ. The *testimonium* does not supply an *a priori* certainty regarding Scripture, which afterwards is supplemented with and through its message.

The problem of the doctrine of the *testimonium* is also especially illuminated by the way in which Kuyper has handled it. He proceeds from the assumption that the *testimonium* directly addresses itself to us personally, but that it is no magical event or supernatural message from God that says, "This Scripture is My Word."[18] According to him, such a notion is definitely "uninformed" and inevitably leads to a false mysticism that ultimately minimizes the authority of Scripture. Rather, the inseparable connection between belief in Scripture and certainty of faith must be emphasized. Referring to Article IX of the Belgic Confession ("All this we know as well from the testimonies of Holy Writ as from their operations, and chiefly by those we feel in ourselves"), Kuyper speaks of the "melody of redemption." Belief in the divine nature of Holy Scripture "rests upon the experience of spiritual life." Hence the *testimonium* usually works "gradually and unobserved."[19] The Spirit's witness begins by binding us to the center of Scripture, namely, Jesus Christ. The extent of this authority is of no significance at first. Only by degrees does Scripture begin to fascinate us by its organic composition in a gradual assimilation process regarding its content and its message. Hence, Kuyper rejects what Heim later called an *a priori*, formal "assurance," for with faith in Scripture the only thing that counts is faith in the promise. Experiencing the *divinitas* of Scripture takes place

---

[16]Ibid., pp. 565–69.
[17]Regarding the witness and canonicity, see H. N. Ridderbos, *The Authority of the New Testament Scriptures* (Grand Rapids, 1963), pp. 10ff., 39–40.
[18]Kuyper, p. 557.
[19]Ibid., pp. 558–59.

through experiencing God's *benevolentia*. In spite of the many complicating factors in Kuyper's theology, there are clear similarities between his and Bavinck's, because both reject isolation of the *testimonium*. Kuyper insists that the connection between the *testimonium Spiritus Sancti* and faith in Christ[20] is so close that the *testimonium* is a part of every conversion.[21] Hence his strong rejection of a "magical" *testimonium* separate from the Christian life, which can easily lead to religious fanaticism.[22] When one is in contact with Holy Scripture, the testimony of the Spirit shows him as the sinner and shows the marvelous way of deliverance. It is in this way that the Spirit witnesses concerning the Word, as "Holy Scripture in divine splendor commences to scintillate before our eyes."[23]

It is important that both Bavinck and Kuyper reject the idea that Scripture is the object of the *testimonium* apart from its message, for as Kuyper points out, such a view is contrary to the way in which faith works, which excludes such a formalization. Furthermore, this separation fails to do full justice to the fact that there is the closest connection between the words of Holy Scripture and that about which they speak and witness. To formalize Holy Scripture in this way is as nonsensical as to praise a book without reading it; to do so violates the word-character of Holy Scripture. Whoever envisions the Spirit's testimony as an independent, isolated witness affording *a priori* certainty about the quality of Scripture cannot escape voiding the words of Holy Scripture itself. For on such a view the way of faith splits into two parts: first, the way to certainty regarding Scripture, and then the way to the message. Such an abstract division does not coincide with the correct understanding of the way expressed in the church's confession that the "Holy Scriptures fully contain the will of God and that whatsoever man ought to believe unto salvation is sufficiently taught therein" (*Belgic Confession*, VII). Whoever makes a distinction regarding certainty at this point must inevitably view the *testimonium* as a mysterious event, as "a supernatural factor of an incomprehensible nature that is added

---

[20]Cf. Bavinck, *GD*, I, 569, on the increase and decrease of faith in Scripture, and the cited part in Kuyper's "Locus de Sacra Scriptura," *Dictaten Dogmatiek*, Vol. 2 (Kampen, 1910), p. 197, on the differences in rapidity and clarity of the process of the *testimonium*.

[21]Kuyper, *Dictaten*, p. 199.

[22]Kuyper, *The Work of the Holy Spirit* (New York and London, 1900), p. 192.

[23]Ibid., p. 193.

to the Word and its impotence."[24] No added recognition of the self-authentication of Scripture can change this, for the mystery of the witness has already preceded the message of Holy Scripture; and thus it becomes impossible to recognize how Scripture itself speaks concerning the words that come to us. Scripture deals with "words" in their relation to the message of salvation, as Peter says to Christ: "Lord, to whom shall we go? You have the words of eternal life; and we have believed, and have come to know, that you are the Holy One of God" (John 6:68–69).[25] In spite of its seemingly greater objectivity, all formalizing of the *testimonium* and certainty violates the true meaning and intent of Holy Scripture.

The crucial nature of the subject under discussion makes it important to examine whether Bavinck's opinion that Calvin was too one-sided is indeed justified, especially since Calvin's influence on the confession is unmistakable. This, in turn, is important for a correct understanding of Article V, which states that the Holy Spirit witnesses in our hearts that these books are from God. Did Calvin have in mind a separate and precedent assurance by the witness of the Spirit regarding Holy Scripture in its capacity as writing? Is he concerned with the *divinitas* of Scripture "without thereby bringing the soteriological aspect of faith to the fore?"[26] Krusche is of the opinion that this kind of conclusion might be drawn from the *Institutes*, but that Calvin's commentaries offer an entirely different picture,[27] in which the *testimonium Spiritus Sancti* is not seen as giving prior certainty about the special divine quality of Holy Scripture. However, it is not easy to get a clear picture.

Calvin mentions the testimony of the Spirit in connection with his discussion of Holy Scripture, but later, in his chapter on faith, he does not mention it (*Inst.*, III, ii, 41). This may give the impression that he teaches that faith in Scripture precedes saving faith. However, according to the *Institutes* (I, vi, 2), faith in Scripture and saving faith coincide. Krusche refers to Calvin's exegesis of Ephesians 1:13: "The true conviction which believers have of the Word of God, of their own salvation, and of all religion [springs] . . . from the sealing of the Spirit," who makes their

---

[24]P. Althaus, *Die Prinzipien der deutschen reformierten Dogmatik im Zeitalter der altprotestantischen Theologie* (Leipzig, 1914), p. 209. See "a wholly incomprehensible operation of the Spirit" (pp. 211, 234, 264).

[25]See John 6:63: ". . . the words that I have spoken to you are spirit and life."

[26]W. Krusche, *Das Wirken des Heiligen Geistes nach Calvin* (Göttingen, 1957), p. 216. Krusche answers this question in the negative.

[27]Ibid., p. 217.

consciences more certain and removes all doubt.[28] At crucial points it is clear that Krusche is justified in his conclusion that "Calvin has not torn asunder certainty of Scripture and certainty of faith."[29] Calvin does speak emphatically of the *testimonium* and Holy Scripture, but the manner in which he does so does not warrant the charge of formalizing. Rather, Calvin sees Scripture as the clothes in which Christ comes to us (*Inst.*, III, ii, 6; cf. his commentary on I Pet. 2:8); whereas faith is the knowledge of God's will for us, which is learned from his Word (*Inst.*, III, ii, 6). For this reason there is no isolated objectification in Calvin, nor a mere interest in showing that there is a God, but a concern that we learn to know what his will concerning us is.[30]

In Bavinck's short survey of the history of this confession, he points out that in the course of time it began to lose its place of honor in Reformed theology and to yield to an "enlightenment" that credited the mind with insight into the divine nature of Scripture.[31] This "enlightenment" had no room for a direct correlation between the Word of God and faith, since it interposed between the two all kinds of reasonings and arguments to prove the truth of Holy Scripture. Later, rationalism secularized this position.

According to Bavinck, the doctrine of the *testimonium* was somehow revived again when it was realized that rationalism was untrustworthy and apologetics unfruitful. In this connection he mentions Kant's criticism of the proofs for the existence of God. Once again there was room for the conviction that it is meaningful to speak of a testimony of the Spirit, because it was seen that the ultimate basis of faith cannot lie outside of us in proofs and arguments, the church, or tradition, "but can be found only in man himself, in the religious subject."[32] Bavinck here expresses his appreciation for any insight into the uniqueness of *religious* certainty.

Only the Holy Spirit himself can give certainty and conquer all doubts; even though man himself is directly involved in every aspect of his life, the *auctoritas divina* is all-pervasive.[33] Hence, by saying that the "ultimate basis of faith is in the religious subject,"

---

[28]Ibid. See "firm and steady conviction" and the testimony of his adoption in his commentary on Eph. 1:13.

[29]Ibid.

[30]"For it is not so much our concern to know who he is in himself, as what he wills to be toward us" (*Inst.*, III, ii, 6).

[31]Bavinck, *GD*, I, 553.

[32]Ibid., p. 555.

[33]Ibid., p. 432.

Bavinck does not mean that it is not God but man who creates
certainty; on the contrary, "the subject does not create the truth;
it only recognizes and acknowledges it."[34] That is why he can
say in one breath that the ultimate basis of faith lies in the religious subject and that Holy Scripture is self-authenticating, the
final ground of faith,[35] and add to it that "carefully speaking,"
the testimony of the Spirit is not the ultimate ground.[36] Thus, it
is not the testimony of man's own spirit but the testimony of God
that causes man to rest in his salvation. In this way Bavinck
maintains the correlative connection between faith and revelation
and refuses to proceed from an alleged continuity between man's
own spirit and judgment and the testimony of the Spirit. Bavinck's
rejection of the isolation and supernaturalization of the *testimonium* does not lead him to deny the testimony of the Spirit to and
in man over against man's autonomous judgment.

It is not difficult to see why, in connection with salvation and
certainty, the church's reflection and discussion always centered
on the Holy Spirit. From the Word of God it increasingly learned
to understand better that certainty of faith was by no means a
self-evident human correlate of revelation by natural rational insight. The biblical-pneumatological aspect of faith, knowledge,
trust, and certainty is clearly seen in the fact that faith and knowledge do not come from "flesh and blood" (see Matt. 16:17), and
in the radical and revealing statement that "no one comprehends
the thoughts of God except the Spirit of God" (I Cor. 2:11).
According to the New Testament, certainty can never be explained in terms of the receptivity of the human heart or its
capacity to reassure itself and convince itself of the truth. In the
words of Paul, it is God himself who has revealed it to us through
the Spirit, who "searches everything, even the depths of God"
(I Cor. 2:10). The Spirit is given "that we might understand the
gifts bestowed on us by God" (v. 12). We need to be "taught by
the Spirit" (v. 13), since "the unspiritual man does not receive
the gifts of the Spirit of God" and is thus unable to understand
them (vv. 14, 15).

The consideration of the mystery of the knowledge of God, of
faith, and of complete, limitless trust is not a general epistemo-
logical problem concerning the various ways in which man ar-
rives at certain knowledge, but a confrontation with the marvel
of the gift of being taught and led. Realizing this, the church was

[34]Ibid., p. 557.
[35]Ibid., p. 559.
[36]Ibid., p. 569.

prompted to proceed with care in its own life and in its witness and exhortation, avoiding the use of force or coercion. At the same time, it is clear that a realization of the necessity of the decisive and exclusive significance of the Spirit's work for true knowledge and understanding does not mean an esoteric acceptance of an uncontrollable and irrational event that surprises a person in the darkness and isolation of his uncomprehending life, but instead points to the operation of the Spirit in its convincing nature. The wonder of faith and certainty may not be described as an irrational event or fact unapproachable except through individual experiences like that of the healed man born blind: ". . . one thing I know, that though I was blind, now I see" (John 9:25). Rather, the New Testament depicts the wonder of faith in a wealth of essential contexts. Christ promises that the Holy Spirit "will guide you into all the truth" (John 16:13). As the Spirit of truth, he bears witness to Christ (John 15:26), and in direct relationship with him he "convinces the world of sin, of righteousness, and of judgment" (John 16:8).

The powerful operation of the testimony of the Spirit centers in the salvation that has appeared in Christ. It is impressive how the New Testament speaks of the way that leads to faith and certainty as a testimony of Christ bearing witness to himself, and of the Father bearing witness to him (John 8:18–19).[37] This legitimating is taken up and secured by the Holy Spirit and carried out into the world. The Spirit speaks, proclaims, and bears witness to this truth of all opposition, and his testimony is trustworthy. The New Testament presents a unique connection between the Holy Spirit and the truth: "And the Spirit is the witness, because the Spirit is the truth" (I John 5:7).

The New Testament does not, however, envision an isolated

---

[37]Note the reference that the witness of two persons is true (v. 17; cf. Deut. 17:6; 19:15). When the legitimacy of Christ's statements are at stake, he also says that his witness would not be true if he would bear witness to himself. Someone else bears witness to him, and that testimony is true (John 5:32). Cf. the Pharisees' accusation: "You are bearing witness to yourself; your testimony is not true" (John 8:13), and Christ's answer: "Even if I do bear witness to myself, my testimony is true." It is obvious that the variation is determined by the different situations and is not contradictory (John 5:31; 8:14–18), because in the one instance where he does not bear witness to himself, he takes into account "the people and their manner of thinking" regarding a profound testimony of oneself (N. Brox, *Zeuge und Märtyrer. Untersuchungen zur frühchristlicher Zeugnis-terminologie* [1961], p. 73). Cf. also John 7:18 on speaking on one's own authority and seeking glory by doing so, and on being true in seeking the glory of one's sender. See also C. H. Dodd, *The Interpretation of the Fourth Gospel* (Cambridge, 1953), p. 329 and Bultmann's *The Gospel of John: A Commentary* (ET Philadelphia, 1971), pp. 263–64, 280–81.

and supernatural testimony of the Spirit present in the human world of lies as a fact that cannot be further described. Rather, his testimony is the foundation and ferment of the witness of the apostles, who received the promise that the Spirit of the Father would speak through them at the time that they were called to bear witness to the Gentiles (Matt. 10:18; cf. Acts 1:8). Their witness came into being under the authorization and blessing of the Spirit to the extent that it could be said that it was not they who spoke, but the Spirit of the Father in them, who engaged their witness in his service (Acts 5:32; John 15:27; Acts 22:20). From the world of men—amidst all its uncertainty—the testimony of God resounds as a true and trustworthy word of man, as the human witness concerning Christ. Because of this concrete content of the testimony of the Spirit and of eyewitnesses, this testimony cannot be understood as an errant, mysterious, irrational event.[38] Rather, its structure is thus so that it is recognizable; and because this testimony can be recognized, the church warns the believers not to believe every spirit, but to "test the spirits whether they are of God" (I John 4:1; cf. I Cor. 12:10). This warning does not imply any sort of higher criterion by which the Spirit himself can be tested, but it is meant to criticize arbitrary appeals to the Spirit. The definitive criterion is the coming of Jesus Christ in the flesh (I John 4:6). Only thereby can the Holy Spirit's testimony in the correlation between man's confession and man's witness be recognized.[39]

The testimony of the Spirit does not exclude man, but wins his inner consent. This is evident above all in Romans, where the Spirit's witness is directly related to man's being a child of God: ". . . it is the Spirit himself bearing witness with our spirit that we are children of God" (8:16). Because Paul's statement is so specific, it is obvious how necessary it is to give further explanation whenever we describe the Spirit's testimony by the term "formal." For the concrete content of this testimony is the *adoptio* in direct relation to the receiving of the Spirit "by whom we cry,

---

[38]Cf. Preiss, p. 28.

[39]The application of this criterion is clearly evident in I Cor. 12:3 in the contrast of "Jesus be cursed!" and "Jesus is Lord." Cf. W. Schmithals, *Gnosticism in Corinth* (ET Nashville, 1971), pp. 124ff. Schmithals specifically answers the question how anyone in the church could say *anathema Iesous*, considering this a Gnostic separation between the heavenly pneuma-Christ and the man Jesus (pp. 127–28). He says that he finds this exegesis already with Godet. For a different opinion, see F. W. Grosheide, *Commentary on the First Epistle to the Corinthians* (Grand Rapids, 1953), p. 281, who does not think that this text has reference to an actual event in the church. Schmithals especially points out the connection between I Cor. 12 and I John (p. 126).

'Abba! Father!' " (v. 15). It is by means of a testimony that this
unassailable certainty, with all its concomitant eschatological
perspective, grows (v. 17). This testimony of the Spirit is called
"a bearing witness with" our spirit (Rom. 8:16). This description
of it points out how much this testimony touches man, without
being in immediate continuity with the natural heart or explic-
able on the basis of anything in man himself. One could speak
of being filled with words by the mystery, citing a great variety
of references (Rom. 8:15; Gal 4:6; Rom. 8:26– 27). Such Scripture passages are an urgent exhortation to carefulness in theological formulation and a warning against simplistic biblicism.

All this shows a concentration on the believer's filial relationship to God. It is no wonder that Paul's statement on the Spirit's
witness to the believer's sonship has played an important role in
many discussions of the *testimonium* and Holy Scripture. Theologians have always sensed intuitively that one cannot dualisti-
cally place the confession of the Reformation alongside the
certainty concerning one's sonship. Bavinck declares emphatically that, regarding the Spirit's testimony, one must first of all
think of this filial relationship, calling it "the central truth, the
core and focus of this testimony."[40] Furthermore, realizing the
necessity for this doctrine to be based on the pronouncements of
the Bible, theologians had to continually take into account its
explicit statement regarding man's sonship, particularly when
they discussed the *testimonium* in connection with Holy Scripture.
The Reformed confession can be correctly understood and function only in connection with this testimony regarding the believer's sonship.

There can be no splitting of the *testimonium* into two separate
testimonia, namely, one regarding our sonship, and another concerning the truth of Scripture. In the light of the New Testament
we clearly see the victorious nature of the Spirit's witness. It is
a witness concerning Christ and his salvation that reaches to the
depths of the heart in the face of all former estrangement, bond-
age, doubt, and uncertainty. Although Bavinck does not examine
the New Testament witness terminology exclusively, he nevertheless clearly reflects its tenor when he calls the *testimonium* "the
triumph of the Holy Spirit in the world," "the victory of the
foolishness of the cross over the wisdom of the world," and "the
triumph of the thoughts of God over the deliberations of men."[41]
This triumph does not manifest an independent illumination of

[40]Bavinck, *GD*, I, 564.
[41]Ibid., p. 570.

the Spirit. Whenever the doctrine of the *testimonium* went in that direction, the Word of God was devaluated. But neither is the confession of the *testimonium* a theoretical explanation of certainty on the basis of an established cause. Rather, it is a confessing declaration, an account of the way that leads from the Word to faith and its certainty.[42]

This has often been expressed in a way that seems to be a subtle differentiation at first glance, but which nevertheless has something essential in view: that the witness of the Spirit is not the ultimate basis of faith and that we believe Scripture "not *because* of but *through* the Spirit's testimony."[43] These formulations can be understood correctly only if they are not regarded as theoretical constructs but rather as part of a believing understanding of the miracle of certainty, which does not originate in man himself amid all his uncertainty and doubt. The Reformed confession is the discovery, already reflected in Jeremiah: "O Lord, thou hast deceived[44] me, and I was deceived; thou art stronger than I, and thou hast prevailed" (Jer. 20:7). This prevailing power of God has nothing to do with coercion; nevertheless, in faith it is understood as divine force and triumph, with the attendant subjective correlate of capitulation, which in turn becomes the source of the greatest freedom and certainty.

On the basis of the New Testament, the confession of the Spirit is first of all related to salvation in Christ; and *then* the Word of God is discussed. It has often been noted that Scripture itself speaks of a testimony of the Spirit, but not in direct relation to Holy Scripture. This argument seemed to be quite powerful, especially over against the Reformation's emphasis on *sola Scriptura* in the foundation of its dogma. It is obvious, however, that precisely because of the *sola Scriptura* principle Reformed theology was not confronted with the dilemma of a dualism between authoritative Scripture and the message it brings, because Reformed theology hears the message of salvation precisely in the witness of Scripture. Hence, there can be no objection to the expression "faith in Scripture" (except for the possible misunderstanding of it), and it is incorrect to say that this is the same as a trivial faith in a book. To deduce a contradiction from this is nothing but an abstraction in which one no longer understands the power and the miracle of the testimony. This miracle is the

---

[42]Cf. G. W. Locher, *Testimonium internum: Calvins Lehre vom Heiligen Geist und das hermeneutische Problem* (Zurich, 1964), p. 6.

[43]Bavinck, *GD*, I, 568; cf. Krusche, p. 208.

[44]The Dutch Nieuwe Vertaling, which Berkouwer uses, has the word "overwhelmed" or "liberally overridden" here (tr. note).

miracle of the burning heart about which the disciples on the road to Emmaus speak in inescapable connection with Christ's testimony: "Did not our hearts burn within us while he talked to us on the road, while he opened to us the scriptures?" (Luke 24:32). This is no irrational fact that as an immediate and direct event is disconnected from the message of Scripture.[45] On the contrary, just when we speak about the Spirit's testimony and the heart, we are warned against devaluating the written and spoken Word. The question is not whether faith in Scripture can be joined with true Christian faith, but only in what way there can be such a combination or harmony.

This question is of decisive significance for understanding the confession of the *testimonium Spiritus Sancti*. Central to this question is the meaning of "faith" in the expression "faith in Scripture," especially as it comes to a head in Question 21 of the Heidelberg Catechism: "What is true faith?" The Catechism then speaks of holding for truth all that God has revealed in his Word — which is a "sure knowledge" — and it speaks of a "firm confidence which the Holy Spirit works in my heart by the gospel." The wording strongly emphasizes the "for me" aspect.

Theologians have long discussed the relationship between "knowledge" and "firm confidence." Many have preferred to solve the problem by resorting to a less dualistic terminology such as found in Calvin's definition of faith as "a firm and certain knowledge of God's benevolence toward us" (*Inst.*, III, ii, 7). We need not go further into this matter of wording, since it is generally agreed that Calvin on the one hand does not mean by *cognitio* a purely intellectual knowledge, and that the Catechism on the other is not referring to a combination of intellectual *fides historica* and trusting *fides salvifica*. Common to all attempts at formulating the essence of Christian faith was the conviction that Christian faith is not — as it has been expressed — an act of the mind as *cum assensu cogitare*, as assent to all those things that God sets forth to be believed.[46] Neither in Calvin ("toward us" and "God's benevolence") nor in the Catechism is there an isolation or autonomizing of belief in Scripture. True belief in Scripture is possible and real only in relation to the message of Scripture. According to Bavinck, the Reformation theologians presented "an idea of the object and essence of faith" totally different from an intellec-

---

[45]Cf. Heidegger's opposition to the "irrational movement of the heart" in H. Heppe, *Reformed Dogmatics* (ET London, 1950), p. 25.
[46]Bavinck, *GD*, IV, 85.

tual "assent."[47] In fact, they opposed the notion that soon became predominant in the church of "an intellectual assent to revealed truth,"[48] a notion that "had very negative results" in practical life.[49] The Reformation theologians discovered the religious nature of faith. They did not merely add the *fides historica* and the *fides salvifica* to a mechanical total, for even though they spoke of knowledge and trust, nevertheless the knowledge they had in mind was "totally different from that of historical faith."[50] It is good to recall all these things when reflecting on the nature of belief in Scripture. When the "acceptance" of Holy Scripture as the Word of God is separated from a living faith in Christ, it is meaningless and confusing to call this acceptance belief in Scripture or an "element" of the Christian faith.[51] This does not imply an underestimation of Scripture or of belief in it, but rather a great respect for Scripture, which in its testimony addresses itself to our faith. Hence, it is of great importance that the Reformed confessions definitely do not view faith in Scripture as a preparation for true faith, or as a component of it which, if so desired, can be considered independent of it; but they connect faith in Scripture with the testimony of the Holy Spirit. They thereby do full justice to the profoundness of the biblical concept of faith, because this implies that faith in Scripture is possible and real only in connection with the witness of the Spirit to Christ and his salvation. Calvin's "toward us" and the Catechism's "firm confidence" are not an anthropocentric departure from the "objective" truth of Scripture, but instead point to the purpose of Scripture: ". . . these [signs] are written that you may believe that Jesus is the Christ, the Son of God, and that believing you may have life in his name" (John 20:31). The true meaning of faith in Scripture can be understood only in the full stature of the one true and living faith, as this is described in various words, such as: accepting, holding for truth, knowing and trusting, embracing and relying. The confession of the *testimonium Spiritus Sancti* once and for all precludes every separation of faith in Christ from faith in Scripture. Faith in Scripture is not a separate belief

[47]Ibid., p. 87.
[48]Ibid., I, 540.
[49]Ibid., IV, 85. According to Bavinck, no justice was done to the grand teaching of Scripture "because theologians proceeded from the everyday meaning of the word and lost sight of the religious meaning which it had in Scripture."
[50]Ibid., I, 541.
[51]Cf. Calvin's critical reminder that if someone believes that God exists, and that the recorded history of Christ is true, such belief is worth nothing and does not deserve the name of faith (*ita indigna est fidei appellatione*), with reference to Jas. 2:19 (*Opera Selecta*, I, 68, 69).

that must be complemented by trust.[52] The Reformation, by its confession of the testimony of the Holy Spirit, has freed faith in Scripture from its isolation and impoverishment and thus pointed out the way to a true acceptance of the prophetic-apostolic witness.

If the true confession of the testimony of the Spirit precludes the method of supplementing one kind of faith with another, neither can later critics be correct in saying that this confession leads its defenders into a vicious circle because they simultaneously confess the self-authentication of Holy Scripture.[53]

The Reformers linked the confession of the Spirit's testimony harmoniously with a great concentration on the witness of Holy Scripture. They did so because they were fully convinced that the testimony of Scripture, which addressed itself to faith, did not automatically evoke faith by way of a natural self-evidence of the written Word. In this connection Calvin writes that the Word can at best touch the ears but not the heart (Inst., III, i, 4). With this anthropological presentation he means to point out that there is not a single thing that can convince man, in his estrangement and isolation, of the truth of this message except God himself.[54] That is why the Reformers never devaluated the message on the basis of a misunderstood testimony of the Spirit that in essence is no more than a mystical and immediate revelation; on the contrary, it is exactly by means of this confession that they evoke and stimulate attention for this message. This confession is not a theoretical, causal explanation, but one that at the same time comprises confession of guilt and confidence in the Word. Calvin is concerned with the reality of faith and its inviolable certainty through the spirit of Christ,[55] and it is in this connection that he speaks of the blindness of our eyes which

[52]Cf. Bavinck's objection to the concept that the *fides informis* must be complemented until it becomes *fides formata* (*GD*, I, 541). Cf. also Kuyper, *E Voto Dordraceno*, Vol. I (Kampen, 1895), p. 129.

[53]Bavinck discusses the critics who claim that their opponents appeal to the testimony of the Spirit while at the same time insisting on the self-authentication of Scripture and then believe in revelation because there is a revelation (the *testimonium*) *concerning* revelation (*GD*, I, 550, 568). Bavinck says that this is a misinterpretation of the confession because its intent is not to point out a final basis for testing and justifying Holy Scripture.

[54]Besides many similar statements by Calvin, we refer to Luther's: "One can preach the Word to me, but to put it in my heart nobody can but God only; He must speak in my heart, otherwise nothing will come of it" (quoted in P. Althaus, *Die Christliche Wahrheit: Lehrbuch der Dogmatik*, Vol. I (Gütersloh, 1947), p. 221.

[55]Cf. Calvin on I Cor. 2:10, where he refers to the Spirit, and adds "for the encouragement of believers" as if we were told: "Let it be enough for us that we have the Spirit of God as witness." Cf. also *posse comprehendi Evangelii doctrinam* through the testimony of the Spirit (Locher, p. 19).

prevents us from seeing the riches of Christ that the gospel offers us.

Calvin can then approach the marvel of faith on the basis of the "secret efficacy of the Spirit" and his illumination and renovation,[56] in order to express, in a halting anthropological distinction, that the decision does not fall in the mind but in the heart (*Inst.*, III, ii, 33). By thus pointing to the heart, the confession of the testimony of the Spirit does not devaluate the Word of God; neither does it allow the inward witness to prevail over the outward, since the *testimonium* certifies the words of none other than human witnesses.[57]

We are not dealing with an isolated testimony that can afford certainty concerning the authority of Scripture apart from trust, but with one that binds us to the message, to the testimony of Scripture itself. Krusche has pointed out many places in Calvin's commentaries where he relates the testimony of the Spirit and the sealing by the Spirit to the resurrection of Christ, the gospel, the promise, and the adoption as being the contents of the prophetic-apostolic witness.[58] Wholly in line with this is Calvin's rejection of a spiritualism that makes great display of the superiority of the Spirit, but rejects all reading of Scripture itself, and derides the simplicity of "those who, as they express it, still follow the dead and killing letter" (*Inst.*, I, ix, 1). These men tear asunder what is indissolubly joined in union.[59] For the Spirit does not give new and hitherto unheard revelations,[60] but confirms the teaching of the gospel in our hearts. Within the concrete situation at the time of the Reformation, this meant the rejection of the appeal to the Spirit which inevitably and always must lead to the triumph of subjectivism, and hence it would be incorrect to view Calvin's doctrine of the *testimonium* and the self-authentication of

[56]Locher, p. 19.

[57]"Let this point therefore stand: that those whom the Holy Spirit has inwardly taught truly rest upon Scripture" (*Inst.*, I, vii, 5). See also what follows in connection with Scripture's authentication. It is not fair to lift Calvin's statements on the outward preaching as being "useless and vain unless the teaching of the Spirit is added to it" (in his commentary on John 14:26) out of their context, because it is exactly his opposition to abstraction that governs his polemical thinking. Cf. his commentary on Rom. 10:17, on the voice of man being his virtue.

[58]Cf. Krusche, p. 212, and Calvin's commentary on Rom. 1:4; I Cor. 1:6; Eph. 1:4; and I Cor. 2:12.

[59]*Inst.*, I, ix, 1. Calvin quotes here (as in I, vii, 4) Isa. 59:21: "My Spirit which is upon you, and my words which I have put in your mouth."

[60]Cf. Calvin's commentary on John 14:26: the Spirit is not "a constructor of new revelations." Cf. also on John 16:12: against blasphemy.

Scripture as a one-sided reaction against spiritualism.[61] He is concerned with the meaning of Old Testament prophecy — the Spirit and the Word — and with the connection between the witnessing Spirit of Christ and the apostolic witness which he himself has called forth. For that reason Calvin rejects the contextless contrasts between *pneuma* and *gramma*, between spirit and letter, since Scripture is not merely outward and hence unreal *gramma* — worthless and insufficient. Calvin does not abstract the letters and words of Holy Scripture from the context and relatedness in which they serve and function, and he calls attention to the "living oracles" that Moses received to give to the people (Acts 7:38). To speak of Scripture as, and to reduce it to, mere *gramma* is nothing else than an abstraction of the letters of a book as such, because then the phrase "as such" points up the illegitimacy of the abstraction. On the basis of the context of the written and spoken word, Calvin can answer the question why Stephen calls the law "living oracles": Christ himself is contained therein.[62]

When it is thus clear from the nature and the contents of the scriptural witness that the work of the Spirit by no means relativizes it, then it is also obvious that there are not two separate kinds of witness, one that must be called the outer and the other the inner testimony. Only robbing the written words of their meaning can lead to such dualism and in the end to a spiritualism that always thrives on dualism and exerts its suggestive power.[63]

---

[61]Cf. Peter Brunner, *Vom Glauben bei Calvin* (Tübingen, 1925), p. 98, against Karl Heim. Prenter's *Spiritus Creator*, pp. 105ff., points out that Luther's position is already noticeable before his attack on spiritualism. It only increases to greater polemic intensity.

[62]Cf. Calvin's commentary on Acts 7:38: "But it is asked, 'Why does he call the Law a living word?' " This does not contradict II Cor. 3, Calvin correctly says, because Paul does not view the word and preaching as a dead letter and sound, and is not speaking of a dead letter, but of a letter that works death, of an active *gramma*, for example, when the law is divorced from the gospel and presented as the way to salvation (II Cor. 3:6). Cf. Calvin's commentary on II Cor. and *Inst.*, I, ix, 3, with reference to the disciples on the way to Emmaus and to I Thess. 5:19-20 (the warning against quenching the Spirit and despising prophesying). Calvin's views are still very valuable, especially over against the interpretation of II Cor. 3:6 (the killing written code) which has become tradition. On the *pneuma-gramma* antithesis, cf. Gerhard Kittel, ed., *Theological Dictionary of the New Testament*, Vol. I (ET Grand Rapids, 1964), pp. 65-68.

[63]Cf. Prenter, p. 104, who describes the background of the problem with which the Reformation wrestled as follows: "On the one side there is such a strong emphasis on the sovereignty of the Spirit that the outward Word seems to be reduced to a comparatively insignificant accompanying phenomenon of the free work of the Spirit. On the other side there is so strong an emphasis on the connection of the Spirit to the outward Word, on its being a necessary consequence of the Word, that the Spirit seems to become a mere attribute to the Word."

For that reason Calvin calls faith "the principal work of the Holy Spirit" and the Spirit "the inner teacher," and thus he conquers the contrast between figurative and real (*Inst.*, III, i, 4). The action of the Spirit of Christ, the Paraclete himself, calls forth the human testimony. Hence, the Spirit does not minimize this testimony but only man's reasoning, which he exposes to the light of the ultimate proof of the truth of Scripture, which is derived from the person of God himself.[64] So the *testimonium Spiritus Sancti* does not oppose the self-authentication of Scripture, but forms a unity with it when it is received as directed towards Christ and his salvation.

From all the aspects of the confession of the *testimonium Spiritus Sancti*, it is evident that the problem of ultimate certainty is at stake here. The Reformers, surrounded as they were by Roman Catholicism and spiritualism, fully realized that what was at stake was "the hearing of God's very own Word,"[65] with certainty and comfort as the goal of that which was written (cf. Rom. 15:4).

This confession of the testimony of the Spirit was not intended to give a rational and theoretical solution or explanation to the relationship between Word and Spirit. The Reformers realized that it is impossible to ascribe all kinds of human experiences to the Spirit's operation. For those who do so, the function of Scripture and of preaching is to illustrate what is experienced in the depths of subjectivity and not the confrontation of man with the authoritative testimony of God. But even subsequent to the rejection of such an exclusion of the Word, the mystery of Word and Spirit remains unfathomable. When confronted with the Word, we cannot by means of a solution or technique trace or circumscribe the way from the Word to faith. Every attempt to somehow clarify the mystery remains revealingly unsatisfactory. This becomes evident as soon as we try to express this mystery in all kinds of exclusive terminology, and to express the operation, power, and conviction of the Spirit as *with* the Word or as *through* the Word. We can observe that in this history of the Reformed churches, theologians were of the opinion that the mystery could be expressed both as *with* and as *through* without doing

[64] *Inst.*, I, vii, 4: "Thus, the highest proof of Scripture derives in general from the fact that God in person speaks in it." Cf. I, vii, 1: ". . . the Scriptures obtain full authority among believers only when men regard them as having sprung from heaven, as if there the living words of God were heard."

[65] K. Holl, "Luther und die Schwärmer," *Luther* (1923), p. 431, in connection with the Holy Spirit. See also Calvin, *Inst.*, I, vii, 4: ". . . God alone is a fit witness of himself in his Word. . . ." Cf. W. Niesel, *The Theology of Calvin* (ET Philadelphia, 1956), p. 33.

injustice to it by emphasizing both the significance and power of
the Word, which deals with this "absolutely incomparable matter"[66] and the witnessing and convincing Spirit who wins the
hearts over to Christ.

The mystery cuts across every exclusive formulation[67] and
itself points out the way from the Word to faith, a way in which
we can walk only in fear and trembling. It is remarkable that all
kinds of seemingly logical arguments and conclusions may lead
to an impasse that leaves no more room for the ministry and
man's responsibility. To sense and emphasize this is not a flight
into an irrationalism that prefers vagueness rather than clarity
of insight and confession, but directly results from the nature of
the witness of God and the mystery of the Spirit which can be
understood only by faith. Rationalization of this mystery always
leads to conclusions which in the preaching reveal themselves as
illegitimate foreign elements. Men have given rational explanations of the relation between the Word and the Spirit such that
the testimony of Scripture and of preaching were suddenly placed
in a vacuum and reduced to powerless and hence meaningless
"outward" things. By misinterpreting the striving of the Spirit
that calls the human witness into his service, they finally ended
up in the direction of spiritualism. Thus, Holy Scripture became
merely a "revelation" that was confirmed by an added testimony
of the Holy Spirit, and thus the connection with the human testimony regarding salvation in history became obscured. This
opened the way to an appeal to the Spirit as *privatus Spiritus*, and
he was used as a criterion that cast its shadow of doubt on the
trustworthiness and persuasiveness of the prophetic-apostolic testimony. The relation between faith and revelation took on more
and more formal traits, and men became ignorant of the way in
which Scripture itself speaks of the claim of the gospel as the
power of God (I Cor. 1:18 — the word of the cross) and the sword
of the Spirit (Eph. 6:17). The protest (which in itself is justifiable)
against externalization and literalism could thus develop into a
denial of the meaningful language of Scripture by abstracting the
testimony that comes to us in words into mere "word" and "let-

[66]Weber, *Foundations*, I, 244.

[67]No doubt that is what the Augsburg Confession is referring to when it says,
"For by the Word and Sacraments, as by instruments, the Holy Spirit is given:
who worketh faith, where and when it pleaseth God, in those that hear the gospel
. . ." (Schaff, *Creeds*, III, 10). Cf. Berkouwer, *Sin* (ET Grand Rapids, 1971),
pp. 214ff., where I have extensively discussed the matter that it is incorrect to
say that the Reformed position exclusively sees it as "with the Word."

ters."[68] Individualism and subjectivism misinterpreted the meaning and intent of the Spirit's words, with the result that the emphasis on "for us" (and "for me") narrowed down and reduced the divine to one's own existential experiences. A more serious caricature of the Spirit's witness is hardly imaginable, and the Reformers, although in groping and halting language, clearly saw and proclaimed this. Exactly in view of these errors, the Reformed confession of the testimony of the Spirit is the definitive defense,[69] because in the controversy regarding certainty—in the midst of many and varied kinds of "spirits"—it points to the way of faith that removes all autonomy, both theoretical and practical, from every reflection on the criteria. To those traveling the way of faith, the testimony of the Spirit does not merely "compensate" for the Word that "as such" (the "as such" of an abstraction) is inoperative and powerless, but binds them increasingly to the witness concerning Christ. Hence, we are confronted with the fact that, by precluding every mechanical "certification," all dogmatic reflection of its own nature must remind us of the prayer, "Come, Creator Spirit!" We are not concerned here with an edifying and practical application of the doctrine, but with its own structure and contents. This also implies a serious warning against the idea that a traditional belief in Scripture can be retained when a living subjection to the message of Scripture no longer governs life to the depths of the heart. For belief in Scripture conforms to the will of God only when it is the response to the preaching of the mystery which "now is disclosed and through the prophetic writings is made known . . . according to the command of the eternal God, to bring about the obedience of faith" (Rom. 16:26). Belief in Scripture is inseparably connected with this testimony—with the gospel. Without this gospel it is doomed to rigidity.

In a cultural surrounding which engulfs the "controversial Bible" with disquietude and various attacks, the preaching of the gospel is itself the only way in which we can speak about Scrip-

[68]Remarkably revealing is Paul's statement that his gospel preaching had come to the church "not only in word, but also in power and in the Holy Spirit" (I Thess. 1:5). This has nothing to do with spiritualism. Cf. the antithesis in I Cor. 1:17 (the wisdom of words) and I Cor. 4:20 (power versus words)—a clear *polemic.* Cf. further many expressions in I Thess., such as receiving the Word with joy in the Holy Spirit (1:6), the sounding forth of the Word (1:8), the active Word (2:13), speaking to save (2:16), and the glorification of the Word (II Thess. 3:1).

[69]According to Weber (I, 242), this confession is "the only really new development which Reformed theology has contributed regarding the basis of the authority of Scripture," i.e., this discovery in connection with "a new encounter with Scripture" which is so characteristic of the Reformation.

ture, not in whispers but with thankfulness and songs of praise. In this we follow the Israelite when he spoke of God's Word as his lamp and light and testified to his love for the law (Ps. 119:105, 113). In this way we come to understand the witness of the Paraclete and through this in turn the secret of true piety — the divine command to pay attention to the witness of Scripture (Rom. 16:26). These then become "spotlights illuminating the magnificent drama of God's saving acts."[70]

In a noteworthy formulation appended to the confession regarding the *testimonium*, the Belgic Confession expressly states that a recognition of the witness of the Spirit does not endanger or belittle the testimony of Scripture: ". . . whereof they carry the evidence in themselves. For the very blind are able to perceive that the things foretold in them are fulfilling" (*Belgic Confession*, V; Schaff, *Creeds*, III, 387). It can readily be understood that these words occasioned much debate. This becomes evident when we take note of the manner in which Calvin spoke of the testimony of the Holy Spirit. He separated it from all proofs or rational arguments for the trustworthiness of Scripture. Questions have been raised whether these words of the Belgic Confession agreed with the real intention of the confession regarding the testimony of the Spirit. For does not this confession speak of the mysterious nature of faith in Scripture in the sense that Scripture is not matter-of-fact and not readily apparent to human understanding? Is this decisive perspective not contradicted by adducing "evidence," and by giving it a function parallel to the internal witness in establishing certainty? The striking assertion that even the blind are able to perceive[71] appeared to support such objections, especially in the light of later attempts to posit various "proofs" for the trustworthiness of Scripture alongside the testimony of the Spirit. Was it not the real intention of the confession of the testimony of the Spirit to point out that the heart was blind and closed to this very witness of God and through this to posit the need for prayer for continuing illumination so that man might receive the miracle of vision and understanding?

It is not easy in this discussion to arrive at a conclusion by means of the words which really stand out — the "evidence" and the "very blind" being able to perceive. He who recognizes the human side and the incomplete nature of confessional statements and wishes to guard himself against mere harmonization must

[70]H. N. Ridderbos, *Aan De Romeinen* (Kampen, 1959), p. 354.
[71]The Dutch version, which Berkouwer cites, has an even stronger expression. It states that the blind can "touch" the evidence (tr. note).

confront the distinct fact that the "evidence" adduced here differs
from the proofs and arguments which were later coordinated with
the *testimonium Spiritus Sancti*. For, while Article V does not mention the varied qualities of Scripture itself, it distinctly approaches the Word of God on the basis of its contents. The writers
clearly did not wish to isolate the *testimonium Spiritus Sancti* from
the message of Scripture, and in the same breath they mentioned
the self-authenticating nature of Scripture's witness. They did so
by relating this self-authenticating element to the content and
message of Scripture. The fact that the "evidence" of this authority and trustworthiness is inherent in Scripture was pointed
out by a reference to the fulfillment of God's Word in history.
Polman's heavy emphasis on this aspect is quite correct. A merely
natural recognition of Scripture as a supernatural phenomenon
with the consequent "rational" proofs is not possible. Scripture
authenticates itself, especially where its message is concerned.
This then is Polman's intention when he forbids us to look upon
Scripture as a "precious document with a certain quantity of
truths" in separation from the continuing mighty acts of God.[72]
We must rather focus our attention on the fulfillment of that
Word. We must see the promises of God as words which do not
fall to the ground nor return to him empty (I Sam. 3:19 and
Isa. 55:11). It is my opinion that such a view does not proceed
from an outlook on history that circumvents faith. The formulation, "even the very blind are able to perceive," does not intend
to replace the uniqueness of the *testimonium Spiritus Sancti* by mere
rational insight and intrinsically convincing evidence. It rather
seeks to manifest the confidence of a faith that knows that the
acts of God are not esoteric mysteries. The problem that Article V wishes to comment on is not the completion of the testimony of the Holy Spirit; it gives us a perspective on that testimony
and the acts of God. This is in itself an important indication that
although the confession is diametrically opposed to every attempt
to formalize the Word, it yet refers to Scripture as the mighty
oracles and the acts of God himself. Its reference to the fact that
even the blind can touch reminds us of Paul's retort to Festus's
criticism of his defense. When accused of madness, he did not
fall back on being privy to an esoteric mystery open only to
initiates, but rather affirms that he is speaking the "sober truth"

---

[72]A. D. R. Polman, *Woord en Belijdenis*, Vol. I (Franeker, n.d.), p. 111. See also
his *Onze Nederlandse Geloofsbelijdenis*, Vol. I (Franeker, n.d.), pp. 226ff. Polman's
emphasis is on Scripture's focus on God's mighty deeds and on the redemptive-
historical character of God's Word.

and accurately indicates that what happened "was not done in a corner" (Acts 26:25–27). Speaking about the "evidence" inherent in Scripture, evidence which culminates in a reference to the truth and the power of God's Word, adds no "arguments" to the witness of the Spirit, but rather proffers a perspective on a nonreactionary confession of this testimony, a confession which does not alienate us from the message of Scripture but rather allows us to rest on it.

We have noted in passing that Bavinck answered Strauss's contention that the confession of the *testimonium Spiritus Sancti* is "the Achilles' heel of the Protestant system."[73] Bavinck countered by asserting that what here seems to be weakness or indefensibility is in reality a sign of power, indeed the cornerstone of the Christian confession of the Spirit's triumph in the world. Besides evincing a remarkable parallel to Barth on this point,[74] this answer, at first glance, seems to be not much more than a rather easy piece of apologetic one-upmanship which does not really do justice to Strauss's objection. Only recently was such a transposition — moving from weakness to strength — brought sharply to the fore in H. A. Smit's critique of Kierkegaard. Smit sees this turning of what has always been considered Christianity's weakest point into its point of strength as "the key to his defense of Christianity," and describes this method as "this judo-like ability to turn weakness into strength."[75] Without examining the structure of Kierkegaard's apologetics any further, we can readily see that a similar parallel is conspicuously present in Bavinck's answer to Strauss. He formulates it in the context of his apologetic for the Christian faith and the testimony of the Holy Spirit. It is exactly this testimony which is for him "the crown and seal of all Christian truth, the triumph of the Spirit in the world."[76] By

---

[73]Strauss, I, 136. In his opinion this weakness becomes apparent in two possible perversions. It can lead to fanaticism (which treats the Spirit as a source of new revelation and opposes it to Scripture) and to rationalism. For he asks, "Who then assures me that my experience derives from the working of the Holy Spirit in me?" It does not help, according to Strauss, to "posit between the Scripture and the human spirit a 'divine something' testifying in my spirit to the former, for who then witnesses to me of the divinity of such a testimony?"

[74]Compare Barth's answer to Strauss: "Indeed who does attest the divinity of this witness? What Strauss failed to see is that there is no Protestant 'system,' but that the Protestant church and Protestant doctrine has necessarily and gladly to leave this question unanswered; because at its weakest point, where it can only acknowledge and confess, it has all its indestructible strength" (*CD*, I/2, 537). Cf. also Weber, I, 243.

[75]H. A. Smit, *Kierkegaard's Pilgrimage of Man. The Road of Self-positing and Self-abdication* (Delft, 1965), pp. 37ff.

[76]Bavinck, *GD*, I, 570.

transposing in his answer from the weak to the strong, he is not indulging in mere rhetorical technique which reveals its own weakness in a meaningless shift of words. He instead draws attention to the depth of certainty, a depth which does not and cannot find its origin in human reason, but which can only come about through the testimony of the Spirit. Bavinck sees such a formulation as clearly and essentially related to the manner in which Paul discusses strength and weakness: the foolish and the weak things of God which are stronger and wiser than men (I Cor. 1:25). Human reason holds them to be madness because they are spiritually discerned (I Cor. 2:14). Bavinck does not by mere technique transpose them into strength and glory; for they are *in reality* "the essence and glory of Christianity."[77] This power is the reverse side of the secret, which is revealed not to the wise and understanding but to babes (Matt. 11:25; cf. 16:17), a secret for which Christ thanked the Father. Bavinck's argument versus Strauss[78] reminds one of the deepest motifs of Luther's *theologia crucis*, when it denies to rational and autonomous man a way to God outside the cross. This apologetic does not therefore glorify a weakness into an ode to uncertainty or a protest against assurance. In a pastoral-theological examination it rather seeks to point out the only way in which an answer is found to the deepest quest for certainty.

The strong language which Bavinck uses to express the confession of the testimony of the Spirit could lead to the understanding that this confession provides us with one simple and sufficient answer to the manifold questions which are so often denoted as "problems regarding Scripture." This is not at all the case. We can instead see that many important questions concerning this confession will continue to engage our attention. For instance, if we take this Reformation confession to definitively exclude every attempt at formalizing and mechanizing the testimony while we focus our attention on the message of Scripture in its peculiar authority, we are directly confronted with the question regarding the subjection of our faith to the entire Bible. How must we

---

[77]Cf. Smit's characterization of Kierkegaard: "Here is an apologetic which need not be ashamed. It does not betray the Christian faith of subjecting it to Reason; instead Reason is brought into subjection and becomes the servant of faith" (p. 39). This certainly cannot be labeled a "technique."

[78]One could question whether Bavinck's answer meets Strauss's criticism *precisely*. The latter saw in this confession an untenable antinomy. Yet it must be granted that Bavinck met it in its very core. By saying that the "preceding demonstration" is not necessary when one is in communion with God, he robs Strauss's contention of its basis. Cf. R. Rothe's *Zur Dogmatik* (Gotha, 1869), pp. 151ff.

consider the testimony of the Spirit when it confronts us with God's message as the message of Holy Scripture? Keeping the concrete Scripture in mind, the holy and canonical books listed in the Belgic Confession, does not our confession of the *testimonium Spiritus Sancti*, despite its focus on the message of Scripture, ultimately lead to an interpretation of this *testimonium* as an autonomous witness to the canonicity of the several books? We are faced with the fact that precisely this question, even though the answer is negative, in turn raises numerous new queries, which have always played a large part in the reflection upon Scripture as the Word of God. How do we go from Article V, in speaking of concrete canonical books "for the regulation, foundation, and confirmation of our faith," to a believing study of God's Word as a prophetic-apostolic witness?

These questions bring us to a new and important aspect of the doctrine of Holy Scripture. It has been the starting point of many discussions and has occupied, especially in our time, a dominant place. We refer to the specific and determined manner in which the church has confessed Holy Scripture as *canon*.

10 THE INSPIRATION AND AUTHORITY OF HOLY SCRIPTURE

H. N. RIDDERBOS

When speaking about the authority of the Scriptures, one must distinguish sharply from the beginning between this authority itself and our *doctrine about* Scripture, its authority, infallibility, and all qualifications and concepts concerning Holy Scripture that have proceeded from theological reflection and discussion over the years. The Bible itself gives no systematic doctrine of its attributes, of the relationship in it of the divine and human. Its point of view is other than that of theology.

This does not mean, of course, that the Bible has nothing to say about its authority and infallibility. The authority of the Scripture is the great presupposition of the whole of the biblical preaching and doctrine. This appears most clearly in the way the New Testament speaks about the Old Testament. That which appears in the Old Testament is cited in the New Testament with formulas like "God says," "the Holy Spirit says," and so on (cf., for instance, Acts 3:24, 25; II Cor. 6:16; Acts 1:16). What "the Scripture says" and what "God says" is the same thing. The Scripture may be personified, as if it were God himself (Gal. 3:8; Rom. 9:17). This "indicates a certain confusion in current speech between 'Scripture' and 'God,' the outgrowth of a deep-seated conviction that the word of Scripture is the Word of God. It was not 'Scripture' that spoke to Pharaoh (Rom. 9:17), or gave his great promise to Abraham (Gal. 3:8), but God. But 'Scripture' and 'God' lay so close together in the minds of the writers of the New Testament that they could naturally speak of 'Scripture' doing what Scripture records God as doing" (B. B. Warfield). And this naturally implies *authority*. "It is written" (Greek, *gegraptai*) in the New Testament puts an end to all contradiction.

This authority of the Scriptures of the Old Testament is no other than that which the apostles ascribe to themselves, namely as heralds, witnesses, ambassadors of God and Christ (Rom.

From Herman N. Ridderbos, Studies in Scripture and its Authority, *pp. 20-36. Copyright © 1978 by Wm. B. Eerdmans Publishing Co.*

1:1, 5; I Tim. 2:7; Gal. 1:8, 9; I Thess. 2:13). They attach that authority in the same manner to their writings as to their words (I Cor. 15:1f.; II Thess. 2:15; 3:14). In the New Testament the apostolic writings are already placed on a par with those of the Old Testament (II Pet. 3:15, 16; Rev. 1:3). *Gegraptai* is already used of the writings of the New Testament (John 20:31). And the New Testament concept of faith is in accord with that: it is *obedience* to the apostolic witness (Rom. 1:5; 16:26; 10:3). This apostolic witness is fundamentally distinguished in this respect from other manifestations of the Spirit, which demand of the congregation (*ekklesia*) not only obedience, but also a critical discernment between the true and the false (cf. I Thess. 5:21; I John 4:1). For this witness deserves unconditional faith and obedience, in its written as well as in its oral form.

Similarly for infallibility. Although, as far as I am aware, the equivalent of our word "infallibility" as attribute of the Scripture is not found in biblical terminology, yet in agreement with Scripture's divine origin and content, great emphasis is repeatedly placed on its *trustworthiness*. The prophetic word is sure (*bebaios*) (II Pet. 1:19). In the Pastoral Epistles Paul does not tire of assuring his readers that the word he has handed down is trustworthy (*pistos*) and worthy of full acceptance (I Tim. 1:15; 3:1; 4:9; II Tim. 2:11; Titus 3:8). In Hebrews 2:3 the author writes that salvation was declared at first by the Lord and it was attested (made *bebaios*) to us by those who heard him. While it must be said of man that "all flesh is grass," it is true of the word of God that "it abides forever." And "that word is the good news, *which was preached to you*" (I Pet. 1:24, 25).

The abiding and trustworthy word of God has thus entered into the spoken and written word of the apostles. As Luke tells Theophilus, the tradition of what was heard and seen by those who were from the beginning eyewitnesses and ministers of the word has been written down so that he might recognize the trustworthiness (*asphaleia*) of that of which he has been informed (Luke 1:1–4). The whole of Scripture is full of declarations that the one who builds on the word and promise of God will not be ashamed (Isa. 28:16; Rom. 9:33; I Pet. 2:6); this applies to the spoken as well as to the written word of the apostles (John 19:35; 20:31; I John 1:1–3). The Scripture is infallible, so we may summarize, because it does not fail, because it has the significance of a foundation on which the *ekklesia* has been established and on which it must increasingly establish itself (Col. 2:6, 7). The whole concept of *tradition*, as it is used by Paul, for example, has this connotation of authority, certainty, irrefutability. Protestants thus do well not to give up this concept out of reaction against its use in Roman Catholicism. The authority and infallibility of the Scriptures are thus two sides of the same coin; namely, that the Scripture is of God.

The second thing we have to observe from the beginning is that all attributes which the Scripture ascribes to itself stand in close relationship to its purpose and nature. And so our way of thinking about Scripture and our theological definitions must also be related to this purpose.

It is obvious that Scripture is given us for a definite purpose. Paul says that it "was written for our instruction, that by steadfastness and by the encouragement of the scriptures we might have hope" (Rom. 15:4). The famous pronouncement of II Timothy 3:15–16 is to the same effect: the sacred writings "are able to instruct you for salvation through faith in Christ Jesus." Not only are the nature and force of the Scriptures to be found in their providing instruction for salvation, so are the means and key for understanding them — faith in Jesus Christ. Only by the light of such faith is the treasure of wisdom and knowledge of the Scriptures unlocked.

This purpose of Scripture (of the Old Testament as well as the New) and the use which corresponds to it must always be borne in mind when framing a theological definition of the attributes of the Scripture. That is the thrust of Calvin's comment on II Timothy 3:15: "In order that it may be profitable to salvation to us, we have to learn to make right use of it. . . . He has good reason to recall us to the faith of Christ, which is the center and sum of Scripture." What follows in verse 16 is in complete accord with this: "All Scripture is inspired by God" — and the predicative significance of *theopneustos* is not in my opinion disputable — "and profitable for teaching, for reproof, for correction and for training in righteousness." The purpose and the nature of Scripture lie thus in that qualified sort of teaching and instruction which is able to make us wise to salvation, which gives God's people this "completeness" and equips them for every good work.

That we cannot speak about Scripture and its qualities apart from this scope, purpose, and nature should also be the point of departure of every theological evaluation and definition of biblical authority. This authority is not to be separated from the content and purpose of Scripture thus qualified, nor can it be recognized apart from this content and the specific character of the Scripture. No matter to what extent we reject the dualistic doctrine of inspiration, which holds that only the religious-ethical sections of Scripture are inspired and authoritative, this does not remove the fact that, in Herman Bavinck's words, "Holy Scripture has a thoroughly religious-ethical purpose (designation, intention) and is not intended to be a handbook for the various sciences." We may not apply to Scripture standards which do not suit it. Not only does it give no exact knowledge of mathematics or biology, but it also presents no history of Israel or biography of Jesus that accords with the standards of historical science. Therefore, one must not transfer biblical authority.

God speaks to us through the Scriptures not in order to make us scholars, but to make us Christians. To be sure, to make us Christians in our science, too, but not in such a way as to make human science superfluous or to teach us in a supernatural way all sorts of things that could and would otherwise be learned by scientific training and research.

What Scripture does intend is to place us as humans in a right position to God, even in our scientific studies and efforts. Scripture is not concerned only with persons' *religious* needs in a pietistic or existentialistic sense of that word. On the contrary, its purpose and authority is that it teaches us to understand everything *sub specie Dei* — humanity, the world, nature, history, their origin and their destination, their past and their future. Therefore the Bible is not only the book of conversion, but also the book of history and the book of creation. But it is the book of history of salvation; and it is this point of view that represents and defines the authority of Scripture.

But when one connects the theological definition of authority and infallibility as attributes of Scripture so closely with Scripture's purpose and nature, does one not run the danger of falling into a kind of subjectivism? Who will establish precisely the boundaries between that which does and that which does not pertain to the purpose of the Scripture? And is the way not thus opened for subjectivism and arbitrariness in the matter of the authority of the Scripture, as has been so detrimental to the authority of the Scripture in the history of the church? I should like in this connection to point out the following:

First, the misuse of the Scripture does not abolish the good and correct use. The Scripture is not a book of separate divine oracles, but is from Genesis to Revelation an organic unity, insofar as it is the book of the history of God's redeeming and judging acts, of which the advent and work of Christ is the all-dominating center and focus. The testimony of Jesus is the spirit of prophecy (Rev. 19:10), and Scripture has the power to save by faith in Christ Jesus (II Tim. 3:15). This is the center to which everything in Scripture stands in relationship and through which it is bound together — beginning and end, creation and re-creation, humanity, the world, history, and the future, as all of these have a place in the Scripture. Therefore, there is also a correlation between Scripture and faith, namely, as faith in Jesus Christ. If you take that unity away from Scripture and this correlation of Scripture and faith, you denature Scripture and faith in it; and the authority and infallibility of the Scripture also lose their theological-christological definition and become formal concepts, abstracted from the peculiar nature and content of Scripture.

But in the second place, that does not mean we are permitted to apply all sorts of dualistic operations on Scripture and make distinctions between what is and what is not inspired, what is and what is not from God — to say, for instance, that the content but not the form, or the essence but not the word, was subject to the might and inspiration and authority of God. God gave us the Scripture in this concrete form, in these words and languages. The confession applies to this, and not to specific sections or thoughts, that it is the inspired word of God, that it is given to us as the infallible guide to life, God's light on our path, God's lamp for our feet. But divine inspiration does not necessarily mean that the men who spoke and wrote under inspiration were temporarily stripped of their limitations in knowledge, memory, language, and capability of expressing themselves, as specific human beings in a certain period of history.

We have to be very careful, I think, not to operate as though we know ahead of time to what extent divine inspiration does or does not go together with the human limitations mentioned above. Inspiration does not mean deification. We cannot say everything of Scripture that we say of the word of God, nor can we identify the apostles and prophets during their writing with the Holy Spirit. The word of God exists in eternity, is perfect. But Scripture is neither eternal nor perfect. Inspiration consists in this, that God makes the words for his divine purposes. As such the human words stand in the service of God and participate in the authority and infallibility of the word of God, answer perfectly God's purpose, in short, function as the word of God and therefore can be so called. And it is not up to us; it is up to the free pleasure of God to decide what kind of effect divine inspiration should have in the mind, knowledge, memory, accuracy of those whom he has used in his service, in order that their word really can be accepted and trusted as the inspired word of God. If we deny or ignore this, we dispose of the very nature of the Scriptures as the word of God, and also of the nature of his authority and infallibility. The best way not to fall into such a danger is to study Scripture itself from this point of view.

* * *

In order not to get bogged down in generalities and abstractions I will demonstrate what I mean with a number of examples from the Bible itself.

One of the proofs that the authority and infallibility of the Scripture are to be understood in a qualified sense is the way the Synoptic Gospels present the same material with several different arrangements, sequences, and expressions. Undoubtedly the total picture that these evangelists draw of Jesus is entirely the same, not only in its totality but also in many details. Therefore, when we read the gospels one after another (in the manner and with the intention with which the church may and must read them), nobody will have for even an instant the impression that the Christ of the one gospel is a different one in comparison with the image of Christ in another gospel.

Yet this does not mean that there are no differences in historical details, or in the tendency of two or three evangelists' telling the same story, or in the reproduction of the same words and deeds of Jesus, or in the presentation and interpretation of the good news as a whole. Nor are those differences limited to little details, which one can easily neglect or dismiss. Compare, for instance, the Lord's Prayer in Matthew and Luke. It is apparent that Luke, in addition to recording a shorter address of God, lacks the third petition entirely and for the last petition has only "Lead us not into temptation."

Now, one might suggest that Jesus gave his disciples the Lord's Prayer on two different occasions in two different formulations, thus tracing differences between Matthew and Luke back to Jesus himself and not to the recording of the evangelists. No one can prove that this is impossible. But it is quite another thing to assert that Jesus himself *must* have given the Lord's Prayer twice, in two different forms, or that otherwise the inspiration and infallibility of Scripture have failed. One must be able to realize that on one and the same occasion spoken words of Jesus were recorded in different ways and that often it cannot possibly be established which is the historically exact reproduction. For even if you hesitate about whether the Lord's Prayer was given on one or two occasions (a matter, Calvin says, "about which I will be at odds with no one"), nevertheless, you cannot do this with regard to certain other words of Jesus. The beatitudes of Matthew differ considerably from those of Luke, although surely no one any longer would be willing to accept two Sermons on the

Mount. And the record of the institution of the Lord's supper, while in the substance of the matter much the same, displays, in the tradition of Matthew and Mark on the one side and that of Luke and Paul on the other, various more or less interesting and important differences.

All this has yet nothing to do with *essential* trustworthiness or infallibility. For the gospels, as the basis on which Christ builds his *ekklesia*, all these differences in tradition regarding the Lord's Prayer, the Beatitudes, the words of the Lord's supper, constitute no problem. But if one attempts to design a doctrine concerning Holy Scripture, he must surely not lose sight of this freedom and difference of presentation. One cannot postulate on the basis that the books of the New Testament are God-breathed that "every word then must precisely reproduce the historical situation, for otherwise the Scripture would not be 'infallible.' " The fact is that the infallibility of Scripture has in many respects a character other than that which a theoretical concept of inspiration or infallibility, detached from its purpose and empirical reality, would like to demand. One must be careful when reasoning about what is and what is not possible under inspiration by God. Here too the freedom of the Spirit must be honored; and we shall first have to trace the courses of the Spirit in reverence, rather than come at once to overconfident pronouncements, however proper our intentions.

To mention another, slightly different example which casts light on this so-called organic character: we see occasionally that one evangelist purposely introduces changes into what another has written, sometimes, apparently, in order to correct him. Though there is no absolute certainty about the mutual relationship of Matthew, Mark, and Luke, there is a probability bordering on certainty that Mark was the first to write his gospel and that Matthew and Luke constructed theirs on the basis of Mark's. In Matthew, in any case, we observe a clear systematizing of material which in Mark lies scattered far apart. This indicates a different design and development of common material. It does not necessarily imply that the one is "better" than the other, but does indeed point again to the elbow-room allowed the evangelists in their presentation of the same message.

Occasionally, this leads to remarkable results. In the story of the rich young ruler Jesus says, according to Mark 10:18, "Why do you call me good? No one is good but God alone." In Matthew 19:17, however, we read the same material (from Mark) this way: "Why do you ask me about what is good? One there is who is good." It is possible that there are two traditions here, but one must also take into account the possibility that Matthew expressed in somewhat different words the material used by Mark to avoid the implication that Jesus should not have considered himself "good." This is not to say that Mark indeed meant that, only that Matthew wished to safeguard against a misunderstanding of the version which we meet in Mark.

This remarkable difference between the two furnishes no difficulty whatever for the essential authority of the gospel, but it does enable us to see that a doctrine of "verbal inspiration" which aims at closing off discussion of the historical precision and accuracy of every word in the Bible is exceeding its area of competence. That is not to say that therefore there is inspiration only in respect of the matter and not the word: such a distinction is much too mechanical. But it is indeed to say that inspiration is something other than an elimination of human freedom and human limitation. The Spirit certainly takes care that the church not suffer deficiency and that it may believe and preach on the basis of the *written* word. But the way down which the Spirit travels and the liberty he grants himself and the writers of the Bible are not capable of being expressed in one neat dogmatic formula. It is the liberty of the Spirit; we must approach it with respect and discuss it in our theological statements with caution.

That we must not form an abstract theological concept of the inspiration and authority of the Scripture but instead pay heed to how the writers of the Bible went about their work also appears from another phenomenon that strikes us again and again in the study of the Bible. Although the biblical writers were equipped by the Holy Spirit for the task they had to fulfil in the service of God's special revelation for all times and generations, they were nevertheless in many respects entirely children of their own time; and to this extent they thought and wrote and narrated just as their contemporaries thought and wrote and narrated. This is true not only of the languages in which they wrote, which have become dead languages, but also of their concepts, their ideas, their manner of expression, their methods of communication. All these were in a sense conditioned in various ways by the time and milieu in which they lived. And it cannot be said of all these concepts and ideas that because they have received a place in the Bible, they have also received the significance of infallible revelation.

However difficult — even dangerous — it may be to operate with this form-content schema, no one must be under the illusion that he can avoid it in the theological exegesis and explanation of the message of the Bible. Everything depends on how and why such

a schema is used. Whenever it is used in the service of a naturalistic and evolutionary world view, it is a destructive instrument,
a dissecting knife, which cuts the Scripture off from the roots that
give it life and makes it just another remnant of the ancient Near
Eastern or hellenistic spirit. More than once it has been treated
precisely that way; so it is no wonder that the evangelical view
of Scripture listens with extreme suspicion, raised eyebrows, and
heightened vigilance when modern scholars apply this form-
content schema, these accommodation theories, to the Bible.

But there is another side to the matter. From the standpoint
of faith, the nature of the Scripture and its authority can surely
be more sharply, clearly, and precisely distinguished when we
see the Bible against the background and in the light of the time
in which it was written. Then we come to see on the one hand
the incomparable otherness of Scripture and on the other that
which is bound up with and limited to the time.

In this connection mention is often made of the influence the
ancient Near Eastern conception of the universe had on how the
biblical writers thought and expressed themselves. Some have
wanted to deny this influence by saying that these authors spoke
of such things just as we do in everyday life when we speak of
"sunrise" and the like. But it is surely difficult to maintain this.
If there are said to be three stories in the universe, as for example
in Exodus 20 and still in Philippians 2 (heaven, earth, and that
which is under the earth), this is positively not a scientific, but
still a traditional, generally current representation of the structure of the universe. We can hardly think in such terms anymore.
We can no longer think so "massively" of heaven and so spatially
of the ascension as was possible in the representations of the
biblical writers. It is clear that the "translation" of *this* confronts
us with much greater problems than does the translation of the
Old and New Testaments into a modern language, but this does
not take away the fact that in this respect the Scripture speaks
in images and concepts, exhibiting the stamp and also the relativity of the time in which they were current.

In another respect, too, it is clear that the writers of the Bible
associated themselves with what, by virtue of education or tradition, pertained to the manner of speaking and thinking of their
contemporaries, without enabling one thus to say that since this
or that idea or expression finds a place in the Bible, it thereby
becomes "revelation." This is the more obvious because the content of the Bible doubtless signals a radical breakthrough into all
sorts of contemporary convictions and traditions. To take one
prominent example, Paul's preaching is a continuous antithesis

to the Jewish synagogal schema of redemption. In this fundamental sense Paul is the apostle of Christ and one inspired by
the Spirit. But this does not remove the fact that this same apostle
still betrays some traces of his rabbinical education, for example
in the manner in which he debates, uses rabbinical argumentation and traditional materials, cites the Old Testament.

Certainly even in this "formal" sense the difference between
Paul and the synagogue is greater than the conformity between
them; and the message of Christ signifies in his disciples, too, a
clearing away and purging of all kinds of subtle and casuistical
rabbinical lore. But in some respects the Jewishness and the rabbinical background of New Testament writings are clear enough.
If the second letter to Timothy speaks of Jannes and Jambres as
men who withstood Moses, we cannot recognize in them the
Egyptian magicians of the court of Pharaoh, until we come across
these same names in certain late Jewish writings with a plain
reference to those magicians. Elsewhere, when Paul speaks of the
mediation of angels in giving the law on Sinai (Gal. 3:19), or
when, wishing to indicate Christ's exaltation above all other spiritual powers, he lists a whole series of kinds of angels (Col. 1:16);
or says that the promise was given 430 years before the law (Gal.
3:17) — these are all expressions whose background we are not
able to find in the Old Testament or elsewhere in the New Testament, but which only become clear to us from the late Jewish
writings. How must we now view this? Must we say that because
Paul, the apostle of Christ, who was led by the Spirit, calls the
magicians of Pharaoh Jannes and Jambres, these must have been
their real names? Although there may have been those in times
past who would have answered this affirmatively, it would not
be easy to mention anyone who takes this standpoint today, at
least among those aware of the way these names were probably
brought into vogue in Jewish literature.

Now, of course, the concrete significance of this last example
is particularly slight. From the point of view of faith no one is
interested in the names of Pharaoh's magicians. Nevertheless, as
an example, this case of Jannes and Jambres is not without importance. It lets us see that inspiration can also mean connection
with certain Jewish or non-Christian elements, without these elements at the same time being brought under the sanction of
inspiration and thus belonging to the normative character of the
Scripture.

More is at stake here than a name or a number, as anyone
realizes who has been confronted by these things in his investigation of the Scripture. The nonscholarly reader of the Bible can

understand this, too. This has to do with literary genres, with methods of writing history, with the sometimes fluid boundaries of a parabolic narrative and a historical narrative. When in the Book of Job a marvelous dialogue between Job and his friends is presented in artistic language, everyone can grasp that this is not a stenographic transcription of a number of improvised speeches which an afflicted man and his friends, who had been sitting in ashes silently for seven days and nights, uttered one after another, but rather that here the problem of theodicy, of "justifying God's ways to man," is posed and treated in a dramatic fashion. And when Matthew's genealogy of Jesus is formulated in a series of three sets of fourteen names, one can by comparing this with the data of the Old Testament, which include more names in the same line of descent, come to no other conclusion than that the evangelist has either deliberately "stylized" this himself or has used an already existing stylizing. It will not do to say, "It does not tally," or something like that. One must come to appreciate that there is a difference between our exact Western spirit and the spirit of someone two thousand years ago who, in other circumstances and with other objects in view, recorded his vision of history.

In this same genealogy of Matthew there are more proofs of this. However, our concern here is not with further details but with an overall approach to these things which does as much justice as possible to the particular nature of Scripture and its authority. In this approach we must always be aware that we are dealing with the Scripture as the word of God. So, it would be a denial of the very nature of Scripture if, in view of what we have been discussing here, we were to acknowledge Scripture as only a human attempt to give expression to and interpretation of what some human writers long ago might, by way of their belief, have understood of the word of God; and, in addition, we would consider that our engagement to the Bible would consist only in having to do the same thing as they did: staying in the line of their tradition and passing on what they understood of the word of God, in our language, way of thinking, and by our means of interpretation.

I say this would be perversion of the nature of Scripture. For what we are confronted with in Scripture is not just human beings in their human faith and human efforts to witness to what they understood of God's revelation; it is God *himself*, addressing himself to us by men. This is a real and essential difference, for it is the difference of the real subject and author of Scripture. But at the same time we must always be aware that it is God's speaking his condescension to men, wonderfully adjusting himself to human language and human possibilities of understanding. Therefore what is presented to us in Scripture will always be a matter for listening to in submission to God's divine authority. It may never become a matter of "one's own interpretation" (new in every age), because no prophecy ever came by the impulse of man, but men moved by the Holy Spirit spoke from God (II Pet. 1:20, 21). And at the same time listening to Scripture is listening to a human language, human concepts, human images, which we have to translate, in more than one respect, in order to understand what God is saying to us in and by means of Scripture.

* * *

Let us try to come to a conclusion.

To attempt a theological definition of the Scripture is no easy matter. This results from its unique origin and character. All Scripture is God-breathed. Therefore all our human definitions will remain inadequate. Just because it is divine, it arises above our knowledge, and we shall never fully realize "what is the breadth and length and height and depth" (Eph. 3:18). This applies also to its authority and infallibility. Its authority is much greater than we are able to express in human words. But at the same time we have to acknowledge that this word of God has entered so very much into the human and has so identified itself with it that we shall always again stand before the question as to what the unassailably divine and what the relativity of the human in Scripture mean concretely. We stand before a very deep and mysterious task, transferring thoughts from the life and the world of persons of two thousand years ago and more to the world of today. Here lies the great question of hermeneutics, with which many today are engaged very intensively.

Nevertheless, it remains true that Scripture and its authority, in the most profound and central sense of the word, is not obscure but clear, namely, in the manner in which it teaches persons to understand themselves, the world, history, and the future in the light of the God and Father of Jesus Christ. It is on account of this clarity of the Scripture that it is an everflowing well of knowledge and life and that it teaches wisdom to the simple. And it is on account of this clarity and this purpose of the Scripture that it can be identified with the word of God, that it has unconditional authority, and that it is the infallible foundation for faith.

Finally I should like to say a couple things in response to the claim that the intricate way theology speaks about the authority and infallibility of the Scripture lacks the power and simplicity of a less complicated, more "naive" approach. First, when new light is cast on the Scripture, also through the investigations of historical science, the church has to rejoice, even though this may compel it at the same time to be ready to reconsider and redefine theological concepts related to Scripture.

In the second place, remember that just those who have occasion to come to a more historical approach to the Bible and its authority will be able along the way to understand the unique and incomparable significance of Scripture. The world of the ancient Near East is being increasingly opened to us. We are discovering very ancient "literature" in which the religious feelings of people who were contemporaries of the biblical writers are expressed. There is increasing Jewish background through the Talmud and through insights into the radical movements in the Judaism of Jesus' time through the discovery of the Qumran writings. Of more recent date still is the discovery in Egypt of an entire library of gnostic literature from the second century.

All of this teaches us more strongly than ever to be mindful of the relationship between Scripture and the world out of which it arose. At once we see a striking establishment of the historical correctness of the biblical data and then again are placed before questions in which we cannot always see a priori that "the Bible is right." But something else is far more important: namely, that there is nothing that more clearly brings to the light the unique character of the Scriptures than the qualitative comparison between that which here and that which there steps out to meet us. That difference does not lie in a more advanced human development, or greater accuracy, or another manner of tradition. It inheres in what we have again and again described as the purpose and the qualitative content of the Scripture. On the one side we find legalistic scrupulousness, flight into the speculative, invincible fear of death. On the other side, in the Scripture of the Old and New Testaments, we see a qualitatively different knowledge of God and of nature, faith in forgiveness, the conquest of death, dying with Christ to that which Paul describes as the weak and poor principles of the world.

The difference is not easy to put into words. The expression in one of the Reformation confessions from the sixteenth century is not too strong or too naive: the Scriptures "carry the evidence in themselves" of their divinity and authority (Belgic Confession, V). For where the testimony of Christ appears, there not only does the light arise, but also the darkness is illuminated; as it is said of Jesus, he spoke with authority and not as the scribes did. This is not to imply that the *doctrine concerning* the Holy Scriptures has become a simple matter. But in the light of *this* authority, we can overcome the fear that we may be on a dangerous pathway if we view the ways of the Spirit in recording the word of God more historically, more critically, as more shaded than along the way of an exclusively dogmatic reasoning.

We shall come to stand before more questions, perhaps before more questions without answers. That is the lot of everyone who will gather science to himself: he gathers grief, too. But at the same time, the light that shines in the darkness is so clear and so bright that not only the prophet but even the far more skeptical theologian has to confess, "I have seen a limit to all perfection, but thy commandment is exceedingly broad" (Ps. 119:96).

11 THE CHURCH DOCTRINE OF BIBLICAL AUTHORITY

JACK B. ROGERS

Evangelicals believe that the Bible is the authoritative Word of God. On two closely related questions there is significant disagreement: (1) what is the nature of the Bible's authority? and (2) how is that authority known and accepted? This chapter will examine those two questions at several significant points in the history of the church. If we can discover any patterns on which there is consensus in the church, it may give us perspective on some of our contemporary controversies.

For the earliest Christians the biblical writings were linked to the work of the Holy Spirit in bearing witness to the Savior, Jesus Christ.[1] Jesus said regarding the Old Testament writings, "It is they that bear witness to me" (John 5:39). The central purpose of the New Testament writings, according to the apostle John, was that people might know Christ savingly: "But these are written that you may believe that Jesus is the Christ, the Son of God, and that believing you may have life in his name" (John 20:31).

The first written source of saving knowledge for the early church was the Old Testament. By understanding Jesus as the fulfillment of messianic prophecy the Old Testament became a Christian book. Most early Christians did not read the Old Testament in Hebrew, but in a Greek translation, the Septuagint. It likely included a group of books which Protestants now exclude called the Apocrypha.[2] The canon, setting the limits of the New Testament, was not officially fixed by the church until late in the fourth century. But all of the materials we have in our New Testament seem to have been in general circulation and acceptance by A.D. 200.[3]

---

[1]John 14:26. See Geoffrey W. Bromiley, "The Church Doctrine of Inspiration," *Revelation and the Bible*, ed. Carl F. H. Henry (Grand Rapids, 1958), p. 205. This article is perhaps still the best brief overview of the history of the doctrine of inspiration.

[2]J. N. D. Kelly, *Early Christian Doctrines* (New York, 1960), pp. 52–53.

[3]Bernhard Lohse, *A Short History of Christian Doctrine*, trans. F. Ernest Stoeffler (Philadelphia, 1966), p. 28.

Gradually, the early church had a variety of sources of authority and guidance. It had a body of "teaching" — its history, interpretations of past events and actions, and eventually some creeds. But central for the church was the Bible, containing what had been expressly revealed by God to bring people to salvation and to guide their life of faith. Problems arose when differing individuals or groups used variant texts of Scripture to support their particular "teaching" on certain issues.[4]

Most of the early church was part of a Greek world culture. Christians were influenced by that culture and in turn wished to influence it. They wanted to make Christianity acceptable by putting the Christian message into Greek concepts which educated persons would adopt. Two main schools of thought had been inherited by early Christian culture from the "classical" period of Greek philosophy in the third century before Christ. They were the schools of Plato and Aristotle.

For our purposes we may use the names Platonic and Aristotelian to designate two schools of thought, each of which had significant impact on Christian theology. The Platonic school assumed that the knowledge of great truths, like God as Creator, was born into every person. Knowledge of particular things in this world was known by deduction from those general principles. When applied to theology, the Platonic method assumed that faith preceded and provided a framework to make possible right reasoning.

The Aristotelian school took the opposite view. We are born with blank minds but a capacity for reasoning. All knowledge begins from sense experience of things in the world. We come to general principles by induction from a number of particulars. When applied to theology, the Aristotelian method assumed that reason, based on the evidence of senses, must precede and would lead to faith.

Educated Christians in the first centuries of the Christian era were influenced by these philosophical schools and their offshoots. Platonic influences dominated. In part this was because philosophical speculation in the second century A.D. was largely directed to the problem of Providence. Platonists defended Prov-

---

[4] I am indebted throughout this article to Donald K. McKim for his collaboration. He has shared his insights and much unpublished research material, in this case a paper entitled "The Doctrine of Scripture in Origen and Its Use in the Commentary on John" (1972). See R. P. C. Hanson, *Origen's Doctrine of Tradition* (London, 1954), p. 33.

idence. Aristotelians were regarded as atheists because they denied Providence and the immortality of the soul.[5]

ORIGEN

A man who exemplified the blending of Platonic philosophy and biblical thought was Origen of Alexandria (c. A.D. 186–255), the most influential father of the early church. Origen has been called the first great preacher, devotional writer, biblical commentator, and systematic theologian of Christianity.[6]

The Bible was authoritative for Origen. The Scriptures were "sacred books," "holy documents,"[7] without which we could have no clear knowledge of God. The Scriptures of the Old and New Testaments had an "inseparable unity."[8] The Bible was harmonious throughout and "supernaturally perfect in every particular."[9]

At the same time, Origen was very conscious of the human character of the holy writings. He knew that the New Testament was not written in the best Greek. But to him, that was unimportant because the revelation did not consist in the words but in the things revealed.[10] Indeed, for Origen, the very reason that human beings could know the revelation of God is that God had "condescended" or "accommodated" himself to our human ways of communicating and understanding. According to Origen:

> He condescends and lowers himself, accommodating himself to our weakness like a school master talking "little language" to his children, like a Father caring for his own children and adopting their ways.[11]

Scripture was the work of a single divine author who adjusted himself to human thought in order that his saving message might be understood.[12]

The great preacher John Chrysostom (A.D.347?–407) also held to the principle of accommodation. Chrysostom said:

[5]Jean Danielou, *Origen*, trans. Walter Mitchell (New York, 1955), pp. 74, 80.
[6]Charles Bigg, *The Christian Platonists of Alexandria* (Oxford, 1886), p. 155.
[7]Origen, "De Principiis," trans. F. Crombie, *The Ante-Nicene Fathers*, Vol. IV, ed. Alexander Roberts and James Donaldson (Buffalo, 1885; American reprint of the Edinburgh edition), IV, 9; IV, 8, pp. 356–57.
[8]R. P. C. Hanson, *Allegory and Event* (Richmond, 1959), pp. 198ff.
[9]F. W. Farrar, *History of Interpretation* (New York, 1886), p. 190.
[10]Farrar, p. 190.
[11]Hanson, *Allegory*, p. 226.
[12]Bruce Vawter, *Biblical Inspiration* (Philadelphia, 1972), p. 40.

Christ often checked himself for the sake of the weakness of his hearers when he dealt with lofty doctrines and that he usually did not choose words as were in accord with his glory, but rather those which agreed with the capability of men.[13]

AUGUSTINE

Augustine (A.D. 354–430) served as a link between the ancient church and the Middle Ages. He spoke Latin, not Greek, and was a teacher of rhetoric. His early life is generally well known including the fact that he had dabbled in many religions and philosophies before coming to Christianity.

Preparatory to his conversion to Christianity was a conversion to neo-Platonism. Augustine joined a group of young intellectuals in Milan who were neo-Platonists. With them he heard the preaching of Bishop Ambrose whose sermons were often a synthesis of Scripture and neo-Platonic ideas.[14]

The integration of biblical data and Platonic philosophy can be seen in the famous maxim of Augustine's theological method: "I believe in order that I may understand." The biblical foundation came from the Septuagint translation of Isaiah 7:9: "Unless you believe, you shall not understand." The philosophical foundation was the Platonic concept of innate first principles which enable us to make sense out of particulars. "No one," prayed Augustine, "can call upon Thee without knowing Thee."[15] In "matters of great importance, pertaining to divinity," Augustine declared, "we must first believe before we seek to know."[16]

Almost everyone wants to claim Augustine—Protestants and Roman Catholics, Platonists and even some Aristotelians. There are two citations in Augustine's works which speak of the priority of reason. In these Augustine was presupposing man's capacity for thought. But there are no passages in Augustine's writings where he puts reason before faith as a method of knowing God.[17] Augustine asserted: "But, if they say that we are not even to believe in Christ, unless they can give a reason that cannot be doubted, then they are not Christians."[18]

---

[13]Cited in G. C. Berkouwer, *Holy Scripture*, trans. Jack B. Rogers (Grand Rapids, 1975), pp. 175–76.

[14]Peter Brown, *Augustine of Hippo* (London, 1967), pp. 91–95.

[15]Cited in John E. Smith, *The Analogy of Experience* (New York, 1973), p. 8.

[16]Cited in Robert F. Davidson, ed., *The Search for Meaning in Life* (New York, 1962), p. 292.

[17]Smith, pp. 9–10.

[18]Cited in E. L. Miller, ed., *Classical Statements on Faith and Reason* (New York, 1970), p. 36.

Augustine's understanding of the authority of the Bible flowed from his general method, "I believe in order to understand." Scripture was a divine unity for Augustine. No discordancy of any kind was permitted to exist.[19] Augustine had several ways of handling apparent disharmonies. He claimed variously that the manuscript was faulty, that the translation was wrong, or that the reader had not properly understood.[20] When none of these answers seemed appropriate, Augustine sometimes concluded that the Holy Spirit had "permitted" one of the Scripture writers to compose something at variance from what another biblical author had written. For Augustine, these variances were meant to whet our spiritual appetite for understanding.[21]

Variant readings were not an ultimate problem for Augustine because the truth of Scripture resided ultimately in the thought of the biblical writers and not in their individual words. Augustine commented, "In any man's words the thing which we ought narrowly to regard is only the writer's thought which was meant to be expressed, and to which the words ought to be subservient."[22] To keep to the thoughts and intentions of the biblical writers we must, according to Augustine, remember that their purpose was to bring us, not information in general, but the good news of salvation. For Augustine, Scripture was not a textbook of science, or an academic tract, but the Book of life, written in the language of life. When Felix the Manichean claimed that the Holy Spirit had revealed to Manicheus the orbits of the heavenly bodies, Augustine replied that God desired us to become Christians, not astronomers. Such talk, Augustine said,

> takes up much of our valuable time and thus distracts our attention from more wholesome matters. Although our authors knew the truth about the shape of the heavens, the Spirit of God who spoke by them did not intend to teach men these things, in no way profitable for salvation.[23]

Augustine followed Origen and Chrysostom in accepting the notion that God accommodated himself to fit our abilities. Augustine spoke about "the Holy Scripture, which suits itself to babes."[24] Commenting on the Apostle John, Augustine said:

[19]Vawter, p. 33.

[20]R. M. Grant, *The Letter and the Spirit* (London, 1957), p. 108.

[21]Vawter, pp. 38–39.

[22]Cited in A. D. R. Polman, *The Word of God According to St. Augustine*, trans. A. J. Pomerans (Grand Rapids, 1961), p. 49.

[23]Polman, pp. 59–60.

[24]Ibid., p. 57.

I venture to say, brethren, that not even John himself has presented these things just as they are, but only as best he could, since he was a man who spoke of God—inspired, of course, but still a man. Because he was inspired he was able to say something; but because he who was inspired remained a man, he could not present the full reality, but only what a man could say about it.[25]

THE MIDDLE AGES

Scholasticism, the work of the School Men, was the medieval attempt to harmonize faith and reason. John Scotus Erigena (d. 895) is generally credited with laying the foundation for the medieval synthesis. He said, "Reason and authority come alike from the one source of divine wisdom, and cannot contradict each other. Reason is not to be overruled by authority but the reverse."[26] This putting of reason over faith began a movement which culminated in a decisive philosophical shift in the high Middle Ages. Platonic thought was replaced by Aristotelian reasoning as the basis for theological work.

In the thirteenth century Albertus Magnus determined to make all of a newly rediscovered body of Aristotelian work available by making a philosophical and theological commentary on it. Among Albert's pupils in both Paris and Cologne was a young Dominican monk named Thomas Aquinas. Partly in response to the intellectual, political, and military pressure on Europe from the Arabs, Thomas sought common ground with them by using Aristotle, whom the Arabs accepted, to create a comprehensive and systematic philosophical theology.

For Augustine, following Plato, God was known by a divine illumination of the mind, in a very different way from that in which the world was known by the senses. For Thomas, following Aristotle, all knowledge came from the same source—reason based on the data of our sense experience. Thomas declared, "Beginning with sensible things our intellect is led to the point of knowing about God that He exists."[27] Thomas therefore developed five proofs for the existence of God using reason based on our sense experience. The Thomistic arguments were designed to be persuasive to pagans, Arabs, and Christians.

[25]Augustin Bea, *The Study of the Synoptic Gospels*, ed. Joseph A. Fitzmyer (ET New York, 1965), p. 59.

[26]Cited in Raymond Larry Shelton, "Martin Luther's Concept of Biblical Interpretation in Historical Perspective" (Ph.D. diss., Fuller Theological Seminary, 1974), p. 109.

[27]Miller, p. 41.

CHURCH DOCTRINE OF BIBLICAL AUTHORITY

Certain truths, such as the Trinity, exceeded the ability of reason to know them. But reason, according to Thomas, could bring men to the point where such scriptural truths would be accepted on the authority of the church. Theology now moved away from exegesis and became more closely aligned with philosophy.

The medieval synthesis of reason and faith, of Aristotelian philosophy and scriptural teaching, began to break up in the fourteenth century. Reason was separated from faith by the Nominalists, so called because philosophy, they felt, only arbitrarily gave names to things.

Two British Franciscans, John Duns Scotus (d. 1308) and his pupil, William of Occam (d. 1349), turned away from Aristotle to the older Platonic Augustinian thought and criticized Thomism. Science and theology were separate realms. It was impossible to prove theological doctrines rationally. Since Occam had deep reservations about the authority of the corrupt papacy he observed, he proclaimed the revelation of God in the Bible as the authoritative basis for faith. The Scripture was true for Occam, because inspired by the Holy Spirit.[28]

Occam's follower Gabriel Biel (d. 1495) taught Nominalism in Germany at Tübingen. Martin Luther's philosophy professors at Erfurt were Occamists, and his first theology professors were followers of Biel. Luther, in turn, called Occam "beloved master" and "the most eminent and the most brilliant of the Scholastic doctors."[29] Even after Luther turned against nominalist theology, he retained his respect for the antischolastic Occamist philosophy.

LUTHER

Luther was an Augustinian monk at home in the neo-Platonic philosophical milieu of Augustinianism which put faith before reason. Luther said that he learned more from Augustine and the Bible than all other books.[30] His understanding of Scripture followed in that tradition. Luther said:

> For Isaiah vii makes reason subject to faith, when it says: "except ye believe, ye shall not have understanding or reason." It does not say, "Except you have reason ye shall not believe."[31]

[28]Otto W. Heick, *A History of Christian Thought*, Vol. 1 (Philadelphia, 1965), pp. 300–303.

[29]Shelton, p. 147.

[30]Ibid., pp. 120–21.

[31]Cited in Hugh Thompson Kerr, Jr., ed., *A Compend of Luther's Theology* (Philadelphia, 1943), p. 4.

For Luther, "in spiritual matters, human reasoning certainly is not in order."[32]

Most important of all was Luther's motivation for turning to Scripture—his personal search for salvation. Luther's question was: How may I find a gracious God? In the Bible Luther found a God who justified the ungodly. The purpose of Scripture was to speak to us of personal salvation. The subject matter of Scripture by which all its parts were rightly interpreted was Christ as Savior. Luther proclaimed:

> The Gospel, then, is nothing but the preaching about Christ, Son of God and of David, true God and man, who by His death and resurrection has overcome all men's sin, and death and hell for us who believe in Him.[33]

For Luther, the inner testimony of the Holy Spirit testified to Christ and thus gave authority to the Word. Luther asked:

> How can we know what is God's Word, and what is right or wrong? . . . You must determine this matter yourself, for your very life depends upon it. Therefore God must speak to your heart.[34]

The human form in which the Bible came to us was an example of the miracle of God's gracious condescension, to clothe his Word in an earthly form. Luther said:

> Holy Scripture possesses no external glory, attracts no attention, lacks all beauty and adornment. . . . Yet faith comes from this divine Word, through its inner power without any external loveliness.

Luther concluded:

> It is only the internal working of the Holy Spirit that causes us to place our trust in this Word of God, which is without form or comeliness. . . .[35]

Luther's concept of biblical authority followed from his personal relationship to the Bible. For him, Christ alone was without error and was the essential Word of God. Thus, Luther's faith was in the subject matter of Scripture, not its form, which was the object of scholarly investigation. When Luther said of Scripture, "There is no falsehood in it," he was speaking not about technical accuracy, but the ability of the Word to accomplish righteousness in us. See the context of his words:

---

[32]Ibid., p. 3.
[33]Ibid., p. 9.
[34]Ibid., p. 11.
[35]Willem Jan Kooiman, *Luther and the Bible*, trans. John Schmidt (Philadelphia, 1961), p. 237.

For we are perfect in Him and free from unrighteousness, because we teach the Word of God in its purity, preach about His mercy, and accept the Word in faith. This does away with unrighteousness which does not harm us. In this doctrine there is no falsehood; here we are pure through and through. This doctrine is genuine, for it is a gift of God.[36]

CALVIN

Calvin, like Luther, reacted against the Aristotelian-Thomistic method of the Middle Ages and embraced the older Augustinian tradition. Plato was the best of all the philosophers for Calvin who cited him freely, though not uncritically. Augustine was cited most by Calvin among the church Fathers. Calvin's basic concepts of the relationship of faith and reason followed the Augustinian "faith leads to understanding" pattern.

For Calvin, all persons had an inborn knowledge of God: "There is within the human mind, and indeed by natural instinct, an awareness of divinity."[37] Calvin believed that "God himself has implanted in all men a certain understanding of his divine majesty."[38] He called it a "conviction" which is "naturally inborn in all,"[39] and "the seed of religion" which was "divinely planted in all men."[40]

That innate knowledge of God was suppressed by sinful humans, leaving them responsible for their condition. Calvin said:

Since, therefore, men one and all perceive that there is a God and that he is their Maker, they are condemned by their own testimony because they have failed to honor him and to consecrate their lives to his will.[41]

Because humankind sinfully suppressed this inborn knowledge of its creator, Calvin noted that God gave "another and better help" properly to direct us to God the Creator. The purpose of this revelation of his Word was "to become known unto salvation."[42] The means of this revelation was Scripture which functioned like "spectacles gathering up the otherwise confused knowledge of God in our minds, having dispersed our dullness,

[36]Shelton, p. 179.
[37]John Calvin, *Institutes of the Christian Religion*, ed. J. T. McNeill, trans. F. L. Battles (Philadelphia, 1960), I, iii, 1.
[38]Ibid., I, iii, 1.
[39]Ibid., I, iii, 3.
[40]Ibid., I, iv, 1.
[41]Ibid., I, iii, 1.
[42]Ibid., I, vi, 1.

clearly shows us the true God."[43] It is in this context that Calvin uttered the oft-quoted statement that "God . . . not merely uses mute teachers, but also opens his own most hallowed lips."[44]

How can we know the authority of Scripture? Calvin felt that even to ask such a question was to "mock the Holy Spirit." To ask the question, "Who can convince us that these writings came from God?"[45] was like asking "Whence will we learn to distinguish light from darkness, white from black, sweet from bitter?" The answer for Calvin, as for Augustine, was self-evident: "Indeed, Scripture exhibits fully as clear evidence of its own truth as white and black things do of their color, or sweet and bitter things of their taste."[46]

According to Calvin, the persuasion that God is the author of Scripture was established in us by the internal testimony of the Holy Spirit. He said: "We ought to seek our conviction in a higher place than human reasons, judgments, or conjectures, that is, in the secret testimony of the Spirit."[47] According to Calvin, "human testimonies," which are meant to confirm Scripture's authority, "will not be vain if they follow that chief and highest testimony,"[48] as secondary aids to our feebleness. Scripture cannot be known as authority outside of faith. Calvin said explicitly, "But those who wish to prove to infidels that Scripture is the Word of God are acting foolishly for only by faith can this be known."[49]

Calvin strove for the Augustinian middle way of the church. He fought against two extremes. He rejected the rationalistic Scholasticism on the one side which demanded proofs prior to faith in Scripture. He rejected with equal firmness the spiritualistic sectarians on the other side who claimed leadings of the Spirit apart from the Scripture. For Calvin, "Word and Spirit belong inseparably together."[50] The children of God, said Calvin, "know no other Spirit than him who dwelt and spoke in the apostles."[51]

Calvin accepted the Augustinian view of the authority of Scripture. The central theme of Scripture was Jesus Christ. The

[43] Ibid.
[44] Ibid.
[45] Ibid., I, vii, 1.
[46] Ibid., I, vii, 2.
[47] Ibid., I, vii, 4.
[48] Ibid., I, viii, 13.
[49] Ibid.
[50] Ibid., I, ix, 3.
[51] Ibid.

purpose of Scripture was to know Christ savingly. Calvin wrote, "The object of faith is Christ."[52]

God's humbling of himself in Christ was a model of God's method of accommodating himself to us, according to Calvin.

> All thinking about God without Christ is a vast abyss which immediately swallows up all our thoughts. . . . It is evident from this that we cannot believe in God except through Christ, in whom God in a manner makes Himself little, in order to accommodate Himself to our comprehension.[53]

This incarnational style of communication was evident as well in the language of the Bible, according to Calvin:

> For who, even of slight intelligence, does not understand, as nurses commonly do with infants, God is wont in a measure to 'lisp' in speaking to us? Thus such forms of speaking [i.e., the biblical anthropomorphic expressions] do not so much express what God is like, as accommodate the knowledge of him to our slight capacity. To do this he must descend far beneath his loftiness.[54]

God's method, for Calvin, was "to represent himself to us, not as he is in himself, but as he seems to us."[55]

For Calvin it was not necessary for God to use precise forms of words in Scripture. His saving message was adequately communicated in the varieties of normal human speech.

Calvin noted an inaccuracy in Paul's quotation of Psalm 51:4 in Romans 3:4 and generalized it:

> We know that, in quoting Scripture the apostles often used freer language than the original, since they were content if what they quoted applied to their subject, and therefore they were not overcareful in their use of words.[56]

Similarly, Calvin affirmed in his commentary on Hebrews 10:6 that the saving purpose of the biblical message could come through what we would think of as the human form of words:

> They [the apostles] were not overscrupulous in quoting words provided that they did not misuse Scripture for their convenience.

[52]Ibid., III, ii, 1.

[53]I Peter 1:21 in John Calvin, *Hebrews and the First and Second Epistles of St. Peter*, trans. William B. Johnston, eds. D. W. and T. F. Torrance (Grand Rapids, 1963), p. 250.

[54]Calvin, *Inst.*, I, xiii, 1.

[55]Calvin, *Inst.*, I, xvii, 13. The context here is a passage of Scripture where God is said to repent.

[56]Romans 3:4 in John Calvin, *The Epistles of Paul the Apostle to the Romans and to the Thessalonians*, trans. R. Mackenzie, eds. D. W. and T. F. Torrance (Grand Rapids, 1961), p. 61.

We must always look at the purpose for which quotations are
made . . . but as far as the words are concerned, as in other things
which are not relevant to the present purpose, they allow themselves some indulgence.[57]

Because the purpose of Scripture was to bring us to salvation
in Christ, Calvin did not feel that the Bible's teaching had to be
harmonized with science. Each was valid in its own sphere. In
his commentary on Genesis (1:15, 16), Calvin faced the issue of
the relationship of the science of his day and the Bible. The
problem was that the moon was spoken of in the Bible as being
one of the two great lights with the stars being mentioned only
incidentally. Astronomers of Calvin's day had proved that Sat-
urn, because of its great distance from earth, appeared to be less
than the moon, but really was a greater light. Calvin wrote:

Moses wrote in popular style things which, without instruction,
all ordinary persons, endued with common sense are able to
understand; but astronomers investigate with great labour whatever the sagacity of the human mind can comprehend. . . . Nor [is]
this science to be condemned. . . . Astronomy is not only pleasant,
but also very useful to be known. . . . Nor did Moses truly wish
to withdraw us from this pursuit. . . . Had he spoken of things
generally unknown, the uneducated might have pleaded in excuse
that such subjects were beyond their capacity.[58]

The most recent scholarly biographer of Calvin, T. H. L. Parker, aptly summarized Calvin's views on the authority and interpretation of Scripture: "The creatureliness of the Bible is no
hindrance to hearing God's Word but rather the completely necessary condition."[59]

POST-REFORMATION SCHOLASTICISM

Calvin died in 1564. By that time the Roman Catholic Counter-
Reformation had consolidated and focused its strength in a rejection of Protestant doctrines at the Council of Trent (1545–
1563). In response to Trent, the second generation of Reformers
adopted the methods of their adversaries in order to fight them.
Post-Reformation Protestants tried to prove the authority of the

[57]Hebrews 10:6 in Calvin, *Hebrews*, p. 136.
[58]Genesis 1:15,16 in John Calvin, *The First Book of Moses Called Genesis*, trans.
John King (Grand Rapids, 1948), pp. 86–87. Cited in Arthur Lindsley, "The
Principle of Accommodation" (unpublished paper, Pittsburgh Theological Seminary, 1975), pp. 17–18.
[59]T. H. L. Parker, *John Calvin: A Biography* (Philadelphia, 1975), p. 77.

Bible using the same Aristotelian-Thomistic arguments which Roman Catholics used to prove the authority of the church. Melanchthon, the successor of Luther, and Beza, the successor of Calvin, both endeavored to systematize the work of their masters by casting it into an Aristotelian mold.[60] Thus a significant shift in theological method occurred from the neo-Platonic Augustinianism of Luther and Calvin to the neo-Aristotelian Thomism of their immediate followers. A period of Protestant Scholasticism was thus launched on the European continent in the immediate post-Reformation period.[61]

On the Lutheran side, Melanchthon's work was carried on and crystallized in the *Loci Theologici* of John Gerhard (1582– 1637). Gerhard contended that the Scriptures met Aristotle's qualifications for the principles in any science. The doctrine of Scripture, therefore, was not an article of faith, but the *principium* (foundation) of other articles of faith.[62]

On the Reformed side, Beza's Aristotelian rigidifying was furthered in the mid-seventeenth century by the Genevan Francis Turretin (1623– 1687) in his *Institutio theologiae elencticae*. Scripture was "the sole principle of theology" for Turretin.[63] While the existence and power of God could be known by reason, redemption and grace could be known in the Word only. Accordingly, the authority of Scripture was the most important subject in theology. Turretin asked a twofold question: "Is the Bible truly credible of itself and divine?" and "How do we know that it is such?" His response was to proclaim that the Bible was inerrant in all matters.

According to Turretin, the Bible is "authentic and divine" because the human writers "were so acted upon and inspired by the Holy Spirit, both as to the things themselves, and as to the words, as to be kept free from all error."[64] He specified: "The

[60]For the evidence regarding Beza see Brian G. Armstrong, *Calvinism and the Amyraut Heresy* (Madison, 1969), pp. 38– 42.

[61]Armstrong, p. 32, notes that Protestant Scholasticism "is more a spirit, an attitude of life, than a list of beliefs." He lists, however, four "more-or-less identifiable tendencies." Cf. Bromiley in *Revelation and the Bible*, pp. 213– 14, who points to five "shifts of emphasis" from the teaching of the Reformers which are "slight in themselves but serious in their historical consequences."

[62]Robert P. Scharlemann, *Thomas Aquinas and John Gerhard* (New Haven, 1964), p. 4.

[63]Leon McDill Allison, "The Doctrine of Scripture in the Theology of John Calvin and Francis Turretin" (Th.M. thesis, Princeton Theological Seminary, 1958), p. 57. All citations from Turretin's *Institutio* are taken from this most helpful study.

[64]Ibid., pp. 59– 60.

prophets did not make mistakes in even the smallest particulars. To say that they did would render doubtful the whole of Scripture."[65] And their inerrant words were inerrantly preserved, according to Turretin: "Nor can we readily believe that God, who dictated and inspired each and every word of these inspired men, would not take care of their entire preservation."[66]

Turretin utilized the Aristotelian-Thomistic method of putting reason before faith to develop his theology.

> Before faith can believe, it must have the divinity of the witness, to whom faith is to be given, clearly established, from certain true marks which are apprehended to it, otherwise it cannot believe.[67]

He applied this method to Scripture as well: "The Bible with its own marks is the argument on account of which I believe."[68] Because reasonable proofs must precede faith, Turretin felt it necessary to harmonize every apparent inconsistency in the biblical text. He refused to admit that the sacred writers could slip in memory or err in the smallest matters.[69]

The method used by Turretin was that developed by Thomas Aquinas. Questions were asked, answers given, objections stated and refuted. The result was a work of systematic precision and great clarity. Turretin quoted 175 authorities in his treatment of the doctrine of Scripture, including most of the church Fathers, many of his Roman Catholic opponents, and contemporary Reformed orthodox theologians. But, although he claimed to be expounding Reformed theology, he never quoted Calvin.[70]

Many confessional statements had been prepared during the sixteenth century. Turretin felt that yet another was needed, especially to refute weaknesses in the Reformed doctrines of the School of Samur in France. At Turretin's urging, the four Protestant cantons of Zurich, Basel, Bern, and Schaffhausen agreed to the task. J. H. Heidegger of Zurich undertook the writing. The result, published in 1675, was the Helvetic Consensus Formula.[71] Its section on the Bible is directed against textual criticism of the Old Testament. It declared the inspiration of the "Hebrew Orig-

---

[65] Ibid., p. 60.
[66] Ibid.
[67] Ibid., p. 61.
[68] Ibid.
[69] Ibid., p. 62.
[70] Ibid., p. 92.
[71] Donald D. Grohman, "The Genevan Reactions to the Samur Doctrine of Hypothetical Universalism: 1635–1685" (Th.D. diss., Knox College, Toronto, 1971), pp. 380–84.

inal of the Old Testament." This inspiration was found "not only in its consonants, but in its vowels — either the vowel points themselves, or at least the power of the points." The Bible was inspired "not only in its matter, but in its words," the confession stated. In its third article it announced that textual criticism of the Old Testament would "bring the foundation of our faith and its inviolable authority into perilous hazard."[72]

THE WESTMINSTER CONFESSION OF FAITH

The English Reformation underwent a separate and distinctive development from that on the continent.[73] There was a Church of England which stood between Roman Catholic and Protestant. Within that church was a Puritan party which pressed for reform in a Calvinistic direction theologically and a Presbyterian direction governmentally. Usually in control and opposed to the Puritans were the Anglo-Catholics who maintained an Aristotelian-Thomistic theology and an hierarchical episcopal form of church government. By the seventeenth century these two church parties were identified with political forces — the Puritans with Parliamentarians and the Anglo-Catholics with the King.

The Westminster Assembly of Divines (1643– 1649) was called by the English Parliament to advise them on religious reform. When the English Parliament turned to Scotland for aid in a civil war against King Charles I, Scottish representatives were sent to the English Parliament and to participate in the Assembly.

Eleven persons composed the committee to draft the Westminster Confession of Faith, seven Englishmen and four Scots. The most important outside resources on which the divines drew were the Irish Articles of 1615, prepared by Dublin professor James Usher, and a work of Usher's entitled *A Body of Divinity*, which was a compendium of Reformed theology in use at that time.[74]

Britain was distinctive not only politically, but philosophically. A British anti-Aristotelian Augustinianism was a deep-

[72]Grohman, pp. 432– 33. The English translation of the *Consensus* is by Archibald Alexander Hodge in *Outlines of Theology* (1897; reprint ed. Grand Rapids, 1949) and reprinted in John H. Leith, ed., *Creeds of the Churches*, rev. ed. (Richmond, 1973).

[73]John W. Beardslee, ed. and trans., *Reformed Dogmatics* (New York, 1965), p. 5.

[74]Jack Bartlett Rogers, *Scripture in the Westminster Confession* (Grand Rapids, 1967), ch. 3.

rooted tradition which was carried on in the Puritan party. The other centrally important philosophical influence was that of Peter Ramus (1515–1572), a Protestant martyr in the St. Bartholomew's Day massacre in Paris. Ramus attacked Aristotelian logic as artificial and contrived and the university curriculum based on Aristotle as confused and disorganized. (Beza would not allow Ramus to teach in Geneva because of his anti-Aristotelianism.) Ramus developed a simplified logic based not on syllogisms, but on self-evident propositions — working in a Platonic way from universals to particulars. From these axioms ideas were laid out in pairs in a neat outline organization. Ramism was introduced in England as a counterforce to the Aristotelian domination at the Royalist-controlled universities.[75] The best known English expositor of Ramist logic was William Temple, whose son Thomas chaired the committee which drafted the Westminster Confession. Thomas Temple's preaching showed that he had mastered the Ramist logic which was considered just the outlining preparatory to expository preaching.[76]

Philosophically, the Westminster divines remained in the Augustinian tradition of faith leading to understanding. Samuel Rutherford stated the position: "The believer is the most reasonable man in the world, hee who doth all by faith, doth all by the light of sound reason."[77]

Chapter I of the Westminster Confession is entitled "Of the Holy Scripture." The first five of the ten sections of this chapter are an ascending development on the theme of the Holy Spirit's relationship to Scripture. Section i speaks in Platonic-Augustinian fashion of the "light of nature" which is a direct revelation of God in every person's heart. As with Augustine and Calvin, the divines held that humans suppressed but could never wholly eradicate that sense of the divine within him. The "works of creation and providence" reinforce in persons that knowledge which has been suppressed and because of which a person is inexcusable for his sin. Thus there is no "natural theology" in the Thomistic fashion, asserting that persons can know God by reason based on sense experience prior to God's revelation. When the Westminster divines spoke of "natural theology," they meant the knowledge which God had implanted in their inner nature. Samuel Rutherford spoke of man's "reasonable soul, which to me

[75] Ibid., pp. 87–89. I am also indebted to Donald K. McKim, "Ramist Influence on Amesian Methodology" (unpublished paper, Pittsburgh Theological Seminary, 1975).

[76] Ibid., pp. 90, 237–38.

[77] Cited in ibid., p. 247.

to me is a rare and curious book, on which essentially is written by the immediate finger of God, that natural Theology, that we had in our first creation."[78]

The authority of Scripture in section iv was not made dependent on the testimony of any person or church, but on God, the author of Scripture. There was no recourse, as in Aristotelian Scholasticism, to rationally demonstrable external evidences of the Bible's authority. Edward Reynolds declared that faith is an assent "grounded upon the *authority or authenticalness of a Narrator*, upon whose report . . . we relye without any evidence of the thing itself."[79]

Section v climaxed the development of the first half of the chapter with the statement that, while many arguments for the truth and authority of Holy Scripture can be adduced, only the witness of the Holy Spirit in a person's heart can persuade that person that Scripture is the Word of God. The wording of this section very closely paralleled a work of George Gillespie, one of the Scot commissioners. Gillespie's work was an argument for the union of Word and Spirit against the Antinomians who claimed the Lord speaking to them apart from Scripture. Even in that context Gillespie asserted, "I heartily yeeld that the Spirit of the Lord is a Spirit of Revelation, and it is by the Spirit of God, that we know the things which are freely given us of God."[80]

The last five sections of the Confession dealt especially with how Scripture could be interpreted by a regenerate mind in light of its purpose of bringing us to salvation in Christ. In section vi the saving content of Scripture was clearly delineated: "The whole counsel of God concerning all things necessary for His own glory, man's salvation, faith and life." Scripture was not an encyclopedia of answers to every sort of question for the divines. They asserted that some things are to be ordered by our natural reason and Christian prudence. Those things even included some circumstances of worship and church government.

Scripture was not to be used as a source of information in the sciences to refute what the scholars were discovering. The Westminster divines aligned themselves with the Parliament and supported the idea of a new university in London to teach natural science as the ancient Royalist-dominated universities were not doing. Samuel Rutherford made explicit the fact that Scripture

[78]Ibid., p. 267. A helpful and historically reliable treatment of the Westminster divines' views on the Bible is contained in John H. Leith, *Assembly at Westminster* (Richmond, 1973).

[79]Rogers, p. 312.

[80]Ibid., p. 321.

was to mediate salvation, not communicate information on science. He listed areas in which Scripture is *not* our rule, e.g., "not in things of Art and Science, as to speak Latine, to demonstrate conclusions of Astronomie." But it is our rule, he said, "1. in fundamentall's of salvation."[81]

In the final section of their chapter on Scripture, the Westminster divines ended with an affirmation of the union of the Spirit and the Word. They concluded: "The Supreme judge, by which all controversies of religion are to be determined . . . can be no other but the Holy Spirit speaking in the Scripture." Thomas Gataker used the phrase "the Spirit of God in the Word" in speaking of how people might find happiness and contentment. Robert Harris spoke of the Spirit and the Word as one rule: "If you would have your heart made one, you must go all by one rule, inward, the Spirit; outward, the Word."[82]

Despite the pressure from sectarian appeals to private interpretations of the Spirit, the Westminster divines would not give up their firm conviction that it was the Spirit who brought them to the authority of the Word and guided them in interpreting it. Samuel Rutherford, in a tract against the Roman Catholics, asked, "How do we know that Scripture is the Word of God?" If ever there was a place where one might expect a divine to use the Roman Catholic's own style of rational arguments as later Scholastic Protestants did, it was here. Rutherford instead appealed to the Spirit of Christ speaking in Scripture:

> Sheep are docile creatures, Ioh. 10.27. *My sheep heare my voyce, I know them and they follow me* . . . so the instinct of Grace knoweth the voyce of the Beloved amongst many voyces, *Cant.* 2.8. and this discerning power is *in the Subject.*[83]

For Edward Reynolds, the Spirit is the Spirit of Christ who works in the Word to persuade us.

> Which should teach us, what to look for in the *Ministry of the Word*, namely that which will convince us, that which puts an edge upon the Word, and opens the heart and makes it burn, the Spirit *of Christ; for by that only we can be brought unto the righteousness of Christ.*[84]

For the Westminster divines, the final judge in controversies of religion was not just the bare word of Scripture interpreted by human logic, but the Spirit of Christ leading us in Scripture to its central saving witness to him.

[81] Ibid., pp. 366, 367.
[82] Ibid., pp. 426–27.
[83] Ibid., p. 324.
[84] Ibid., p. 323.

THE PRINCETON THEOLOGY

The Westminster divines still belonged to the Reformation era in England. Until the middle of the seventeenth century the "Age of Faith" prevailed. The "Age of Reason" came quickly but unexpectedly thereafter.

Soon after the Westminster Assembly, John Owen, a younger contemporary of the Westminster divines, moved English Reformed theology in the same direction as that taken by Francis Turretin and the continental Scholastics. The threat in both cases was the rise of biblical criticism. In 1659 Brian Walton published a Polyglott Bible in England. It introduced variant readings of the Old Testament text and questioned the antiquity of Hebrew punctuation. Owen, similarly to Turretin, held that the Hebrew vowel points were an ancient, sacred, and inspired part of the Hebrew Bible. Walton was able to hold Owen up to ridicule as the evidence became clearer that the Hebrew vowel points were a later addition to the text.[85]

In Scotland, an unofficial and anonymous commentary on the Westminster Confession appeared in 1650. It manifested a much more restrictive spirit than the Westminster Confession. It was, however, often published in the same volume as the Confession, and many thought it was a product of the Assembly.[86]

Reformed theology moved to the New World in several separate streams. New England Calvinism was brought and developed by the Congregationalists, or Independents, as they were known in England. Scotch-Irish immigration brought another stream of Calvinism, also modified since the Westminster Assembly. Elements of these two slightly divergent traditions merged to form the Presbyterian Church in its first American presbytery in 1706. The significant differences between the traditions have been responsible for splits and reunions which have marked Presbyterian history since that time.[87]

The Presbyterian Church had no center of theological training until the founding of Princeton in 1812. Until that time it was customary for young men to study with pastors as their tutors in preparation for ordination examination by the presbytery. One such young man was Archibald Alexander, born in 1772 of Scotch-

---

[85]Donald K. McKim, "John Owen's Doctrine of Scripture in Historical Perspective," *The Evangelical Quarterly* (Oct.-Dec., 1973), pp. 195–207. McKim points out that Owen was a transitional figure, in most ways maintaining a Reformation stance, while at points giving in to rationalist tendencies.

[86]Rogers, p. 149.

[87]Lefferts A. Loetscher, *The Broadening Church* (Philadelphia, 1954), ch. 1.

Irish parents.[88] In preparation for ordination he studied Jonathan Edwards, John Owen, John Witherspoon's *Lectures on Moral Philosophy*, and Francis Turretin's *Loci* in a Latin compendium.[89] In 1812, Archibald Alexander was named the first professor of Princeton Seminary and given the task of planning the curriculum. He centered that curriculum in the works of Francis Turretin and the Scottish Common Sense philosophy brought to America by John Witherspoon.

The *Institutio theologiae elencticae* of Francis Turretin was the principal textbook in systematic theology at Princeton Seminary for sixty years until Charles Hodge's *Systematic Theology* replaced it in 1872. Dr. Alexander's biographer reports:

> Dr. Alexander . . . conceived that theology was best taught by a wise union of the text book with the free lecture. Finding no work in English which entirely met his demands he placed in the hands of his pupils the Institutions of Francis Turretin.[90]

Alexander would assign twenty to forty pages of Turretin in Latin and at the next class would ask the students for an exact repetition of what they had read.

Charles Hodge pronounced Turretin's *Institutio* "one of the most perspicuous books ever written." When Hodge replaced Alexander as Professor of Exegetical and Didactic Theology, he continued to use Turretin. Hodge met both the Middler and Senior classes once a week.

> Before the first meeting of either class for the week, the Professor assigned a topic and a corresponding section of Turretin's Institutes of Theology in Latin for previous study. When they met the hour was occupied by a thorough discussion of this subject in the form of question and answer.[91]

Both Alexander and Hodge wrote commentaries on Turretin for classroom use. The influence of Turretin's scholastic theology continued at Princeton until it was reorganized in the 1930s.

The professors at Princeton Seminary vowed to "receive and subscribe" the Westminster Confession of Faith and Catechisms. But the terms used in the Confession's chapter on Scripture were

---

[88]I have been helped in developing this section by Donald K. McKim, "Archibald Alexander and the Doctrine of Scripture," *Journal of Presbyterian History* 54, no. 3 (Fall 1976), 355–75.

[89]James W. Alexander, *The Life of Archibald Alexander, D.D.* (New York, 1854), pp. 108–109.

[90]Ibid., p. 368.

[91]A. A. Hodge, *The Life of Charles Hodge, D.D., LL.D.* (New York, 1880), p. 323.

defined by concepts taken from Turretin's *Institutio*.[92] In Hodge's commentary on Turretin in 1833 he wrote that the "authenticity and trustworthiness of the [biblical] narratives" is necessary for a "true faith."[93] Hodge then indicated rational evidences which would demonstrate that authenticity.

The question of errors in the Bible arose in this connection. There is some development within the thought of each of the Princeton theologians on this question. And there is an increasing rigidification from one theologian to another with the passage of years. But, in keeping with their roots in Turretin, when faced with problems, each of them postulated the inerrancy of the Bible in all things. Archibald Alexander wrote:

> And could it be shown that the evangelists had fallen into palpable mistakes in facts of minor importance, it would be impossible to demonstrate that they wrote anything by inspiration.[94]

In his *Systematic Theology*, Hodge declared that the Bible was "free from all error whether of doctrine, fact or precept."[95] Hodge further stated that inspiration was "not confined to moral and religious truths, but extends to the statements of facts, whether scientific, historical, or geographical."[96]

Later Princeton theologians Archibald Alexander Hodge and B. B. Warfield refined the doctrine of inerrancy still further. As their contribution to a series of articles in *The Presbyterian Review* dealing with biblical criticism, they wrote on "Inspiration" in 1881. Hodge, in his part of the article, after admitting the fallibility of human language and judgment, stated:

> Nevertheless the historical faith of the church has always been, that all the affirmations of Scripture of all kinds whether of spiritual doctrine or duty, or of physical or historical fact, or of psychological or philosophical principle, are without any error, when the *ipsissima verba* of the original autographs are ascertained and interpreted in their natural and intended sense.[97]

---

[92] I have been immeasurably helped in understanding the theological and especially the philosophical background of A. A. Alexander and Charles Hodge by an unpublished paper of John W. Stewart, "The Princeton Theologians: The Tethered Theology" (dissertation research in preparation for the Department of History at the University of Michigan, 1975).

[93] Ibid., p. 9.

[94] Archibald Alexander, *Evidences of the Authenticity, Inspiration, and Canonical Authority of the Holy Scriptures* (Philadelphia, 1836), p. 229.

[95] Charles Hodge, *Systematic Theology*, Vol. 1 (New York, 1872–73), p. 152.

[96] Ibid., p. 163.

[97] Archibald A. Hodge and Benjamin B. Warfield, "Inspiration," *The Presbyterian Review* (April 1881), p. 238.

Thus errorlessness was confined to the original (lost) manuscripts of the Bible. Warfield, in his part of the article, narrowed the burden of proof to one demonstrated error: "A proved error in Scripture contradicts not only our doctrine, but the Scripture claims and, therefore, its inspiration in making those claims."[98] Warfield then added several provisos, one of which was that "no 'error' can be asserted, therefore, which cannot be proved to have been aboriginal in the text."[99] Since the original texts were not available, Warfield seemed to have an unassailable apologetic stance.

Charles Hodge once wrote that "every theology is in one sense a form of philosophy. To understand any theological system, we must understand the philosophy that underlies it and gives it form."[100] That axiom was certainly true of the Princeton theology in its reliance on Scottish Common Sense philosophy.

The founder of Scottish Realism, or Scottish Common Sense philosophy, was Thomas Reid (1710–1796). Developed in an attempt to refute David Hume and Immanuel Kant, this philosophy was brought to America in a fully developed form by John Witherspoon (1722–1794) when he became President of the College of New Jersey (later Princeton College) in 1768. Witherspoon's moral philosophy seems to have been taken over intact by Alexander and Hodge. It influenced generations of students at Princeton Seminary. Between 1830 and 1860, Princeton theologians produced at least fourteen articles endorsing and interpreting the views of Scottish Common Sense philosophers.[101] Archibald Alexander, in a lecture entitled "The Nature and Evidence of Truth," proposed Common Sense philosophy as philosophical "orthodoxy" for succeeding generations of Princeton seminarians.[102]

The principles of Scottish Common Sense philosophy are directly reflected in the principles of biblical interpretation of the Princeton theologians. The first principle of Scottish Realism is that our sense experience is reliable and certain. Witherspoon begins, as all Aristotelians do, with sense experience: "That our senses are to be trusted in the information they give us seems to me to be a first principle because they are the foundation of all

[98]Ibid., p. 245.
[99]Ibid.
[100]Charles Hodge, "What Is Christianity?" *The Biblical Repertory and Princeton Review* (January 1860), p. 121.
[101]Stewart, p. 17.
[102]Ibid., pp. 17–18.

our reasonings."[103] What we perceive with our senses really exists. Furthermore, the mind perceives not merely ideas (versus Hume) or appearances (versus Kant) but external objects in themselves.

Influenced by this principle, Hodge showed no trace of the theory of accommodation held by Origen, Chrysostom, Augustine, and Calvin to explain that we do not know God as he is but only his saving mercy adapted to our understanding. For Hodge: "We are certain, therefore, that our ideas of God, founded on the testimony of his Word, correspond to what He really is, and constitute true knowledge."[104]

A second axiom of Scottish Realism was the principle of universality. Thomas Reid held that the first principles of common sense were endorsed by the "universal consent of mankind, not of philosophers only, but of the rude and unlearned and vulgar."[105] Hodge therefore could deal with problem passages in Scripture simply by appealing to "those principles which are in everyman's heart which is fitly called the common sense of mankind." This principle of universality pitted the Princeton theologians against the higher critics who maintained that the ancient world view of biblical times was different from a nineteenth-century view. The critics assumed, as the Princeton theologians did not, that presuppositions and world views varied with historical periods and cultures.

It was natural that a prime antagonist of the Princeton theologians should be Professor Charles Augustus Briggs, whose chief mission in life was to introduce the views of German higher criticism into the Presbyterian Church. Briggs had studied in Germany and joined the faculty of Union Seminary in New York in 1874. He was concerned that "the new conclusions be accepted and interpreted by evangelical Christians and not become a monopoly of the enemies of historic Christianity.[106] The conflict between Briggs and Warfield over the understanding of Scripture in the Westminster Confession is a fascinating and tragic one which has been detailed elsewhere.[107]

Briggs was historically correct in claiming that the *Institutio* of Francis Turretin had become the textbook at Princeton and that

---

[103] *The Works of John Witherspoon, D.D.*, Vol. VI (Edinburgh, 1815), p. 22; cited in McKim, "Alexander," p. 359.

[104] Hodge, *Systematic Theology*, p. 134.

[105] Stewart, p. 25.

[106] Rogers, p. 29.

[107] See Rogers, *Scripture in the Westminster Confession*, pp. 28–43, and Loetscher, *The Broadening Church*, pp. 29–62.

"the Westminster Divines were ignored."[108] But the majority of ministers, and through them members, of the Presbyterian Church had been trained for decades to equate Turretin with Westminster and the Reformers. In 1893, the General Assembly of the Presbyterian Church upheld the Hodge-Warfield position on the inerrancy of the original autographs and asserted that this "has always been the belief of the Church."[109] Briggs was suspended from the Presbyterian ministry.

Tensions over the issue of the inerrancy of Scripture increased over the next three decades. Some contended that inerrancy was an "essential and necessary doctrine."[110] Increasing numbers of ministers, however, felt that the doctrine of inerrancy "intended to enhance the authority of the Scriptures in fact impaired their supreme authority for faith and life."[111] In 1927, a special theological commission of the denomination declared that the General Assembly did not have the constitutional power to issue binding definitions of "essential and necessary doctrines."[112]

Thus, the false equation of the theory of inerrancy with the position of the Westminster Confession was never repudiated. Rather, the church simply agreed not to make any interpretation of the Westminster Confession binding.

A CONTINUING REFORMED TRADITION

Nineteenth-century theology was not marked only by those who tried to hold onto a scholastic orthodoxy and by those who reacted against it and embraced liberalism. There were others who continued in the Augustinian tradition of the Reformation. In England, for example, there were highly respected evangelicals such as James Orr who did not postulate inerrancy.[113]

Another illustration comes from the Dutch Reformed tradition in the Netherlands in the work of Herman Bavinck (1854– 1921) and Abraham Kuyper (1837– 1920).

Bavinck and Kuyper both were respected as evangelical and Calvinist theologians by their nineteenth-century counterparts in America. Both were guest lecturers at Princeton Seminary, and

[108]Rogers, p. 31.
[109]Loetscher, p. 61.
[110]Rogers, p. 49.
[111]Maurice Armstrong et al., eds., *The Presbyterian Enterprise* (Philadelphia, 1956), p. 286.
[112]Loetscher, p. 135.
[113]See James Orr, *Revelation and Inspiration* (New York, 1910; republished 1952), pp. 199, 212– 17.

Warfield contributed an enthusiastic introduction to the English translation of Kuyper's *Principles of Sacred Theology*. Their recent successor in the chair of Dogmatics at the Free University of Amsterdam was G. C. Berkouwer, who attempted to bring this tradition into dialogue with ongoing discussions in contemporary theology. This group of Reformed theologians followed the Platonic-Augustinian tradition of beginning in faith and then seeking understanding. Berkouwer declared that it was not theologically appropriate "to discuss Scripture apart from a personal relationship of belief in it."[114] Berkouwer thus reflected Bavinck's attitude that no formal theological method guarantees faith in Scripture. Bavinck wrote: "In the period of dead orthodoxy unbelief in Scripture was in principle just as powerful as in our historico-critical age."[115]

In the nineteenth century, while Hodge and Warfield were rejecting biblical criticism, Kuyper and Bavinck were meeting the issues openly and constructively. Kuyper, for example, wrote,

If in the four Gospels, words are put in the mouth of Jesus on the same occasion which are dissimilar in form of expression, Jesus naturally cannot have used four forms at the same time, but the Holy Spirit only intended to create an impression for the church which perfectly answers to what went out from Jesus.[116]

Bavinck, like Calvin, recognized a necessary accommodation in the anthropomorphisms of Scripture. He noted, "Even in historical reports there is sometimes distinction between the fact that has taken place and the form in which it is set forth."[117]

This did not detract from the truth of Scripture for Bavinck: "Then finally it appears that Scripture is certainly true in everything, but this truth is absolutely not of the same nature in all its component parts."[118]

The purpose of Scripture was a central concern in this Reformed tradition. Biblical criticism became a problem, according to Bavinck, only when the critics lost sight of the purpose of Scripture. That purpose, goal, or "destination" of Scripture was "none other than that it should make us wise to salvation." According to Bavinck, Scripture was not meant to give us technically correct scientific information:

---

[114]Berkouwer, *Holy Scripture*, p. 9.
[115]Herman Bavinck, *Gereformeerde Dogmatiek*, Vol. 1 (Kampen, 1928), p. 411. All translations are mine from the Dutch fourth edition.
[116]Bavinck, p. 415.
[117]Ibid., p. 420.
[118]Ibid., p. 419.

The writers of Holy Scripture probably knew no more than their contemporaries in all these sciences, geology, zoology, physiology, medicine, etc. And it was not necessary either. For Holy Scripture uses the language of daily experience which is always true and remains so. If the Scripture had in place of it used the language of the school and had spoken with scientific exactness, it would have stood in the way of its own authority.[119]

The authority of Scripture is affirmed to us by the internal testimony of the Holy Spirit, according to this Dutch tradition. Kuyper, speaking in a Platonic-Augustinian fashion, said:

The Reformers wisely appealed on principle to the "witness of the Holy Spirit." By this they understood a testimony that went out directly from the Holy Spirit, as author of the Scripture, to our personal *ego*.[120]

Bavinck became even more specific:

The real object to which the Holy Spirit gives witness in the hearts of the believers is no other than the *divinitas* of the truth, poured out on us in Christ. Historical, chronological, and geographical data are never in themselves the object of the witness of the Holy Spirit.[121]

This understanding of the saving purpose of the Bible led Bavinck to deny the post-Reformation emphasis on each word and letter in Scripture.

In the thought are included the words, and in the words the vowels. But from this it does not follow that the vowel points in our Hebrew manuscripts are from the writers themselves. And it also does not follow that all is full of divine wisdom, that each jot and tittle has an infinite content. All has its meaning and significance very certainly, but there in the place and in the context in which it comes forth.[122]

It is in this tradition that Berkouwer confronted the question of error in Scripture. He first defined "error" in its biblical context. He commented that when error in the sense of incorrectness is used on the same level as error in the biblical sense of sin and deception "we are quite far removed from the serious manner in which error is dealt with in Scripture." In the Bible, what is meant by error is "not the result of a limited degree of knowledge, but it is a swerving from the truth and upsetting the faith (II Tim.

---

[119]Ibid., p. 417.
[120]Abraham Kuyper, *Principles of Sacred Theology*, trans. J. Hendrik DeVries (Grand Rapids, 1968), pp. 556–57.
[121]Bavinck, p. 414.
[122]Ibid., p. 409.

2:18)."[123] Berkouwer acknowledged the "serious motivation" of advocates of scientific and historical inerrancy, but concluded, "In the end it will damage reverence for Scripture more than it will further it."[124]

Berkouwer summarized the developed thought of his tradition: "It is not that Scripture offers us no information but that the nature of this information is unique. It is governed by the *purpose* of God's revelation."[125] The essential fact to remember, according to Berkouwer, was that "the purpose of the God-breathed Scripture is not at all to provide a scientific *gnosis* in order to convey and increase human knowledge and wisdom, but to witness of the salvation of God unto faith."[126]

CONCLUSION

What can this study contribute to current discussion about the nature of the Bible's authority and how that authority is known? First, it is historically irresponsible to claim that for two thousand years Christians have believed that the authority of the Bible entails a modern concept of inerrancy in scientific and historical details.[127]

Augustine, Calvin, Rutherford, and Bavinck, for example, all specifically deny that the Bible should be looked to as an authority in matters of science. To claim them in support of modern inerrancy theory is to trivialize their central concern that the Bible is our sole authority on salvation and the living of a Christian life. Christian theologians in the Augustinian tradition have been persons of faith in accepting the authority of Scripture and of devout scholarship in understanding it. The theologians cited above did not claim that the Bible was some kind of direct, unmediated speech of God, like the Koran or Book of Mormon. As Christian scholars, Origen, Chrysostom, Augustine, Calvin, Bavinck all stressed that God accommodated his Word to the language and thought forms of limited human beings. We can adequately know God's saving will for us in our human forms of thought and speech.

Second, it is equally irresponsible to claim that the old Princeton theology of Alexander, Hodge, and Warfield is the only le-

---

[123]Berkouwer, p. 181.
[124]Ibid., p. 183.
[125]Ibid.
[126]Ibid., p. 180.
[127]See Harold Lindsell, *The Battle for the Bible* (Grand Rapids, 1976), pp. 18, 19, 27, for such a claim.

gitimate evangelical, or Reformed, theological tradition in America.[128] The old Princeton tradition clearly has its roots in the scholasticism of Turretin and Thomas Aquinas. This tradition is a reactionary one developed to refute attacks on the Bible, especially by the science of biblical criticism. The demand for reasons prior to faith in the authority of the Bible seems wedded to a prior commitment to Aristotelian philosophy.[129] In contrast, Origen, Augustine, Luther, Calvin, the Westminster divines, and Bavinck were decidedly anti-Aristotelian in their theological method. Theologians of the Augustinian tradition accepted the authority of Scripture through the testimony of the Holy Spirit within them. For this Reformation tradition the saving authority of Christ's person known in Scripture authenticates the Bible's authority prior to all human evidences and reasonings.

Third, it is no doubt possible to define the meaning of biblical inerrancy according to the Bible's saving purpose while taking into account the human forms through which God condescended to reveal himself. Inerrancy thus defined could be heartily affirmed by those in the Augustinian tradition. However, the word *inerrancy* has been so identified with the Aristotelian notions of accuracy imposed on it by the old Princeton theology that to redefine it in American culture would be a major task.

Finally, to confuse "error" in the sense of technical accuracy with the biblical notion of error as willful deception diverts us from the serious intent of Scripture. The purpose of the Bible is not to substitute for human science. The purpose of the Bible is to warn against human sin and offer us God's salvation in Christ. Scripture infallibly achieves that purpose. We are called, not to argue Scripture's scientific accuracy, but to accept its saving message. Our faith is not in human proofs but in a divine Person whose Word persuades us.

[128]See John Gerstner, "The Theological Boundaries of Evangelical Faith," *The Evangelicals*, ed. David F. Wells and John D. Woodbridge (Nashville, 1975), pp. 21–37, for such a claim.
[129]See Francis Schaeffer, *Escape from Reason* (London, 1968), p. 35, for an example of this kind of uncritical commitment to Aristotelian thought forms.

AUTHORITY:
Current Views

12 THE THEOLOGICAL SIGNIFICANCE OF HISTORICAL CRITICISM

JAMES D. SMART

We have been attempting to diagnose a breakdown in communication between the Bible and the church and have found the source of the breakdown in a kind of ecclesiastical schizophrenia. With one lobe of its brain, the scholarly lobe, the church has moved out of the precritical era to an acceptance, albeit at times a grudging acceptance, of historical criticism, but with the other lobe of its brain, which extends widely through its membership, it remains in the precritical era. The hiatus between the two has been sharpened by the inability of historical criticism, at least in the form that has been widely accepted, to take adequate account of the theological content of Scripture. And now, when a new development has taken place in interpretation which would extend the scope of historical criticism in order to let the theological content have its full significance, and with the prospect in sight of overcoming the hiatus in the mind of the church, biblical scholarship in America, in fear of losing its scientific character, resists any extensive modification of its hermeneutic.

It is a mistake, however, to think that a spectator hermeneutic is more scientific than a responsibly theological one. A scientific methodology for the investigation of any subject matter must be determined by the character of the subject matter. The inadequacy of historical criticism in its earlier form became evident in its inability to deal with Scripture as witness to a unique and life-transforming revelation of God to humanity. In order to bring the subject matter under control it had to reduce it to a complex of literary and historical traditions exhibiting a series of developments in human religion. But that reduction removed from sight the one element in the Bible that has been responsible for its centrality and authority in the Christian church. The subject

---

matter in Scripture is more than literature, history, and religion; it is a witness that extends over more than a thousand years to a relationship between God and humans in which, first in Israel, then in Jesus Christ and his church, the deepest mysteries of humanity's life in time and beyond time were revealed. The Scriptures are a theological as well as a historical entity and they demand for their scientific investigation a methodology that is as responsible theologically as it is historically. We must guard, however, against thinking of the historical and theological elements in interpretation as though they existed in separate compartments, the theological being an additional compartment added on to an untheological historical one. The theological and the historical content of Scripture are not two separate realities but are one reality with two aspects, each inseparable from the other and interfused with it. The historical scholar who disclaims theological responsibility is simply closing his eyes to the theological aspects and implications of his research. Because the text upon which historical criticism is focused is theological in character, the investigation of it has had profound theological significance even when it has been most avowedly untheological.

A valid criticism of Karl Barth's approach to Scripture is that he makes too sharp a separation between historical and theological interpretation.[1] The former he assigns only a preparatory function, a kind of clearing of the deck for the essential interpretation which is theological. He has always made explicit his acceptance of the basic principles of historical criticism. His one objection was to its failure to transcend its preparatory function and so its neglect of the theological content which alone has caused the biblical documents to survive the centuries. His own concern, therefore, was to get on with what to him was the primary task of exegesis, the exposition of the theological content. The preparatory stage was being sufficiently cared for by others. But the effect of this approach, and especially of the categorizing of historical and literary research as merely preparatory, was to create the impression that the historical and theological aspects of interpretation could exist in separation from each other. It was only a short step from this, for some who came under Barth's

---

[1] A similar criticism may be made of Bultmann, who, as Norman J. Young, *History and Existential Theology* (Philadelphia, 1969), has shown so clearly, makes a sharp division between two levels in history — the outer, factual level, which is accessible to historians (the *historische*), and the inner, personal, existential level, accessible only to faith (the *geschichtliche*). Only the second has theological significance. Barth sees these two levels as intimately related. His separation of the two seems more practical than theological.

influence but had not his thorough training in historical critical scholarship, or who had grown up in an atmosphere hostile to such scholarship, to assume that now a happy era had arrived in which, unencumbered by the problems of historical and literary criticism or comparative religion, they could proceed directly to the excavation of the theological content of the text. They were further encouraged by Barth's use of analogy and typology in his interpretation to reintroduce not only analogy and typology but also allegory as legitimate devices in extracting an edifying meaning from the text,[2] so that theological interpretation seemed to be on the way backward toward the Middle Ages.

One can understand the effect of this in creating a reaction against theological interpretation, and a renewed emphasis upon the importance of the historical task. But among Old and New Testament scholars who have been foremost in the recognition of their theological responsibility there has been no sign of any inclination to separate the theological from the historical or to depreciate the importance of literary and historical research. The relation between the two aspects of interpretation is one of the primary problems of hermeneutics at which we shall have to look more closely. It is still in need of exploration and illustrates the unfinished character of the new development. It needs always to be kept in mind that old and new forms of hermeneutics do not as yet stand over against each other, clearly defined. We see the earlier one with greater clarity because it has been at work in our midst for some time in a fully matured form. We can evaluate its successes and its failures, its positive and its negative contributions in the life of the church. But the later, more recent, developments are still in process, and the hermeneutical discussion today is the attempt to find the way from a hermeneutic that has demonstrated certain crucial inadequacies to one that will let the Bible recover its living voice in the church and, through the church, in the world. Every angle of the problem has to be explored but always with the realization that ultimately a new methodology will be hammered out, tested, and perfected not primarily in discussions of hermeneutical principles but in the exegesis of the text of Scripture itself.[3]

[2]See the chapter "Typology, Allegory, and Analogy," in my *The Interpretation of Scripture* (Philadelphia, 1961), pp. 93–133.

[3]It is significant that the hermeneutical discussion that has been so vigorous among the post-Bultmannians has produced so little in the way of commentaries. Exegesis is the acid test of any methodology. The Old Testament development has been highly productive in commentaries in Europe.

One of the first demands of historical criticism is respect for the text of Scripture and a determination to get at not only the earliest form of the text but the original meaning of that earliest text. Textual criticism in its search for the earliest form of the text has since the time of Origen commanded the interest of scholars but has received fresh impetus from the discovery at Qumran of texts a thousand years more ancient than any that were formerly available. Already in textual criticism when a comparison is made between variant texts, as, for instance, between the Greek and the Hebrew texts of the Old Testament, a theological element becomes evident. Subtle shifts in meaning took place as the translators who lived in a Hellenistic world prepared the biblical text for its appearance in a Hellenistic costume. So also, the translation of the Bible into Latin shows at certain points an accommodation of the text, which was not necessarily conscious, to the forms, the doctrines, and the practices of the church. The translations had a context. We see it more clearly in translations that were made at a distance from us such as the Greek and Latin and less clearly in translations whose context is closest to our own. Translation is always in some degree interpretation and is then followed by an exegesis in which the mind of the interpreter meets and seeks to understand the mind of the author.

In the past there has always been in exegesis a struggle between the theology of the biblical author and the theology of the interpreter. In the Middle Ages the authors were worsted since the interpreters by the use of allegory were able to find in the text almost any meaning that they desired. Luther, Calvin, and other Reformers, while they cannot be called historical critics, can, however, be regarded as forerunners, along with Erasmus, because of their respect for the original Hebrew and Greek text and their zeal to uncover the meaning of the original text from under the heap of misinterpretations that the centuries had placed upon it. In many instances a new translation from the Hebrew or Greek was the equivalent of a new interpretation and was sufficient to let the text speak with revolutionary power. But none of the Reformers saw the danger of their own interpretation becoming a new form of imprisonment for the text or the need to establish a methodology in interpretation that would safeguard the freedom of the text. It was not until two centuries later, when the Bible had become largely a reservoir of proof texts for the doctrinal systems that had been extracted from it and was no longer allowed to speak for itself, that a renewed respect for the text began to bring historical criticism into existence. Pietism and the evangelical revival had turned men back to the Bible to find in it what they could not find in the rigid doctrinal formulations of the various orthodoxies of the time but had given no attention to the problem of how to guard against misinterpretation. That was left to more coldly rational scholars who saw that only the most careful study of the biblical language and the unearthing of the original meaning from beneath the traditional interpretations could provide the text with its freedom and the scholar with a criterion for distinguishing between interpretation and misinterpretation.

The problem was much more complex than was realized at first, or, for that matter, for long afterward. It was expected that with the application of a scientific methodology it would be possible to establish the literal meaning of Scripture with a finality that would be incontestable. We have seen how that expectation was disappointed. Albert Schweitzer, in his *The Quest of the Historical Jesus*, has illustrated for us vividly the limitations that historical criticism experienced in its first century.[4] Nevertheless, principles were being established to safeguard the text against manipulation, principles that cannot be disregarded or neglected without opening the door to a flood of irresponsible interpretation. One of the most important consequences of this respect for the text and guarding of its freedom was the recognition that there must ever be a distance between the text and the interpretation that is placed upon it. Before the rise of historical criticism, biblical theology and systematic theology were all of a piece. The church's theology, based on the Scriptures, was assumed to be the theology of the Scriptures. But now the distance between the two came into sight. The biblical authors were freed to be people of their own time in their theology, and the systematic theologian was freed to be a person of his own time in his theology.[5]

A second major contribution of historical criticism theologically to the church has been its demonstration of the humanity of the Scriptures. Just as the misunderstanding of the divinity of Jesus leads to an obscuring of his humanity, so the misunderstanding of the sacredness of the Scriptures obscures the full human character of the text and removes it into a world other than the one that we inhabit. Docetism gives us a Jesus who is no longer one of us and can no longer make us one with him for

[4]Albert Schweitzer, *The Quest of the Historical Jesus*, trans. W. Montgomery (London, 1910).
    [5]Credit for liberating biblical theology from systematic theology is usually assigned to J. S. Semler. By 1800 the principle was well established.

our redemption. And parallel with that, it gives us a Bible before which we stand in such awe that we fail to enter into intimate converse with those who speak to us by means of it. The text becomes a static formulation of divine truth rather than the human historical words of men like ourselves.

The tendency in the church toward docetism has always been strong because of the elements in Scripture that encourage it. There is an externalizing of the divine presence and action that takes place in the traditions in both Testaments, a describing of events that occurred in the personal relation between God and humanity as though they had been visible events. God walks the earth in visible form and holds conversations with people. He appears to Moses in a burning bush that the reader assumes anyone could have seen had he been present. The descent of the Spirit upon Jesus at baptism becomes in John's gospel a visible movement in space which the prophet John observes. Miraculous interventions are constantly occurring. The difference between that world and ours is obvious. We live in a realm where Jesus was crucified and God did not intervene, where six million Jews were burned in gas ovens and there was no miracle to save them, where God is hidden from the eyes of humans so completely that only faith can know his presence, and where nothing ever interrupts the order of nature. In short, we live in the flow of history, and unless the people who meet us and speak to us in the Scriptures lived in the same flow of history, we have nothing in common with them and they have nothing in common with us. Docetism breaks the continuity between biblical history and our history, removes that uniquely important segment of human history into a realm of its own, and thereby destroys the possibility of effective communication from there to here. Historical criticism, therefore, performs an invaluable service theologically when it strips away all mythological concealment from Israelite and early Christian history and, placing it firmly in its context in the larger history of the ancient Near Eastern world, establishes its continuity with our world and our history.

Closely related to this is the relativizing of everything human and historical that puts an end to even the subtlest form of idolatry. Idolatry results from a confusion of the temporal with the eternal, the human and earthly with the divine. In its crude forms it long ago ceased to be a problem of the church, only to reappear in a more deceptive form in the direct identification of the truth of God with some human phenomenon: the dogmas of the church, the words of a pope, or a sacred book. There is a powerful urge in people, even in Christian people, to give God visibility, to have something in their human world and in their hands that is divine. It is not enough for them that absolute truth resides in God; they must have a portion of it in their own hands and at their disposal: God visible and available, God securely installed within the human institution to make its authority over humans absolute and unchallengeable. There have been both Protestant and Catholic forms of this idolatry. But historical scholarship, when it is allowed its full exercise, exposes ruthlessly the relativity of everything historical, puts an end to the absolutizing of anything human, and restores the distance beween God and humanity, between the temporal and the eternal. There are no absolutes in time. From the beginning to the end of time all is time-conditioned.

The Christian is reluctant to include Jesus in this "all." Is he not for us the one point of absolute truth in the whole of history? How we answer is important, for even here at this point we can fall into idolatry. The absolute truth of God in Jesus Christ is hidden in his history to be revealed to faith. In his humanity Jesus of Nazareth participates in the relativities of history. He was a Jew of the first century A.D., conditioned in his speech and conduct by the language and customs of his time and place. He observed the Jewish festivals, worshiped in the Jewish synagogue, and could argue at times like a rabbi. He can be understood adequately only when his words and actions are observed in their Jewish setting. But that in no way contradicts the Christian faith in him as uniquely one with God or the reality of the divine action in him for humanity's redemption.

The ruthlessness with which the historian exposes the relativity of everything human has been and still is a source of great distress to many churchmen. To them it seems as though the Christian faith were without any solid foundation unless somewhere in the sea of historical relativity they can put their hands with assurance on absolute truth. But different churches have located their formulation of absolute truth at different points in history, and wherever they have located it they have anchored the church to the mentality and spirit of that time. The foundation of the church according to the New Testament was nothing visible or tangible but was the risen Lord, a spiritual presence in the midst of his people to provoke in them, as they remembered his earthly ministry, a renewal of his spirit and his mission. He left behind no formulations of doctrine, no structures of church life, no sacred writings, that a later age could absolutize, for he had himself grown up in a static religious order that had become an obstacle to the progress of God's redemptive purpose for humanity. And yet his church again and again in its history was to reproduce that static religious order, and, paralyzed by it, lose its freedom to move out in the service of God into an uncharted future. Therefore, the historian's relativizing of everything human, in Scripture and far beyond the Scriptures, far from being a threat to the church, can actually be a liberation of the church from outworn formulas of the past to let itself be led by the word and spirit of God into a new stage in the unfolding of its destiny.

An aspect of historical criticism which might not at first be reckoned as theological but which actually is the very soul of theology is its demand for honesty, intellectual integrity, in all our dealings with Scripture. We must let the facts be what they are.[6] Dishonesty takes subtle forms: a closing of the eyes at certain moments or to certain elements in the phenomena that are before us, a twisting of the facts to make them fit our theory or support our practice, a coloring of the facts to make them appear other than they are. It happens in personal relationships and destroys the integrity of the relationships. It happens in society and leaves one segment of it blind to the injustices it has for years been inflicting on another segment. And it happens in the use of Scripture far too often as we protect ourselves against those elements in Scripture which contradict our cherished convictions, our way of life, and our religious establishment. But where people stand before God their eyes are opened to the truth no matter how painful and distressing that truth may be. God is truth, and to be open to his presence is to be receptive to the truth from whatever quarter it may appear. Honesty and integrity thus belong to the very essence of faith in God, and theology as the attempt to define the realities to which faith bears witness can live only in the atmosphere of unconditional truthfulness.

How serious, then, are the consequences for faith if Christians are something less than unconditionally honest in their dealings with Scripture! A little more than a century ago the novelist George Eliot, who had a keen if skeptical interest in theology, took the trouble to read through a number of books of sermons of a prominent evangelical preacher in London by the name of Dr. Cumming. She then published an essay on them which is still worth reading today.[7] What aggravated her in Dr. Cumming was his unwillingness to let the facts be the facts. He seemed to

---

[6]It is Bultmann, and in succession to him Ernst Käsemann, who has been most ruthless in insisting upon this responsibility of critical scholarship; Rudolf Bultmann, *Glauben und Verstehen*, Vol. 1 (Tübingen, 1954), p. 2, expresses his gratitude to liberal theology for imparting to him a sense of the necessity for a radical integrity in theological scholarship.

[7]George Eliot, *Miscellaneous Essays* (Garden City, N.J., 1901), pp. 105ff.

think that he needed to come to God's help with "little white lies." He had a theory about God's truth to which he had to make all the phenomena of Scripture conform. The church of today has in a great measure left the crudity and literalism of Dr. Cumming behind, but there is still frequently a protectiveness that surrounds the use of Scripture and a caution in the approach to its problems that are dangerously close to dishonesty. And just as honesty is the atmosphere in which truth thrives, so dishonesty is the atmosphere in which truth withers and dies and men become blind not just to what meets them in Scripture but to the realities of their own lives and of the society of which they are a part. Historical criticism, therefore, as it insists upon laying bare all that can be known concerning the text of Scripture, probing every problem to its depths, and disregarding what effect its findings may have for established traditions of the church, performs a highly important theological service to the church. It exposes both conscious and unconscious dishonesties in the church's interpretation of Scripture that rob the church's voice of its integrity, and it sets a standard of honesty that is bound to affect every aspect of the church's life. A church that is afraid to look into the Scriptures with open eyes lest it thereby lose something it considers essential to its life is not likely to have the courage or the faith to let its formulation of the gospel, its institutional existence, and the whole social order of which it is a part come under the really searching and disturbing scrutiny of the word of God that is to be heard at the heart of Scripture.

One achievement of historical criticism that was thought by some scholars to spell the end of all endeavors to find a unity in the theology of the Scriptures was the demonstration of the diversity that exists among the authors. As one of my teachers put it, "There are theologies of the Old Testament but no theology of the Old Testament." He would have said the same of the New Testament, and, of course, of the Bible as a whole. But this conclusion was, perhaps, a little hasty. There is a difference between unity and unanimity. Augustine, Thomas Aquinas, Luther, Calvin, and John Wesley have each of them a distinctive theology. There is no unanimity among them, but no one would dare to say that there is not unity. They belong together in a community of faith that is not destroyed but is enriched by the distinctive contribution of each. It would not have enhanced their unity if they all had spoken with a single voice. So also with the biblical authors. When they were all pressed into a single pattern and spoke with an enforced unanimity, violence was done to the individual authors. Since the text was all of it the direct utterance

of deity, to find divergence or contradiction in it was to posit a
confusion of mind in God. But it is a basic characteristic of people
who stand before God and bear witness to his truth that each in
a specific historical situation speaks with the integrity of a distinctive person who could never be confused with anyone else.
That is true both in the Scriptures and beyond the Scriptures.
Those who merely parrot someone else's words bear witness
thereby that they have never as yet stood alone before God.

We do not have to expel Ecclesiastes from the Old Testament,
then, because it speaks with a very different tone from Second
Isaiah, nor the Letter of James because we doubt if Paul would
have approved its doctrine, nor the Gospel of John because its
description of Jesus' ministry fails to follow the pattern common
to the other Gospels. We can let each author be himself and bear
witness in his own way. Amos, Hosea, Isaiah, Jeremiah, Second
Isaiah, and Ezekiel become as real to us as people who lived only
yesterday. We could no more confuse the voice of Second Isaiah
with that of eighth-century Isaiah than we could mistake the
poetry of Robert Frost for that of William Wordsworth. Then
there are those powerful figures who have come out of the mists
of the past and taken definite form, each with a distinctive theology, whom we name so colorlessly J and P and D. In the New
Testament, where for a long time Paul and Peter were the only
salient figures apart from Jesus who appeared with any clarity,
redactional criticism is now making us familiar with the authors
of each of the Gospels as distinctive theologians, giving to each
of them a particular character. Also, the reconstruction of early
church history has brought the whole human scene in the first-
century church before us with a new clarity and in startling diversity from its first stages on. In the apostolic church there was
certainly a unity but no theological unanimity. Unity and diversity were constantly in tension, sometimes explosive tension, with
each other.

This penetration historically to the persons and situations behind the text has sometimes led to a so-called biographical approach to Scripture, as though this acquaintance with the persons
provided us with the essence of Scripture and made close attention to their words superfluous. But we know the persons only
in their words, and our acquaintance with them as individual
persons is valuable only as it enables us to hear more clearly
what they say as they bear witness to the word that was their
life. They become for us as we listen to them a wonderfully rich
and diverse community of faith, prophets and apostles, psalmists

and evangelists, with Jesus Christ at their center, and they invite us into their company. The goal of our biblical studies becomes, not just that we may know and understand the text of Scripture, but that through the text this community of faith may become the primary context of our existence. Historical criticism helps to lay the very foundation of all our theology as it opens to us what is known in the creed as the communion of saints. That communion reaches far beyond the Scriptures. It spans the ages. But its fundamental rootage and the perennial source of its renewal is in the pages of the Scriptures, so that when the Scriptures lose their voice it begins to wither and die.

13 SCRIPTURE: RECENT PROTESTANT AND CATHOLIC VIEWS

AVERY DULLES, S.J.

"The documents of Vatican II and those of the Faith and Order Commission, while they do not totally overcome all the historic disputes between Catholics and Protestants, go a long way toward reconciliation. As a result, it is no longer safe to assume that either Protestants or Catholics adhere to the classical orthodoxies of their own churches, as expressed in past centuries."

For a hundred years or more it has been customary for authors writing on the subject to lament that the Bible has been losing its central position in the lives of Christians. Pannenberg, writing on "The Crisis of the Scripture Problem," remarks: "The development of historical research . . . led to the dissolution of the Scripture principle in the form Protestant scholasticism had given to it, and thereby brought on the crisis in the foundations of evangelical theology which has become more and more acute during the past century or so."[1] According to Gordon Kaufman, "Only in rare and isolated pockets — and surely these are rapidly disappearing forever — has the Bible anything like the kind of existential authority and significance which it once enjoyed throughout much of western culture and certainly among believers."[2] In the opinion of James Barr, doubt about the status of the Bible may well come to be regarded as normal in the churches.[3] The Catholic review, *Concilium*, published in 1969 an editorial with the thought-provoking title, "Is Scripture Becoming Less Important?"[4] In 1971 the Faith and Order study on "The Authority of the Bible" observed: "The automatic acceptance of

[1]W. Pannenberg, *Basic Questions in Theology*, Vol. I (Philadelphia, 1970), p. 6.
[2]G. D. Kaufman, "What Shall We Do with the Bible?" *Interpretation* 25 (1971), 96.
[3]J. Barr, *The Bible in the Modern World* (New York, 1973), p. 8.
[4]*Concilium* 50 (*The Presence of God*) (New York, 1969), 157−75.

From Theology Today, *April 1980, pp. 7 − 26. Reprinted by permission of the publisher and the author.*

the Bible as the basis and standard has in many places been severely shaken of late."[5]

However this may be, the Bible continues to hold great interest and attraction for scholars and theologians. As Patrick Henry points out, there are at least 450 books a year in New Testament studies alone, and articles appear at a rate of a thousand or more in about four hundred journals.[6] It would seem, indeed, that the fascination with the Bible is, if anything, increased by its problematic status. No longer viewed simply as a "divine armory" providing God-given precepts and theological premises, it is perceived as having a multiplicity of uses in the Christian community. Protestant and Catholic theologians are collaborating as never before in seeking to clarify these uses.

The contemporary theological situation, with which we are concerned in the present essay, must be viewed against the background of the previous four centuries, including the Reformation controversies about the sufficiency of Scripture, the authoritarian use of Scripture by Protestant and Catholic scholastics of the "orthodox" period, and, finally, the questioning of biblical authority by the liberal theologians of the late nineteenth and early twentieth centuries. Presupposing a general awareness of this background, we may turn immediately to the more modern views of Karl Barth and Karl Rahner.

BARTH AND NEO-ORTHODOX BIBLICAL THEOLOGY

The period between the two world wars was marked by a return to the authority of the Bible without the dogmatic rigidities of classical orthodoxy. The prevailing mood was best expressed by the neo-orthodoxy of Karl Barth and his associates, who developed a highly Christocentric view of revelation. According to this school, the word of God was to be identified with Jesus Christ and him alone. The Bible was not itself the word of God but a witness to that word. Christ, however, could address the community through the word of Scripture, and when he did so, the Bible became, in a genuine sense, the word of God. The believing community could encounter Christ personally through that word.

In Barthian neo-orthodoxy the classical theses of Protestant orthodoxy were notably modified. Inspiration was no longer a property of the biblical authors or of the books taken in them-

[5]*Faith and Order Louvain 1971*, Faith and Order Paper 59 (Geneva, 1971), p. 9.
[6]P. Henry, *New Directions in New Testament Study* (Philadelphia, 1979), p. 13.

selves. Rather, it was "the promise of God and the Holy Spirit to be present among the faithful when these writings are used in the common life of the church."[7] Inerrancy, as a property of the texts, was vigorously denied, yet a genuine authority was ascribed to the Bible insofar as it became, on occasion, the word of God. In spite of the errors of the human writers, God acts with sovereign efficacy to lead the believing reader to an authentic faith-encounter.[8]

The canon, according to the Barthians, was a free decision of the church, but not an autonomous assertion of church authority. On the contrary it was, as Oscar Cullmann eloquently contended, a supreme act of obedience whereby the church humbly submitted its own witness to the norm of apostolic teaching.[9] For Barth himself, the canon was charismatically determined. In certain books the church heard God speaking; in others it did not.[10] The decision concerning the canon, for Barth, is simply a matter of confession; no human reasons can be given for it. The decision, however, is not irrevocable. In the sixteenth century, Barth admits, the Reformation churches changed the canon by excluding certain books (the "deuterocanonicals") that had previously been accepted. Conceivably the church might decide to change the limits of the canon again at some future time.[11]

Barth's principles of interpretation were consonant with his charismatic approach to the Bible. As appears from the preface to the first edition of his *Epistle to the Romans* (1918), he set little store by the historical-critical method. He wished to "see through and beyond history into the Spirit of the Bible, which is the Eternal Spirit."[12] The task of the exegete in the church is to recreate the biblical message for Christians of a later age, with the help of the Holy Spirit who continues to speak through the Bible.

Finally, regarding the sufficiency of Scripture, Barth castigated both liberal Protestants and Catholics for claiming to have access to God through religious experience rather than through Scripture alone. Against Catholics he held that "unwritten tradition" is an elusive thing, which in practice coincides with the

[7]Barth is thus paraphrased by D. H. Kelsey, *The Uses of Scripture in Recent Theology* (Philadelphia, 1975), p. 212.

[8]K. Barth, *Church Dogmatics* (ET Edinburgh, 1956), I/2, 532.

[9]O. Cullmann, "The Tradition" in his *The Early Church* (ET Philadelphia, 1956), pp. 55–99, especially pp. 87–98.

[10]Barth, *Church Dogmatics*, I/1, 120–21; I/2, 474.

[11]Ibid., 476.

[12]*Epistle to the Romans* (London, 1968), p. 1.

inner life of the church. By spinning tradition out of its own bosom, Catholicism fails in obedience to the word of God.[13] The Bible must be free to assert its claims against all human traditions.[14]

In the years immediately following World War II, Europe and the United States witnessed a remarkable flourishing of what was called "biblical theology." Largely inspired by neo-orthodoxy, the movement included many who were not theologically close to Barth. Among the leaders in the United States, George Ernest Wright, John Bright, Paul Minear, and James D. Smart are generally mentioned, as well as a few Catholics such as John L. McKenzie. The common program of the movement was to construct a theology with the help of biblical terms, categories, and themes — all of which were deemed incomparably superior to Greek thought-forms, described as metaphysical, static, and dualistic. By entering the "strange new world of the Bible," it was felt, one could encounter in a direct and exhilarating way the Lord of history.

During the 1960s and 1970s the biblical theology of the previous two decades was severely criticized. Its real and supposed weaknesses were set forth by Langdon Gilkey,[15] Brevard Childs,[16] and James Barr.[17] Carl Henry, who writes from a conservative evangelical viewpoint, made many of the same criticisms.[18] Walter Wink and Sandra Schneiders, in works we will discuss below, praised the neo-orthodox biblical theologians for having seen the inadequacies of the historico-critical approach, but faulted them for not having sufficiently freed themselves from objectivistic paradigms.

Among the criticisms directed against the biblical theology of the past generation the following are central. The authors are accused of vague and overblown jargon about encounter, God's saving acts, and eschatological events. It is questioned whether terms such as these, as employed by modern authors, are either authentically biblical or authentically theological. Can one regard terms and concepts of ancient Israel as authorized by rev-

[13] *Church Dogmatics*, I/1, 117–18.

[14] Ibid., 119.

[15] L. Gilkey, "Cosmology, Ontology, and the Travail of Biblical Language," *Journal of Religion* 41 (1961), 194–204. Cf. his *Naming the Whirlwind* (Indianapolis, 1969), pp. 91–106.

[16] B. S. Childs, *Biblical Theology in Crisis* (Philadelphia, 1970).

[17] J. Barr, *The Bible in the Modern World*.

[18] C. F. H. Henry, *God, Revelation, and Authority*, Vol. 4 (Waco, Texas, 1979), pp. 454–57.

elation? Can one really do theology in words and categories borrowed from the Bible? Is the Israelite thought-world in fact so special, so different from its environment? Is it possible to achieve a unified approach to the Bible through any one set of categories, such as promise and fulfillment, covenant, salvation history, or "elusive presence"? In sum, the critics call for a more critical approach to the biblical materials, and one that takes better account of the full diversity found in the Bible itself.[19]

KARL RAHNER

Just as Protestant neo-orthodoxy found ways of preserving the authority of the Bible without the rigidities of the old scholastic dogmatism, a parallel movement in Catholic theology managed to retrieve the main intentions of Counter Reformation orthodoxy while respecting the modern historical consciousness. As an example of this turn, we may consider Karl Rahner's theology of the Bible.[20] For Rahner, revelation is the noetic aspect of God's gracious self-communication. Revelation reaches its culmination in Jesus Christ, the supreme self-communication of God. The apostolic church, as the initial recipient of God's self-revelation in Christ, is the irreplaceable foundation of all later Christianity. The history of Israel, as the phylum of religious history leading up to Christ, is the prehistory of the church itself. Ancient Israel and the apostolic church constitute the two major phases of the people of God in its formative period.

For the apostolic church to fulfill its necessary function as the historic basis for the church of future centuries, it was necessary for that church to express its faith in an abiding and dependable form. God brought this about by seeing to it that the apostolic church purely expressed its faith in apostolic writings which could be preserved as a standard for posterity. These writings, together with those of ancient Israel that were judged to point forward to God's revelation in Christ, constitute the Christian Scriptures. The Bible, then, is the literary objectification of the faith of the people of God in its foundational period — the period when the revelation was being initially communicated.

The inspiration of Scripture, according to Rahner, is simply

[19]For a recent defense of "biblical theology" see J. D. Smart, *The Past, Present, and Future of Biblical Theology* (Philadelphia, 1979).

[20]K. Rahner, *Inspiration in the Bible*, rev. trans. (New York, 1964). For a restatement of Rahner's position after Vatican II, see his article, "Bible. I.B. Theology," *Encyclopedia of Theology: The Concise "Sacramentum Mundi"* (New York, 1975), pp. 99–108.

an aspect of God's action in forming the apostolic church. It is the dynamism of the faith of the people of God, insofar as this faith is divinely empowered to express itself in written form. The Bible, for Rahner, is in some sense infallible, for it embodies the normative apostolic witness. By analogy, the Old Testament, too, is infallible, insofar as the church guarantees it as an authentic crystallization of its own prehistory.

The canon, for Rahner, is the necessary correlative of inspiration, which is given precisely in order that there may be canonical books. The revelation of the canon is not an act distinct from the inspiration of the Bible. In reaching a decision concerning the canon, the church of the early centuries did not have to rely on apostolic authorship or on explicit apostolic testimonies. Gifted with the Spirit of Christ, the church was able to recognize through "connaturality" those writings of the foundational period that purely expressed its own faith. In drawing up the canon of the Old Testament, the church had a certain independence from the synagogue. It was not definitively bound by any Jewish canon, but it could profit from what the ancient Jews, by the Spirit of God, were already able to recognize as authentic distillations of their faith.

The interpretation of Scripture, according to Rahner, is the work of the church. Possessing an innate affinity with the God who is revealed in Scripture, the church is able to perceive what God is saying through the canonical books to the questions of the day. Since the church is the community of God's definitive (or eschatological) revelation, it has the power and the responsibility to protect the Scriptures from any corruption that would confuse or obscure their meaning. The infallibility of the church in interpreting comes to expression through the ecclesiastical magisterium, which has the task of formulating the public faith of the church. In its formulations of the faith, however, the church remains permanently dependent on its apostolic origins, and hence on the Scriptures as the normative objectification of the apostolic faith.

In the framework of Rahner's theory, the Bible must be viewed as materially sufficient. Since the purpose of inspiration is that the church may remain faithful to its apostolic origins, one cannot suppose that the biblical sedimentation of the apostolic faith is incomplete. Furthermore, it is gratuitous to appeal to supposedly apostolic traditions not attested by the Bible, for no such traditions are factually verifiable. The church, meditating on the total import of the Bible in the light of new situations, can at times grasp implications not deducible from any particular statements in the Bible. But any Christian doctrine must in some way be radicated in the apostolic faith as attested by the Bible.

Rahner's synthesis differs from that of Barth in being more ecclesiocentric. He grounds the authority of Scripture directly in the mystery of the church, indirectly in God's revelatory action in Christ. Both see the entire Bible, and not simply the New Testament, as oriented to the Christian witness. Neither accepts supernaturalistic hypotheses that would focus on the Bible as a miraculous book. They concur, moreover, in recognizing the charismatic or pneumatic dimension of inspiration, canonization, and interpretation. For Catholics, Rahner's theory functioned in a way similar to Barth's for many Protestants. It enabled them to accept and profit from modern exegetical advances without compromising their biblical faith. Barth and Rahner, ably seconded by many less celebrated theologians, prepared the way for the Protestant-Catholic convergences of the 1960s.

ECUMENICAL CONVERGENCES

Although it would be an exaggeration to speak of an ecumenical consensus, since confessional differences still remain, the decade of the 1960s achieved a significant rapprochement, registered in numerous ecumenical statements of an official or quasi-official character. Generally speaking, the Eastern Orthodox are a party to the new convergence, but the conservative evangelicals have continued to stand by the essentials of the Protestant orthodox position.

The convergence may be illustrated from the documents of Vatican Council II and those of the Faith and Order Commission of the World Council of Churches. Vatican II's Constitution on Divine Revelation, *Dei Verbum*, is in some respects an ecumenical document, for it was composed by a mixed commission including members of Cardinal Bea's Secretariat for Promoting Christian Unity who were keenly sensitive to the demands of ecumenism. The Fourth World Conference on Faith and Order, meeting at Montreal in 1963, issued a remarkable report on "Scripture, Tradition, and Traditions," expressing the common views of Protestant and Orthodox representatives. This was followed up by a report to the Bristol Faith and Order meeting of 1967 on "The Significance of the Hermeneutical Problem for the Ecumenical Movement" and by a report to the Louvain meeting of 1971 on "The Authority of the Bible." This last document was drawn up with Catholic, as well as Protestant and Orthodox, participation.

With reference to the questions central to the present essay, the main features of the ecumenical convergence may be outlined somewhat as follows:

The divine inspiration of Scripture continues to be affirmed, but it is "depsychologized." *Dei Verbum*, while repeating the essential teaching of Vatican I, does not follow Leo XIII in his description of the effects of inspiration on the intellect, will, and executive faculties of the sacred writers; rather, it is content to depict inspiration functionally, in terms of the canonical book which was to be the result (*DV* 11).

Louvain, in its report on "The Authority of the Bible," prefers not to deduce the authority of the Bible from its inspiration, as was done in the dogmatic tradition. Rather, it establishes the authority of the Bible on the ground of its religious value for the church, and then proceeds to postulate inspiration as the source of that authority. "If God's claim is experienced in the compelling way it undoubtedly is in the Bible, does this not mean that beyond the Bible is the activity of God himself, i.e., of his Spirit?"[21] While the method of argument differs from that of Vatican II, the result is substantially similar.

The term "inerrancy," though present in the original 1962 schema, was dropped in the final text of *Dei Verbum*. The Council makes the rather ambiguous statement that "the books of Scripture" teach "firmly, faithfully, and without error that truth which God wanted to put into the sacred writings for the sake of our salvation" (*DV* 11). While some commentators interpret this sentence as excluding all error from the Bible, it may be read as asserting that, while there may be erroneous statements here or there, they are corrected elsewhere or do not affect the meaning of the whole. Further, the Council's statement might seem to allow for errors in matters without importance for our salvation.[22]

Louvain likewise avoids any mention of inerrancy. But the fundamental idea is not entirely absent. The report states that the Bible is "a critical court of appeal to which the church must constantly defer and from whose judgment not even the developments taking place in our world are exempted."[23] Since the report presumably does not mean that the church should defer to error, it seems to imply a certain guarantee of truth in the

---

[21]*Louvain 1971*, p. 20.

[22]For interpretation of the teaching of *Dei Verbum* on inerrancy, see A. Grillmeier in H. Vorgrimler, ed., *Commentary on the Documents of Vatican II*, Vol. 3 (New York, 1969), pp. 231–37; B. Vawter, *Biblical Inspiration* (Philadelphia, 1972), pp. 143–55; N. Lohfink, "The Truth of the Bible and Historicity," *Theology Digest* 15/1 (Spring 1967), 26-29.

[23]*Louvain 1971*, p. 22.

Bible. This of course does not deny that there may be respects
in which the Bible could be subject to error, and the possibility
of incidental misstatements in Scripture seems to be allowed for
elsewhere in the report.[24]

The contents of the canon are not discussed in *Dei Verbum*, but
the footnote reference in *Dei Verbum* 11 to Vatican I's statement
on the subject (DS 3006) indicates an acceptance of all the books
in the ancient Latin Vulgate as belonging to the Bible. As for the
basis, *Dei Verbum* 8 declares that the full canon of the sacred books
becomes known to the church through tradition, which is said to
be present in "the practice and life of the believing and praying
church." Although some Catholic biblical scholars have held that
the canon rested on explicit apostolic testimonies, the Council
gives this opinion no positive support.

Louvain does not explicitly mention the disagreements among
Protestants, Catholics, and Orthodox regarding the Old Testament canon, but it manifests awareness of this problem. It states
that the dividing line between canonical and noncanonical books
is fluid, and that not all canonical books have the same weight.
Further, the intertestamental books are said to be important for
the understanding of the biblical period. Still, the canon cannot
be dismissed as unimportant, for by accepting a canon the church
made the books into a literary unity in which different voices
must be heard as authoritative.[25]

With regard to the idea of a "canon within the canon" recently
promoted by Ernst Käsemann and others, the Louvain report
expresses reserve. "We cannot attribute permanent authority to
an inner circle of biblical writings or biblical statements and
interpret the rest in terms of this inner circle."[26] Yet Louvain
recognizes that some statements and passages are more directly
related to the central saving events than others are.[27] In a similar
vein, Vatican II acknowledges that the four Gospels have a certain preeminence within the New Testament (*DV* 18).

As to the relations between the Old Testament and the New,
Dei Verbum, while unequivocally affirming the abiding value of
the Old Testament (*DV* 15), tends to subordinate the Old Testament to the New. After citing the Augustinian formula to the
effect that God "wisely arranged that the New Testament be
hidden in the Old and the Old be made manifest in the New,"

[24]Ibid., p. 16.
[25]Ibid., pp. 18–19.
[26]Ibid., p. 17.
[27]Ibid.

the Constitution goes on to declare that the Old Testament, "caught up into the proclamation of the gospel," acquires a fullness of meaning that it would not have in itself (*DV* 16). The Louvain statement, without rejecting Vatican II's prioritization, declines to pronounce on the relative merits of the two Testaments. It mentions a division of opinion between some who hold that the Old Testament has authority equal to that of the New and others who hold that the Old Testament receives its authority for Christians only through its relationship to the New Testament.[28]

With regard to the problem of biblical interpretation, Vatican II's statements should be read against the background of recent Catholic controversies. After Pius XII, in *Divino afflante Spiritu* (1943), encouraged scholars to take cognizance of the literary forms and conventions prevalent in the ancient Near East, there was widespread fear that Catholic exegetes, by embracing the novelties of form criticism, might subvert the historicity of the Gospels. In 1964 the Biblical Commission issued an important instruction "On the Historical Truth of the Gospels" which reaffirmed and carried further the directives of Pius XII.[29] The Biblical Commission distinguished three stages in the gospel tradition. At the lowest stratum are the words and acts of Jesus himself. At a second stage the church interprets what Jesus said and did in the light of the Resurrection and Pentecost, which provide a richer understanding. And finally, at a third stage, the Evangelists further interpret the tradition by selecting, synthesizing, and adapting the data in accordance with the particular purposes of their respective Gospels.

Vatican II, in *Dei Verbum*, reproduces the teaching of the 1964 Instruction in very concise form, sufficient, however, to give conciliar authorization to the discreet use of form criticism and redaction criticism (*DV* 19). In so doing, Vatican II fully committed the church to modern methods of biblical scholarship, thus repudiating the rather fundamentalistic approach commonly found in earlier twentieth-century Catholic exegesis.

The hermeneutical principles set forth in *Dei Verbum* 12 distinguish between two levels of interpretation. At the first level, historical and literary analysis seeks to reconstruct the meaning intended and expressed by the original writer, whose work is to be interpreted in its own sociocultural setting. At the second

---

[28]Ibid., p. 19.

[29]*Acta apostolicae sedis*, 56 (1964), 712–18; ET in *Catholic Biblical Quarterly* 26 (1964), 305-12; commentary by J. A. Fitzmyer, *Theological Studies* 25 (1964), 386-408.

level, theological exegesis seeks out the divinely intended meaning in the light of church tradition. All exegesis is ultimately
subject to the judgment of the magisterium, which can reject or
approve a given interpretation in view of its divinely given man-
date (*DV* 10). But the relationship between exegetes and the
magisterium is reciprocal. The exegetes, while subject to the
magisterium, help by their work to mature the judgment of the
church (*DV* 12). The magisterium, for its part, is subject to the
word of God (*DV* 10). For the harmony between theological exegesis and ecclesiastical doctrine, it is important that the Bible
be read "according to the same Spirit by whom it was written"
(*DV* 12).

While the third chapter of *Dei Verbum* is chiefly concerned with
the Bible as a source of doctrine, chapter 6 treats of Scripture in
a wider context. It discusses the uses of Scripture in the life of
the church — in liturgy, in preaching, and in prayer. In this section, Protestants will find many familiar themes. According to
the Council, "in the sacred books, the Father who is in heaven
meets his children with great love and speaks with them; and the
force and power of the word of God is so great that it remains
the support and energy of the church, the strength of faith for
her sons, the food of the soul, the pure and perennial source of
spiritual life" (*DV* 21).

The Bristol report on hermeneutics is rather tentative in tone,
but it clearly recommends both literary and historical criticism
in the study of biblical texts and traditions.[30] The Louvain report
in its closing paragraphs addresses the problem of theological
interpretation.[31] The Bible, it states, remains vital and relevant
if its message is constantly reinterpreted in relation to the questions and controversies of the present day. The right interpretation cannot be achieved without the help of the Holy Spirit.
Scripture, moreover, does not disclose its full meaning except to
those who read it with faith and within the community of the
church. Even though these Faith and Order reports contain no
specific discussion of the role of the magisterium, their positive
principles of interpretation are fully consonant with Vatican II.

With respect to the material sufficiency of the Bible, the ecumenical rapprochement is still more striking. *Dei Verbum*, de-
parting from the preconciliar schema "On the Sources of
Revelation," refused to affirm that there are "two sources" or

---

[30]*New Directions in Faith and Order. Bristol 1967*, Faith and Order Paper 50
(Geneva, 1968), p. 33.
[31]*Louvain 1971*, pp. 21–23.

that some revealed truths are contained in tradition alone. Instead the Constitution accented the living and dynamic character
of tradition as the process of handing on the word of God, which
is indivisibly present both in Scripture and in tradition (*DV*
7– 10). On the other hand, the Council refused to demote tradition to a merely secondary position, as though everything had
to be tested by the Bible alone as the final rule of faith. "It is not
from sacred Scripture alone that the church draws her certainty
about everything which has been revealed. Therefore both sacred
tradition and sacred Scripture are to be accepted and venerated
with the same sense of devotion and reverence" (*DV* 9).

Just as Vatican II broke with the standard Catholic two-source
theory, so the Montreal Conference on Faith and Order, meeting
almost simultaneously, showed a disposition on the part of Protestants as well as Orthodox to assert the primacy and indis-
pensability of tradition as against the *"sola Scriptura"* position.
The report depicts the prophetic and apostolic writings as sedi-
mentations of tradition and holds that even after the Bible became complete, the gospel continued to be transmitted in living
traditions by the power of the Holy Spirit. "Thus we can say that
we exist as Christians by the Tradition of the Gospel (the *paradosis*
of the *kerygma*) testified in Scripture, transmitted in and by the
church through the power of the Holy Spirit."[32] While recognizing that Tradition (with a capital "T") is the word of God, Montreal pointed out that the particular traditions of different churches
may be inadequate and even distorted. As the criterion for genuine Tradition it proposed "the Holy Scriptures rightly interpreted."[33] The report left unsolved the question how the Bible
can judge tradition if its right interpretation depends, in part,
upon tradition. The suggestion would seem to be that there is no
purely objective norm that can deliver the interpreter from the
responsibility to be faithful to the Holy Spirit, whose voice is to
be heard in Scripture and Tradition together.

The documents of Vatican II and those of the Faith and Order
Commission, while they do not totally overcome all the historic
disputes between Catholics and Protestants, go a long way toward reconciliation. As a result, it is no longer safe to assume
that either Protestants or Catholics adhere to the classical orthodoxies of their own churches, as expressed in past centuries. Protestant and Catholic biblical reflection, since the mid-sixties, has

[32] P. C. Rodger and L. Vischer, eds., *The Fourth World Conference on Faith and Order* (New York, 1964), p. 52.
[33] Ibid., p. 53.

embarked on a common history, with certain interconfessional
tensions still remaining.

CURRENT TRENDS

Because of the complexity of the current situation, one cannot
neatly synthesize present-day opinions regarding the Bible in
Protestant and Catholic theology. In general, the mood may be
characterized as open, inductive, and empirical. In much recent
literature, one encounters a certain antipathy to orthodoxy, neo-
orthodoxy, and the biblical theology of the neo-orthodox period.
Many tend to define revelation, as did Schleiermacher and liberal
Protestants, in terms of experience of the transcendent. Schubert
Ogden, for instance, holds that the ultimate sources of religious
authority are two: "specifically Christian experience of God as
decisively revealed in Jesus the Christ" and "universally human
experience of ultimate reality as originally revealed in our existence as such."[34] Edward Schillebeeckx speaks of two sources of
theology: "on the one hand the entire traditional experience of
the great Jewish-Christian movement, and on the other hand the
new, contemporary human experiences of Christians and non-
Christians."[35]

Authors such as Willi Marxsen and Schubert Ogden stress the
importance of the New Testament as a source and norm of specifically Christian experience, since it contains the apostolic witness to Jesus. They emphasize, however, that the real norm is
Jesus himself, whose place cannot be usurped by either church
or Bible.[36] Inspired by the "new quest for the historical Jesus,"
these writers look particularly to what they call the "Jesus-
kerygma" as discoverable in the earliest strata of Christian witness. This, they believe, is the norm by which the appropriateness
of all explicitly Christological assertions is to be tested.[37]

Against this idea of a "canon within the canon," others maintain that the earliest testimony is not necessarily the best. The
first witnesses may have been too close to the revelatory events
to evaluate their real significance. According to D. E. Nineham,

[34]S. Ogden, "Sources of Religious Authority in Liberal Protestantism," *Journal
of the American Academy of Religion* 44 (1976), 411.
    [35]E. Schillebeeckx, *Die Auferstehung Jesu als Grund der Erlösung*, Quaestiones
Disputatae 78 (Freiburg, 1978), p. 13.
    [36]W. Marxsen, *The New Testament as the Church's Book* (Philadelphia, 1972),
p. 154.
    [37]S. Ogden, "The Authority of Scripture for Theology," *Interpretation* 30 (1976),
259.

"it may seem providential that the Gospels were written a generation or more after the events to which they refer ... by a community which, since the end of Jesus' earthly life, had enjoyed a continuous and deepening experience of him as the risen and exalted Lord, and had achieved increasing insight into the connexion between that experience and the events in the days of his flesh."[38]

Many authors today turn to the Bible not so much for accurate information about the words and deeds of Jesus as to find in it a model or paradigm of the specifically Jewish and Christian experience of God. According to James Barr, the Bible, as "the classic model for the understanding of God," offers paradigms that empower us to interpret our own lives in a new way. "Faith is Christian," he says, "because it relates itself to classically-expressed models."[39] David Tracy proposes a similar ground for the authority of the Bible. "The Scriptures serve for the Christian as the classic judging and transforming all other classics — the *norma normans non normata* of all Christian religious and theological language."[40] Gregory Baum does not substantially disagree when he writes: "The Bible is the test, norm, and judge in the church by purifying and reassuring Christians in their own experience of life."[41]

In this inductive approach, the doctrine of inspiration undergoes a certain permutation. Unlike their "orthodox" forebears, most contemporary theologians see no reason for identifying inspiration exclusively with the canonical Scriptures. Krister Stendahl, Everett Kalin, A. C. Sundberg, and others have abundantly proved that the early church acknowledged the inspiration of many writings which they did not accept as canonical Scripture.[42] These findings harmonize with the earlier contentions of Pierre Benoit regarding the inspiration of the Septuagint[43] and

[38]D. E. Nineham, "Eye-Witness Testimony and Gospel Tradition, III," *JTS* 11 (1960), 262.

[39]Barr, p. 118.

[40]D. Tracy, "The Particularity and Universality of Christian Revelation," in E. Schillebeeckx and B. Van Iersel, eds., *Revelation and Experience* (*Concilium* 113), p. 113.

[41]G. Baum, "The Bible as Norm," *The Ecumenist* 9/5 (July–Aug. 1971), 75.

[42]K. Stendahl, "The Apocalypse of John and the Epistles of Paul in the Muratorian Fragment," in W. Klassen and G. F. Snyder, eds., *Current Issues in New Testament Interpretation* (New York, 1962), pp. 239–45; E. Kalin, "The Inspired Community: A Glance at Canon History," *Concordia Theological Monthly* 42 (1971), 541–49; A. C. Sundberg, "The Bible Canon and Christian Doctrine," *Interpretation* 29 (1975), 352–71, especially 364–71.

those of Gustave Bardy regarding the inspiration of church Fathers and councils.[44]

For many writers the inspiration of the biblical books is not intelligible except in the light of an antecedent inspired tradition and a subsequent inspired church. Barr insists on all three of these stages, and in this context reaffirms the inspiration of the Bible. "The biblical men had a pioneering role in the formulation of our classic model, and this may make it fitting for them to be called 'inspired' in a special sense."[45]

Inspiration, as the quality which enabled the community of faith to produce its classic writings, should not be restricted, as some liberals contended, to the *ideas* of the sacred authors. Luis Alonso Schökel, among others, has shown from the psychology of literary composition that it is impossible to separate an author's ideas from the literary genres and language in which the ideas take shape.[46] Barr, cognizant of these facts, is willing to speak, in a certain sense, of "plenary verbal inspiration," though of course he understands this term quite differently from the earlier orthodox or recent fundamentalist theologians.[47]

While fundamentalists continue to work with the dogmatic idea of inspiration, and to deduce the authority of the Bible from its divine origin, the more inductive theology of our day proceeds in the opposite direction. Kelsey, for example, grounds the authority of the Bible in its power to nurture and reform the identity of the Christian community and its members. Inspiration, he holds, is a second-order doctrine, intended to give a theological explanation of how the Bible, properly used, achieves this kind of effect.[48]

The question of inerrancy, now as at the beginning of the century, remains sharply controverted between fundamentalists and non-fundamentalists. In October 1978, a conference of 284 evangelicals, sponsored by the International Council on Biblical Inerrancy, drafted "The Chicago Statement on Biblical Iner-

[43] P. Benoit, "La Septante est-elle inspirée?" in N. Adler, ed., *Vom Wort des Lebens*, Festschrift Max Mienertz (Münster, 1951), pp. 41–49. Cf. P. Auvray, "Comment se pose le problème de l'inspiration des Septante," *Revue Biblique* 59 (1952), 321–36.

[44] G. Bardy, "L'inspiration des Pères de l'Eglise," *Recherches de science religieuse* 40 (1951-52) (Mélanges Jules Lebreton 2), 7–26.

[45] Barr, p. 132; cf. J. Barr, *Fundamentalism* (Philadelphia, 1978), p. 288.

[46] L. Alonso Schökel, *The Inspired Word* (New York, 1965), especially pp. 177–216.

[47] Barr, *The Bible in the Modern World*, pp. 178–79; cf. his *Fundamentalism*, pp. 298–99.

[48] Kelsey, p. 211.

rancy," which concludes from the doctrine of inspiration the inerrancy of the Bible in all its parts.[49] "We deny that biblical
infallibility and inerrancy are limited to spiritual, religious, or
redemptive themes, exclusive of assertions in the fields of history
and science. We further deny that scientific hypotheses about
earth history may properly be used to overturn the teaching of
Scripture on creation and the flood" (Art. 12). These assertions
are somewhat qualified later in the document, where it is admitted that the Bible uses "non-chronological narration and im-
precise citation" and is not "absolutely precise by modern
standards."

While inerrancy continues to be defended by distinguished
conservatives such as Carl Henry, a few evangelicals, such as
Dewey Beegle, reject the doctrine.[50] In Roman Catholicism, many
prominent theologians still assert inerrancy, but only in a very
qualified manner. Norbert Lohfink, for example, has maintained
that the unity of the Bible demands that each individual statement be interpreted in terms of the whole, so that it no longer
bears the meaning which it would have if read in isolation. Thus
an erroneous statement in one or another of the books of Scripture does not compromise the inerrancy of the Bible.[51] Other
Catholic theologians, as we have seen, insist only on the "salvific
truth" of Scripture, and are willing to admit scientific and historical errors. Oswald Loretz, on the other hand, holds that the
Bible is true in the Hebrew sense of being reliable and faithful,
but not in the Greek, scientific sense, which would demand conformity between statements and the facts they refer to.[52] Hans
Küng, who accepts a fundamentally Barthian notion of inspiration, cheerfully admits that the Bible is not immune to "errors
of the most varied kind."[53]

James Barr, the Scottish Presbyterian, harking back to the
Catholic *école large* of a century ago, pleads for what he calls
"inspiration without inerrancy."[54] David Kelsey maintains that
the admission of error in the Bible does not compromise its authority, for the adequate norm or *discrimen* of the Christian life

[49]*Journal of the Evangelical Theological Society* 21 (1978), 289–96; reprinted in
Henry, *God, Revelation, and Authority*, Vol. 4, pp. 211–19.
[50]D. M. Beegle, *Scripture, Tradition, and Infallibility* (Grand Rapids, 1973).
[51]N. Lohfink, "The Inerrancy of Scripture," reprinted in his *The Christian
Meaning of the Old Testament* (Milwaukee, 1968), ch. 2, pp. 24–51.
[52]O. Loretz, *The Truth of the Bible* (New York, 1968).
[53]H. Küng, *Infallible? An Inquiry* (Garden City, N.Y., 1971), pp. 209–21, quotation from p. 215.
[54]Barr, *Fundamentalism*, p. 287.

is not simply the Bible taken as a book. Rather, the *discrimen* is both the Bible as used in the community and the active presence of God, taken together as reciprocal coefficients. Since the active presence of God is essential, literal conformity with biblical statements is neither necessary nor sufficient to guarantee theological positions.[55]

In contemporary writings about the canon one encounters a widespread rejection, except in fundamentalist circles, of the "orthodox" positions that the canon was explicitly revealed in apostolic times or that the canonical books could be identified by their prophetic or apostolic authorship. Ogden, for instance, asserts: "We now know not only that the Old Testament is not prophetic in the traditional sense of the word but also that the New Testament is not apostolic in the same traditional sense. We know, in fact, that the New Testament canon, both as such and in its individual writings, itself belongs to the tradition of the church, as distinct from the original witness of the apostles with which it has traditionally been identified."[56]

Recent historical investigation has provided ample grounds for the position here expressed. With respect to the Old Testament, Sundberg has forcefully argued that the so-called Alexandrian or Septuagint canon never existed. The church, he says, adopted the full range of what circulated as Scripture throughout Judaism (and not simply in the diaspora) before the rabbinic "council" of Jamnia, which, in the last decade of the first century A.D., drew up a restrictive canon so as to exclude certain tendencies, such as the apocalyptic. In limiting its Old Testament to the Jewish canon, Protestantism, according to Sundberg, was misled by the mistaken belief that Jesus, the apostles, and the New Testament writers would not have recognized the Jewish Scriptures later repudiated by the rabbis. By correcting this historical error, he concludes, Protestants could today unite with Catholics in accepting the undivided canon of the early church.[57]

[55]Kelsey, p. 215.

[56]Ogden, "Sources of Religious Authority," p. 414; cf. Ogden, "The Authority of Scripture for Theology," pp. 248–52.

[57]A. C. Sundberg, *The Old Testament of the Early Church* (Cambridge, 1964); "The 'Old Testament': A Christian Canon," *Catholic Biblical Quarterly* 30 (1968), 143–55, and several other articles. Sounding a note of caution, James C. Turro and R. E. Brown point out that we know of no books that were excluded at Jamnia; they also surmise that the Jewish canon may not have been rigidly fixed until the end of the second or the early part of the third century. "Canonicity," *Jerome Biblical Commentary* (Englewood Cliffs, N.J., 1968), 67:35. B. S. Childs, in his *Introduction to the Old Testament as Scripture* (Philadelphia, 1979), pp. 661–71, still favors the narrower Jewish canon, which in his view was prior to Jamnia.

With regard to the New Testament, it was widely agreed, until recently, that the canon was fixed, in substance, about the middle of the second century. According to Cullmann, this was the time when the church was still near enough to the apostolic age to be able to identify the apostolic writings. "At no other time in the history of the church could the fixing of the canon have been undertaken."[58] Since Harnack, it had become customary to appeal to the Muratorian Fragment as a Roman canon of the late second century, and to the testimony of Origen as indicating the canon of the Greek church in the early third century. Sundberg, however, maintains that these evidences are dubious, at best. He argues that the Muratorian Fragment is an Eastern list of the fourth century and that Eusebius himself was responsible for the list of canonical books ascribed on his authority to Origen. On these and other grounds he concludes that the adoption of a canon, in the sense of a closed list of officially recognized books, was an achievement of the fourth century.[59] If Sundberg is correct, Cullmann seriously erred in maintaining that the church, in the middle of the second century, surrendered the normative status of all traditions "that are not fixed by the apostles in writing."[60]

This does not mean that the church, by its fourth-century decision concerning the canon, set itself as judge over the Scriptures. Recent Catholic authors, following along the general lines of Rahner and Barth, regard the fixation of the canon as an act of obedience to the Holy Spirit. The books, they assert, were recognized by a kind of charismatic discernment, analogous to what Thomas Aquinas called knowledge through connaturality.[61] Contemporary Catholic scholarship seems to assume that the canon drawn up by Trent is definitively binding in faith, and consequently subject to no further revision,[62] but this view could perhaps merit reexamination in the light of a careful scrutiny of the acts of the council with the help of recent work on the scope and nature of conciliar infallibility.

Protestant authors, for their part, tend to hold that the deci-

[58]Cullmann, pp. 91–92.

[59]A. C. Sundberg, "Towards a Revised History of the New Testament Canon," *Studia Evangelica* 4 (1968), 452–61; "Canon Muratori: A Fourth-Century List," *Harvard Theological Review* 66 (1973), 1–41.

[60]Cullmann, p. 90.

[61]Cf. R. Murray, "How Did the Church Determine the Canon of Scripture?" *Heythrop Journal* 11 (1970), 115–26; N. Appel, "The New Testament Canon," *Theological Studies* 32 (1971), 627–46.

[62]Brown and Turro, "Canonicity," *JBC* 67:13, 42–43, 90; Appel, "The NT Canon."

sion concerning the canon was a practical one, which could no doubt have been made otherwise. As a result of this decision the church is able to present its faithful with what Barr calls a manageable body of material representing different genres, periods, and points of view.[63] According to Barr, the canon is de facto settled, since this material is now built into Christian faith through its historical roots. We are no longer in the canon-building phase.[64] According to Kelsey, the church in establishing the canon certifies that these writings function together as a sufficient occasion for that presence of God which preserves and nurtures the church's identity.[65]

Like Kelsey, James Sanders stresses the essential relationship between the identity of the community and the books taken as canonical. He proposes a new approach to Scripture which he calls "canon criticism" on the analogy of source criticism, form criticism, and redaction criticism.[66] Brevard Childs prefers to speak of "canon analysis." Reacting against an exaggerated interest in the provenance of the texts, he advocates concentrating on the final form of the text as we have it in the canonical Scriptures.[67] The adoption of the canon, he says, implies confidence on the part of the church that all the diversity will not lead off into irreconcilable opposites.[68]

Turning from the canon to interpretation, we may observe that biblical interpretation is complicated by a lack of agreement about the goals of exegesis. Barr conveniently distinguishes three approaches: the referential, which aims to discover the historical or theological realities about which the Bible speaks; the intentional, which aims to establish what the original writers intended to say; and the poetic or aesthetic, which aims to explore the images, myths, and literary qualities of the biblical text as it is.[69]

While competent exegetes continue to produce valuable studies on what the biblical authors meant by their words, theological scholarship generally pursues the wider goal of seeking out the realities to which faith is committed. The "new quest of the historical Jesus," launched in the late 1950s, continues to have influence, though the original Heideggerian orientation of that quest is today less pronounced. In the late 1970s Catholic theologians

---

[63]Barr, *The Bible in the Modern World*, pp. 155–56.
[64]Ibid., pp. 154–56.
[65]Kelsey, p. 106.
[66]J. A. Sanders, *Torah and Canon* (Philadelphia, 1972), especially pp. ix-xx.
[67]Childs, *Introduction to the Old Testament*, pp. 73–75.
[68]Childs, *Biblical Theology in Crisis*, p. 181.
[69]Barr, *The Bible in the Modern World*, pp. 61–62.

such as Hans Küng,[70] Edward Schillebeeckx,[71] and Jon Sobrino[72] have produced exciting studies focusing on the public ministry of Jesus as retrieved through historical-critical analysis of the earliest traditions. In these studies the influence of Protestants such as Marxsen, Pannenberg, and Moltmann is easily discerned.

Complaints are still heard — and not simply from the fundamentalist camp — to the effect that the historical-critical approach is theologically sterile. In what was evidently intended as a programmatic essay, Walter Wink of Union Theological Seminary in New York City inveighed against the "biblical critical paradigm" as laboring under a false objectivism, technologism, and isolation from the community of faith.[73] Drawing heavily on the hermeneutical theory of Hans-Georg Gadamer and on the critical sociology of Jürgen Habermas, Wink proposes a new model of biblical study, based on the human sciences, and directed to personal and social transformation.

Gadamer's influence is evident also in the work of Peter Stuhlmacher, a former pupil and assistant of Ernst Käsemann, who advocates a "hermeneutics of consent" which allows the text itself to determine the horizons of the interpreter and thus to generate what Gadamer calls "an effective historical consciousness." Tradition, Stuhlmacher contends, is indispensable for exegesis, for any classic text interprets itself by establishing a continuous but fluid stream of commentary which mediates between the text itself and the contemporary reader.[74]

In a perceptive article, Sandra Schneiders, I.H.M., of the Jesuit School of Theology in Berkeley, California, attempts to integrate hermeneutics with faith and spirituality. Theological exegesis, she maintains, must explain not only what the original author meant to say to the original readers, but also what the word of God says to us today through the text.[75] Every significant text, she holds, has an inexhaustible fullness of meaning. "The text functions like a musical composition, which cannot be rendered except by genuine fidelity to the score but which will be

[70]H. Küng, *On Being a Christian* (Garden City, N.Y., 1976).
[71]E. Schillebeeckx, *Jesus: An Experiment in Christology* (New York, 1979).
[72]J. Sobrino, *Christology at the Crossroads* (Maryknoll, N.Y., 1978).
[73]W. Wink, *The Bible in Human Transformation: Toward a New Paradigm for Biblical Study* (Philadelphia, 1973).
[74]P. Stuhlmacher, *Historical Criticism and Theological Interpretation of Scripture* (Philadelphia, 1977).
[75]"The Literal Sense of Scripture," *Theological Studies* 39 (1978), 719-36.

rendered differently by each artist."[76] In this way Schneiders attempts to retrieve what was valid in the search for a "fuller meaning" (*sensus plenior*) recently pursued by Raymond Brown among others.[77]

Contemporary exegesis in France is strongly influenced by structuralism, and in the United States is affected by a combination of structuralism and the new literary criticism which looks upon texts as having an independent life of their own and thus as having meanings irrespective of the intentions of their authors. Distinguished exegetes such as Norman Perrin, Robert W. Funk, John Dominic Crossan, and Dan O. Via, Jr., have been producing new literary and structural analyses of the metaphors and parables in the New Testament. For an introduction to this type of hermeneutics, and of the hermeneutical theory of philosophers such as Paul Ricoeur, one may consult the periodical, *Semeia*, founded in 1974, which describes itself as "an experimental journal devoted to the exploration of new and emergent methods of biblical criticism."

Studies such as these shy away from any attempt to translate the meaning of the Bible into propositional statements. Instead, they seek to clarify how the biblical language can work on the modern reader. The concern is not so much with interpretation as with use; not so much with what *Dei Verbum* discusses in its third chapter as in its sixth, as described above. In this connection, one is reminded of Kelsey's statement that theology should not be content with exploring what the text says, or even what God is saying through the text, but should inquire rather what God is using the text for.[78] In the church, according to Kelsey, God uses the texts of Scripture to shape, nurture, and reform the church's self-identity. By following up this suggestion, one might find surprising new relevance in the spiritual exegesis of the middle ages.[79]

Finally, how is Scripture related to tradition? Since Vatican II and Montreal there has been a growing ecumenical consensus to the effect that both the "two sources" theory of Counter Reformation Catholicism and the *sola Scriptura* formula of Reformation Protestantism are unsatisfactory. Against the former position it

---

[76]Ibid., p. 731.

[77]R. E. Brown, *The "Sensus Plenior" of Sacred Scripture* (Baltimore, 1955). For Brown's more recent views on the subject see his article, "Hermeneutics," *JBC* 71:57–70.

[78]Kelsey, p. 215.

[79]On this see H. de Lubac, *The Sources of Revelation* (New York, 1968), containing selections from his 4-volume *Exégèse médiévale* (Paris, 1959-64).

is argued that Scripture and tradition are not two distinct reservoirs, each containing a certain portion of revealed truth. Against the latter, it is observed that Scripture is never really alone. The Christian reads it within the church, in the light of the use the church makes of it.

There is rather general agreement, also, that the Bible, rather than tradition, is the fundamental embodiment of the word of God. As Joseph Ratzinger says in his commentary on *Dei Verbum*, Chapter 2: "It is important to note that only Scripture is defined in terms of what it *is*: it is stated that Scripture *is* the word of God consigned to writing. Tradition, however, is described only functionally, in terms of what it *does*: it hands on the word of God, but *is* not the word of God."[80] Kelsey, from a Protestant point of view, says much the same. Scripture and tradition, he declares, cannot properly be viewed as competing authorities. Scripture he defines as "that set of writings whose *proper* use serves as the occasion by God's grace for his presence,"[81] whereas tradition is "the process that embraces both the church's use of Scripture and the presence of God which, in dialectical interrelationship, are together essential to the church's self-identity."[82]

Montreal, as we have seen, acknowledged the possibility of distorting traditions and proposed Scripture, rightly interpreted, as a criterion by which authentic tradition could be distinguished from inauthentic. Ratzinger agrees with this proposal and faults *Dei Verbum* for not having pointed out the critical use of Scripture to adjudicate tradition.[83] But as we have noted, the Faith and Order documents fail to settle the question how the Bible can function as a norm against tradition if the Bible itself must be interpreted in the light of tradition.

Catholics continue to hold, in accordance with Vatican I and Vatican II, that the ecclesiastical magisterium is a divinely given guide that enables the truth of revelation to be authoritatively heralded by the church. But as the Councils also point out, the teaching of the magisterium is not itself the word of God; rather, it is under the word of God, which it serves.[84] Kelsey therefore exaggerates when he says: "For the Roman Catholics, God is present only in the mode of uses of canonical Scripture ruled by the divinely instituted teaching office of the church which is to

---

[80]Vorgrimler, *Commentary*, Vol. 3, p. 194.

[81]Kelsey, p. 96 (italics Kelsey's).

[82]Ibid., p. 95.

[83]Vorgrimler, *Commentary*, Vol. 3, p. 191.

[84]See the discussion above of Vatican I (DS 3011) and *Dei Verbum* 10 and 12.

be identified with 'tradition' unambiguously."[85] Most contemporary Catholic theologians clearly distinguish between tradition and the teaching of the ecclesiastical magisterium, but they recognize in the magisterium a power to judge authoritatively when there is doubt about what the tradition has to say.

Vatican Council II, in its Decree on Ecumenism, pointed out that Protestants and Catholics generally differ in their understanding of the proper role of the magisterium in the interpretation of Scripture. In the Catholic view, according to the Council, "an authentic teaching office plays a special role in the explanation and proclamation of the written word of God."[86] The difference, however, may not be unbridgeable. In point of fact it is doubtful that the Catholic magisterium has ever issued an irreformable decision regarding the literal meaning of any given text, and thus Catholic exegetes may, with proper deference to official teaching, continue to explore exegetical questions according to their own proper methodology.[87] On the other hand, Protestants are generally inclined to interpret Scripture in accordance with the confessional standards and traditions of their own ecclesial bodies. The interconfessional disagreements about biblical interpretation are, on both sides, influenced by official church teaching. And the increasing agreements among exegetes of different confessional traditions may well be the harbingers of future agreements among the churches themselves.

In the preceding sketch I have deliberately focused on centrist positions, which I regard as dominant in the recent Protestant and Catholic literature on the Bible. In a longer survey it would be necessary to give closer attention to radical tendencies, which subordinate Scripture to something else (such as personal experience or political action), and to conservative tendencies, which accord peremptory authority to individual texts taken by themselves. The centrist positions we have examined differ from the "orthodoxy" of recent centuries and from contemporary conservative theology by insisting that the biblical texts must be read in their full historical and literary context and pondered in the light of Christian tradition and present experience. But, unlike radical theology, the centrist positions accept the Bible as a primary embodiment of the word of God and as an indispensable normative source for the church and for theology.

---

[85]Kelsey, p. 97.
[86]*Unitatis redintegratio*, p. 21.
[87]R. E. Brown, "Hermeneutics," *JBC* 71:87.

CONTRIBUTORS

ACHTEMEIER, PAUL J. — Herbert Worth and Annie H. Jackson Professor of Biblical Interpretation at Union Theological Seminary in Richmond, Virginia.

BARRETT, C. K. — Professor of Divinity at Durham University and author of many biblical commentaries and New Testament studies.

BEEGLE, DEWEY M. — Professor of Old Testament at Wesley Theological Seminary in Washington, D.C.

BERKOUWER, G. C. — Professor Emeritus of Systematic Theology at the Free University of Amsterdam, The Netherlands.

BLOESCH, DONALD G. — Professor of Systematic Theology at the University of Dubuque Theological Seminary in Dubuque, Iowa.

BRUCE, F. F. — Formerly Rylands Professor of Biblical Criticism and Exegesis at the University of Manchester, England.

DULLES, AVERY —Professor of Theology at the Catholic University of America in Washington, D.C.

GRANT, ROBERT M. —Professor of New Testament at The Divinity School of the University of Chicago.

McKIM, DONALD K.   — Assistant Professor of Theology at the University of Dubuque Theological Seminary in Dubuque, Iowa.

MILLER, DONALD G.   — Formerly Professor of New Testament at Union Theological Seminary in Richmond, Virginia, and President of Pittsburgh Theological Seminary in Pittsburgh, Pennsylvania.

ROGERS, JACK B.   — Professor of Philosophical Theology at Fuller Theological Seminary in Pasadena, California.

RIDDERBOS, HERMAN N.   — Professor Emeritus of New Testament at the Theological School of the Reformed Churches of the Netherlands at Kampen.

SMART, JAMES D.   — Late Jesup Professor of Biblical Interpretation at Union Theological Seminary in New York.

BIBLIOGRAPHY

DONALD K. McKIM

GENERAL

Barclay, William. *By What Authority?* London: Darton, Longman & Todd, 1974. The popular biblical commentator here surveys biblical material as well as early church through Reformation views of authority. For amount of material presented in a non-technical way with wide-ranging illustrations, Barclay is unsurpassed.

Küng, Hans. *Infallible? An Inquiry.* Garden City, N.Y.: Doubleday, 1971. This book was a bombshell when first published and is crucial still for understanding contemporary Roman Catholic struggles with papal and biblical authority. The controversial Küng must be listened to, and this book introduces us to central issues in the current ferment.

Lloyd-Jones, D. Martyn. *Authority.* Chicago: Inter-Varsity, 1958. The authority of Christ, Scripture, and the Holy Spirit are the three topics tackled by this noted evangelical preacher. The book is popularly written and argues strongly for evangelicals to acknowledge these authoritative sources for faith.

McKenzie, John L. *Authority in the Church.* New York: Image Books, 1971. A Roman Catholic scholar looks at the New Testament concept of authority and decides it is based on "service." Here is much of value for Protestants as well.

Paul, Robert S. *The Church in Search of Its Self.* Grand Rapids: Eerdmans, 1972. This work contains a most helpful section on authority and its relationship to the church. Paul clarifies the channels of authority: church, Bible, Spirit, and reason. These are always appealed to, and the author makes us be honest in recognizing them. It is an important discussion.

Ramm, Bernard. *Patterns of Religious Authority.* Grand Rapids: Eerdmans, 1957. A look at the principle and patterns of authority in Christianity and other religious systems.

Reprinted from TSF Bulletin *(May/June 1982) with permission from* Theological Students Fellowship, 233 Langdon, Madison, WI 53703.

SCRIPTURE

A. Biblical Data

Achtemeier, Paul J. *The Inspiration of Scripture: Problems and Proposals.* Philadelphia: Westminster, 1980. This is an important book by a New Testament scholar who presents a view of inspiration that does justice to the positive insights of contemporary biblical scholarship. A stimulating treatment.

Beegle, Dewey. *Scripture, Tradition, and Infallibility.* Grand Rapids: Eerdmans, 1973. An Old Testament scholar here takes account of the role of tradition in the shaping of Scriptures and ties his discussions of inspiration, infalliblity, and inerrancy into examinations of the biblical texts. Particularly valuable for those concerned to explore the adequacy of these concepts in light of the phenomena of Scripture.

Boer, Harry R. *The Bible and Higher Criticism.* Grand Rapids: Eerdmans, 1981. Formerly published as *Above the Battle*, this book presents a veteran missionary teacher and theologian's attempt to help us see the valid insights to be gained from biblical criticism. Boer is strong on maintaining Scripture's infallibility in light of the humanity of the Bible and the different perspectives of the Gospel writers.

Brown, Colin, ed. *History, Criticism, and Faith.* Downers Grove, Ill.: InterVarsity, 1976. Helpful introductory essays on basic issues in biblical criticism and the relationship of history to faith. These essays are authored by Brown, F. F. Bruce, R. T. France, and Gordon Wenham.

Ridderbos, Herman. *Studies in Scripture and Its Authority.* Grand Rapids: Eerdmans, 1978. Working with issues such as inspiration, Christology, the Kingdom of God, reconciliation, and apocalyptic, this New Testament scholar provides keen theological insight and shows how the scientific study of Scripture can deepen our appreciations of scriptural authority.

B. Historical Dimensions

Bruce, F. F. *Tradition: Old and New.* Grand Rapids: Zondervan, 1970. A fine study of the role of tradition in biblical interpretation, theology, and the church. Of particular interest is the discussion of the canon of Scripture and its development.

Cambridge History of the Bible. 3 vols. Cambridge: Cambridge University Press, 1963-1970. This standard three-volume work is a wealth of information on the Bible, biblical exposition, criticism, versions, etc. from the early church to the present day. A wide variety of scholars have contributed to make these volumes very valuable sources for reference.

Johnson, Robert Clyde. *Authority in Protestant Theology.* Philadelphia: Westminster, 1959. An historical study of scriptural authority from Luther to the 20th century which deals extensively with Tillich and Barth. This makes the volume especially useful.

McDonald, H. D. *Theories of Revelation: An Historical Study 1700-1960.* Grand Rapids: Baker, 1979. An analysis of the presuppositions and teachings of numerous schools of thought relating to Scripture. Particularly helpful in sorting out philosophical influences affecting views of Scripture from the 18th to 20th centuries.

Rogers, Jack B. and Donald K. McKim. *The Authority and Interpretation of the Bible: An Historical Approach.* San Francisco: Harper & Row, 1979. A comprehensive historical survey of the Church's doctrine of Scripture from the early church to the 1980's. Takes account of historical and philosophical contexts with particular attention to the "evangelical" and "Reformed" traditions. Extensive documentation and scholarly apparatus.

Vawter, Bruce. *Biblical Inspiration.* Philadelphia: Westminster, 1972. A very helpful historical treatment of inspiration from the early church onward, with attention to both Roman Catholic and Protestant theologians.

C. Theological Developments

Abraham, William J. *The Divine Inspiration of Holy Scripture.* London: Oxford University Press, 1981. An accurate analysis of both conservative and liberal approaches to inspiration. Abraham also puts forth his own proposal (from the Wesleyan evangelical tradition) for a positive doctrine of inspiration. His criticisms and recommendations must be reckoned with by all evangelicals.

Barr, James. *The Bible in the Modern World.* New York: Harper & Row, 1973. An attempt to view Scripture in light of contemporary questions and issues. Barr's views of the nature of Scripture will not be shared by all, but his arguments must be dealt with by all who want to hold to an authoritative Scripture.

_____. *The Scope and Authority of the Bible.* Philadelphia: Westminster, 1980. This collection of essays touches a number of issues relating to the Bible: its character as literature, authority, the historical-critical method, the place of "story" in biblical theology, etc. The concerns Barr raises are "musts" for discussion. Some of his conclusions need careful scrutiny, but his insights are provocative.

Berkouwer, G. C. *Holy Scripture.* Trans. Jack B. Rogers. Grand Rapids: Eerdmans, 1975. One of the finest theological treatments of Scripture available. Berkouwer is concerned for a constructive dialogue with the church's confessions and traditions as well as with contemporary positions. His solid commitment to Scripture's authority pervades his discussions of all the issues. Excellent.

Bloesch, Donald G. *Essentials of Evangelical Theology.* Vol. 1. New York: Harper & Row, 1978. A widely-respected evangelical scholar gives a solid affirmation of "the primacy of Scripture" (chap. 4). His comments on "infallibility and inerrancy" are particularly on target. Also, in Volume II, seeing Scripture as a sacrament provides some very helpful perspectives.

Coleman, Richard J. *Issues of Theological Conflict.* Rev. ed. Grand Rapids: Eerdmans, 1980. A most useful guide to the issues in question in recent debates about the nature of biblical authority, revelation, and inspiration. Here is a most balanced discussion.

Dulles, Avery. "Scripture: Recent Protestant and Catholic Views." *Theology Today*, April 1980, pp. 7 – 26. A helpful survey of contemporary formulations of the doctrine of Scripture. A basic guide to Barth, Rahner, ecumenical trends, and interpretive schools.

Henry, Carl F. H. *God, Revelation, and Authority.* 4 vols. Waco, Tex.: Word, 1976, 1979. These four volumes offer a detailed, step by step analysis of issues related to Scripture by the founding editor of *Christianity Today*. Particularly clear is Henry's method and commitment to "rational" procedures.

Henry, Carl F. H., ed. *Revelation and the Bible.* Grand Rapids: Baker, 1969. A useful collection of essays from noted evangelical scholars who touch on the many dimensions relating to Scripture. While some essays are now dated, others (such as Bromiley's on "The Church Doctrine of Inspiration") still stand out.

Hodge, Archibald A. and Benjamin B. Warfield. *Inspiration.* 1881. Reprint. Grand Rapids: Baker, 1979. A reprint of a famous 1881 article by two outstanding representatives of the "Old Princeton" theology. Here the argument is that inspiration properly refers to the original copies of Scripture and that a "proved error" in Scripture contradicts inspiration. The classic statement of the inerrancy theory.

Kelsey, David H. *The Uses of Scripture in Recent Theology.* Philadelphia: Fortress, 1975. A very helpful attempt to see how Scripture is actually used by a number of contemporary theologians. Kelsey's prescriptions can get somewhat technical but his analyses and paradigms are intriguing and illuminating.

Kraft, Charles H. *Christianity in Culture.* Maryknoll, N.Y.: Orbis, 1979. An anthropologist and former missionary works with relationships between cultural forms and supracultural norms. His analyses of revelation, inspiration, and the transculturation of the biblical message make this a crucial book for 20th-century Christians to understand. A most stimulating effort.

Miller, Donald G. *The Authority of the Bible.* Grand Rapids: Eerdmans, 1972. A more popularly written volume examining Scripture's actual authority in the church and in the Christian life. Miller focuses directly on the center of Scripture, Jesus Christ, and shows how the Bible can live and breathe.

Ramm, Bernard. *Special Revelation and the Word of God.* Grand Rapids: Eerdmans, 1961. A prominent evangelical defines revelation and looks at the instruments and products of God's special revelation.

Rogers, Jack B., ed. *Biblical Authority.* Waco, Tex.: Word, 1977. A collection of essays by evangelical scholars who wish to affirm the saving purpose of Scripture and its infallibility, and who wrestle with under-standing the meaning of God's messages and the human means through which they come to us. Helpful.

Schökel, Luis Alonso. *The Inspired Word.* New York: Herder and Herder, 1972. A Roman Catholic theologian analyzes inspiration with particular attention to the psychological, sociological, literary, and linguistic dimensions involved. Very interesting approach.

Smart, James D. *The Strange Silence of the Bible in the Church.* Philadelphia: Westminster, 1970. A provocative discussion on the disuse of the Bible in churches and a guide to contemporary hermeneutical discussions. Smart also offers an appraisal of the theological significance of historical criticism and a "reinterpretation" of authority. His approach is most sympathetic to Karl Barth's theology.

Warfield, Benjamin B. *The Inspiration and Authority of the Bible.* Philadelphia: Presbyterian and Reformed, 1970. This book presents some of Warfield's most important writings on revelation and inspiration. As such it is highly significant as background for understanding recent evangelical controversies over Scripture.

BIBLICAL INTERPRETATION

Brown, Raymond E. *The Critical Meaning of the Bible: How a modern reading of the Bible challenges Christians, the Church, and the churches.* New York: Paulist Press, 1981. A Catholic scholar approaches the topic through a discussion of the respective roles of theologians and the magisterium in determining what texts meant and mean. Protestants, with little or no transposition, will find the discussion stimulating — and challenging.

Caird, G. B. *The Language and Imagery of the Bible.* Philadelphia: Westminster, 1981. A very important book, offering literary and theological analyses of the different types of language and literature of Scripture.

Childs, Brevard S. *Biblical Theology in Crisis.* Philadelphia: Westminster, 1970. Childs traces the rise and fall of the Biblical Theology Movement. Required reading for understanding the present lack of consensus on how to use the Bible in the church.

Farrer, Frederic W. *History of Interpretation.* 1886. Reprint. Grand Rapids: Baker, 1979. This classic book surveys the history of biblical interpretation from the early church to the last quarter of the 19th century. There is a wealth of very fascinating data here, and for a panoramic view this is unsurpassed.

Frei, Hans W. *The Eclipse of Biblical Narrative.* New Haven: Yale University Press, 1974. A study of hermeneutics in the 18th and 19th centuries which shows how biblical narratives (particularly the creation story and gospel accounts) lost their authority as "narratives." Frei argues that narrative authority should be regained. A striking and important proposal.

Grant, Robert M. *A Short History of the Interpretation of the Bible.* Rev. ed. New York: Macmillan, 1963. The best, brief survey of scriptural interpretation from the time of Jesus to the 20th century. Written interestingly and clearly.

Marshall, I. Howard, ed. *New Testament Interpretation.* Grand Rapids: Eerdmans, 1977. A very helpful collection of essays that introduces the varieties in biblical criticism and the current issues in biblical interpretation.

Ramm, Bernard. *Hermeneutics.* Grand Rapids: Baker, 1971. Reprints of articles from *Baker's Dictionary of Practical Theology* that cover a wide range of issues in interpretation from the parables to typology to the "new hermeneutic." A handy, introductory guide.

_____. *Protestant Biblical Interpretation.* 3d rev. ed. Grand Rapids: Baker, 1970. A detailed study of principles of biblical interpretation used by Protestants throughout history. Also deals with types, prophecy, and parables.

Smart, James D. *The Interpretation of Scripture.* Philadelphia: Westminster, 1961. A wide variety of sources are used here to address problems of biblical interpretation as well as to pose suggestions about inspiration and authority. Particular attention is given to Barth, and the two chapters outlining the history of biblical interpretation in the last 200 years are quite useful.

Stacey, David. *Interpreting the Bible.* New York: Hawthorn Books, 1977. A popularly written guide to the issues and approaches to biblical interpretation. Some will question Stacey's own interpretations, but he raises important problems.

Stuhlmacher, Peter. *Historical Criticism and Theological Interpretation of Scripture.* Trans. Roy A. Harrisville. Philadelphia: Fortress, 1977. A probe of the question of the relation of theological understanding to the historical investigation of Scripture. Excellent survey of the history of scriptural interpretation to the present and challenging comments on the limits of the historical-critical method.

Thiselton, Anthony C. *The Two Horizons: New Testament Hermeneutics and Philosophical Description.* Grand Rapids: Eerdmans, 1980. A scholarly survey of contemporary hermeneutics that examines the contributions of Heidegger, Bultmann, Gadamer, and Wittgenstein. The interplay of philosophy and New Testament interpretive issues is strongly highlighted.